Games of the XXIIIrd Olympiad
Los Angeles 1984 Commemorative Book

Officially sanctioned by the
International Olympic Committee

Published under license from the LAOOC by
International Sport Publications, Inc.

International Sport Publications, Inc. The Official
Commemorative Book Licensee of the 1984 Olympics

Games of the
XXIIIrd Olympiad
Los Angeles 1984
Commemorative Book

Published by International Sport Publications, Inc.

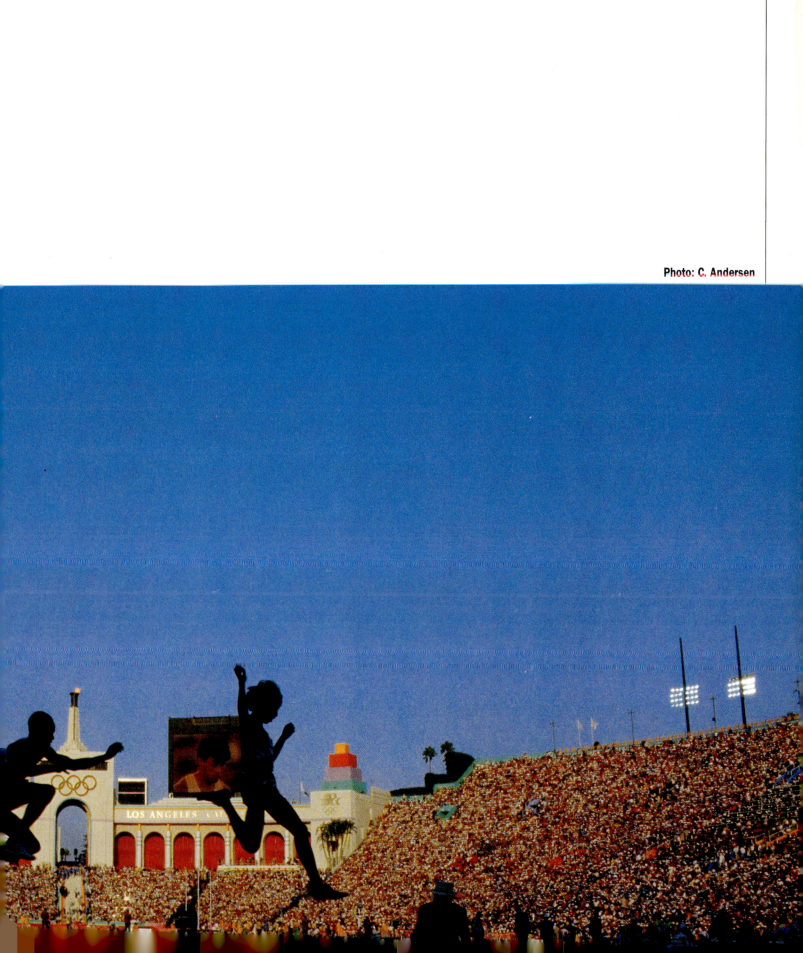

International Olympic Committee

Ancient Greece gave the world the gift of beauty, proclaimed harmony and excellence, and glorified wisdom and heroism, thus achieving the Hellenic miracle. These ideas attained their highest degree of perfection at Olympia, during the festivals celebrated there every four years.

Twenty-five centuries already separate us from the first Olympic Games; soon a hundred years will have elapsed since their revival. Here we are at the dawn of the XXIIIrd Olympiad which has been crowned by the Los Angeles Games.

This work brings the Games back to life in a remarkable way. Both the novice and the initiated will find much pleasure and indeed emotion in looking through this book.

It is a great joy for me to note how well the link with Ancient Olympia has stood the test of time and offered the noble heritage of belief in the Olympic Ideal to civilizations grown more concerned with quantity than quality. May the reader share this joy, in a spirit of brotherhood!

Juan Antonio Samaranch
President

The Olympic Games have traditionally represented much more than athletic competition and the mere winning of medals; more than opening ceremonies and world records. The Olympics are—more than anything else—the expression of the human spirit.

The Los Angeles Olympic Organizing Committee was given a chance to play host to the whole world and through sports have taken a step nearer to world understanding. Perhaps we have moved a little closer to that most important word of all, peace.

This colorful publication should serve as a lasting reminder of one of the truly great sporting events in recent history.

Harry L. Usher
Executive Vice President/General Manager

Paul Ziffren
Chairman

Peter V. Ueberroth
President

President of the United States of America

To Olympic Fans:

It was indeed an honor to officiate at the Opening Ceremonies of the Games of the XXIIIrd Olympiad in Los Angeles and to welcome athletes from other nations who were there to participate. The Olympic Games provide a terrific opportunity for young men and women to experience the importance of honest striving, fair play and the discipline and determination it takes to reach the top.

Thanks to the dedication of the LAOOC, the generosity of millions of Americans, and the help of thousands of volunteers, the 1984 Games were a rousing success.

I would like to congratulate everyone who was involved.

Ronald Reagan

Ronald Reagan

Mayor
City of Los Angeles

As Mayor of Los Angeles, it has been my privilege to be a part of the Games of the XXIIIrd Olympiad. As a former athlete and an ardent lover of sports, I appreciate the color and action that this publication brings to life.

To become an Olympic competitor requires a lifetime of dedication and sacrifice. Even so, it takes a special breed of athlete to challenge the rest of the world and climb to the top of the victory stand. This volume will serve as a lasting reminder of the Games and of the marvelous group of athletes and the Olympic spirit of competition and brotherhood that they represent.

My congratulations to all who helped make these Games a most successful Olympic contest.

Tom Bradley

Tom Bradley

Foreword

George Plimpton

Photo W. Hunt

Almost surely the Games of the XXIIIrd Olympiad would be remembered for the flags. Indeed, at the Opening Ceremonies the huge crowd in the Coliseum was asked to participate in an elaborate card-stunt which actually made everyone there part of a participating country's flag for a stunning instant. Afterwards, long after they had filed out of the Coliseum, those involved tried to figure out what country they had been briefly linked with. "I think I may have been part of Zimbabwe's flag. What were you?"

The preponderance of flags one saw at the various venues were American, of course. Hand-held. Waved at moments of triumph so that the banks of spectator seemed to shiver in patterns of red, white, and blue. These and the Olympic flags with their five linked rings were the only ones for sale at the souvenir shops. Here and there one spotted other nationalities. Japanese. German. Union Jacks. Many Australian pennants. At the women's volleyball matches, a group supporting the Chinese team sat together. They carried little square flags of red silk that at some unseen signal went up as one, as smart as a Rockettes' maneuver, shivered slightly, and then were brought back down again into their bearers' laps.

The athletes themselves were part of it. Most authorities believe that this tradition of spontaneous flagbearing by athletes started with George Foreman, the heavyweight gold-medalist, who carried an American flag into the ring in Mexico City, so small that it could have been pulled out of one of his boxing gloves. Everyone remembers Bruce Jenner's tour of the track in Montreal with his flag. Now the flags are huge. After winning the 100 meters in 9.99 seconds, Carl Lewis grabbed one out of the stands that he had to hold over his head to keep its folds from dragging on the running track. The American 100 meter relay team seemed almost tangled under its flag, like Laocoon and his sons being strangled by the serpents. The practice was by no means restricted to American athletes. At the moment of victory the first impulse seemed to be for the winner to look around for a flag. When he won the 5000 meters, Said Aouita reached into the stands and astonishingly, like a conjuror, produced an enormous flag from his country—Morocco—a lovely vermillion with a five-pointed star in the middle.

Then, at the Closing Ceremonies, an epidemic of flags broke out. The athletes had been urged not to bring flags or banners onto the field, the concept from the organizers being that the teams would walk in intermingled, symbolizing a brotherhood of athletes, and thus nations. Splendid idea. At first, no flags were visible. But then, heralded by homemade "Hi Mom" signs, the flags began to materialize, the larger ones ballooning out like horizontal spinakers. The largest flag carried around the running track was the Australians'—large enough, indeed, to flip a girl, carrying a knapsack for some reason, high in the air as if she were being bounced at the shore on a giant beach-blanket. The athletes' mood was joyous, tumultous, running under their flags with the abandon of a military charge...perhaps compelled by the same mood as the hero of Stephan Crane's The Red Badge of Courage—"as he hurled himself forward was born a love, a dispairing fondness for this flag...a creation of beauty and invulnerability."

And yet, while the flag is thought of as the symbol that induces nationalistic fervor, the Games of the XXIIIrd Olympiad were by no means the chauvinistic occasion one could have expected. From the spectators, even armed as so many of them were with flags, and bellowing "U.S.A! U.S.A!", the support given the athletes of other countries was always gracious, unconstrained, and admiring. The last marathon runner into the Coliseum, bearing a name as lovely as any flag—Dieudonne Lamothe—was a Haitian who received as enthusiastic a welcome as the Portugese runner who won the race. Perhaps the most astonishing statistic of the Olympics was that 101,799 spectators, the largest crowd ever to watch a soccer game in the United States, turned out to watch a final in which the home country was not involved—France versus Brazil.

Naturally, there were a myriad of vignettes that would remain like freeze-frames when the XXIIIrd Olympiad was brought back to memory: the drama of Switzerland's Gabriela Andersen-Scheiss, suffering from heat prostration, and her staggering finish of the first Olympic women's marathon; the tangle during the 3000 meters at the Coliseum and Mary Decker's fall to the infield clutching the number off the back of the little barefoot runner, Zola Budd, originally from South Africa; the tears streaming down the face of Jeff Blatnick winning a gold medal two years after being treated for Hodgkin's disease; the sturdy pertness of Mary Lou Retton, arms aloft on her landing, scoring a perfect 10 with the double-twisting Tsukahara vault, and then doing another, as if to show she was incapable of a fluke; the touching immobility of the giant seven foot center on the Chinese women's basketball team—a looming figure who seemed to be used solely for intimidation. An arm stretched out stiff as if feeling her way through a dark, cobwebby room; the silence of the crowd when Greg

Louganis went to the edge of the 10 meter platform for the last dive of the Olympics—a reverse three-and- a-half tuck, the so-called Dive of Death that had killed Sergei Shalibashvili when the Soviet diver's head hit the platform—and the great roar when (earning an unheard-of 10 from one judge) the American amassed the highest total ever scored in diving competition: 710 points; the incongruous spectacle of the scuba-diver—there to take underwater camera angles—lurking in the corner of the diving pool like a monstrous aquatic predator; the first sight of Carlos Lopes emerging from the darkness of the Coliseum tunnel as the winner of the marathon; the performance of A Touch of Class in the equestrian events and the beauty of her and the other two medalist horses as they were ridden around the Coliseum track at the Closing Ceremonies.

But always the flags. Some of the spectators themselves came decked out in flag patterns—their halters, briefs, jeans spangled and striped. On the last day of the Olympics, the souvenir vendors were selling their flags for a dollar apiece. The sales were brisk—perhaps because people were getting a bargain, but more likely because they wanted a telling memento of the XXIIIrd Olympiad. American flags were not in particular demand. On this last day what everyone wanted was an Olympic flag. . .

Credits

Publisher

International Sport Publications, Inc.
 Keith S Christensen
 G. Reed Petersen
 Michael J. Bray
 Benson L. Hathaway, Jr.

Editorial Staff

Text Editors
 Harvey Frommer
 Myrna Frommer

Managing Editor
 Mary T. Gaddie

Photo Editor
 Sam Locacciato

Assistant Editor
 William Cutting

Art Director
 M.L. Tsumagari
 Vincent Gonzales

Editorial Consultant
 F. Patrick Escobar, LAOOC
 Maurice Louvet, IOC
 Monique Berlioux, IOC

Editorial Assistant
 JaNae Warnock
 Kerry Gonzales
 Sandra Beck

Production

Design
 Penna Gonzales Powers &
 Cutting Inc.

Color Separations
 Earnest D. Miller, Sr.
 International Color Inc.

Production
 Stephen B. Whipple & Associates

Officially sanctioned by the
International Olympic Committee

© 1980 LA Olympic Committee

Published under license from the LAOOC by International Sport Publications, Inc.

International Sport Publications, Inc. The Official Commemorative Book Licensee of the 1984 Olympics

© 1984 by International Sport Publications, Inc.
Salt Lake City, Utah
Library of Congress Catalogue Card Number 84-80729
ISBN 0-913927-03-1

Table of Contents

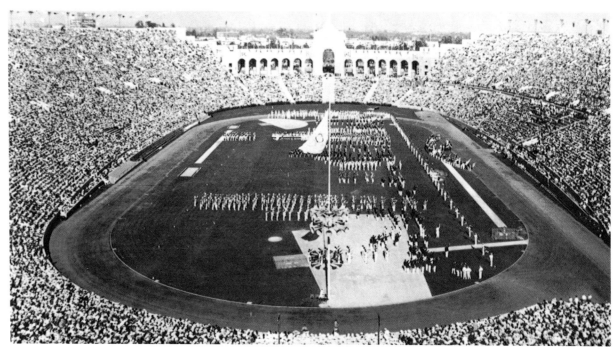

the hard gaze of the Fuhrer, it was a black American, Jesse Owens, who carried off four gold medals in athletics while at the same time beating a world record and three Olympic records. Three years later, the second World War broke out. In the midst of the firing there was no question of organizing the Games planned for 1940 and 1944.

In the period between the wars, Olympism began a new adventure, quite foreign to the hot sun of Elida—the Winter Games. The first, recognized only a posteriori by the I.O.C.—were held at Chamonix, (France) bringing together 294 participants from 16 countries. A discreet beginning! But the importance of the "White Games" grew quickly. Celebrated in the same year as the Olympic Games, the Winter Games were open to every major winter sport with great success. The XVth Winter Games, which took place at Sarajevo (Yugoslavia) in February 1984, brought together 1,490 competitors representing 49 nations.

Let us return to the summer Olympic Games. Their history since the end of the last world conflict may be divided into two parts, the turning point being in 1960. From London (1948) to Melbourne (1956), via Helsinki (1952) the Games rapidly rediscovered their influence and growth. A record number of 58 nations and 4,072 athletes came to London, which had barely recovered from the war. The Soviet Union rejoined the Olympic Movement at the Helsinki games, which, in the eyes of many, were the purest of all.

Olympic universality was affirmed when the Games were held at Melbourne on a third continent, Oceania. The most famous champions of this period are Fanny-Blankers-Koen, Emil Zatopek, Bob Mathias, Wilma Rudolph, Pierre Jonqueres d'Oriola and Vladimir Kutz. In 1952, Avery Brundage was elected President of the International Olympic Committee, a post which he was to hold for twenty years. Pierre de Coubertin retired voluntarily in 1925 and was succeeded by the Belgian, Henri de Baillet Latour, who died in 1942 having heard that his son had been killed in action. His place was taken by the Swede, Sigfrid Edstrom.

Rome in July/August 1960, represented another turning point. Africa with its newly-emancipated nations made its entry into the Games. And for the first time the competitions were broadcast by television, a phenomenon which was to play an ever greater role. The next three celebrations, Tokyo (October 1964), Mexico (October 1968) and Munich (August-September 1972) were in tune with their times when economic growth seemed unbounded. Each of these Games surpassed every kind of record.

The athletes' performances, the infrastructures, broadcasting by the mass media, all of these continued to spiral up-wards. Munich brought together 7,465 participants representing 123 nations, and its program covered 21 sports. Host cities devoted increasingly enormous budgets to organization and set up splendid integrated sports and communication complexes which brought them years ahead in terms of progress. Dawn Fraser, Mark Spitz and Roland Matthes in swimming; Al Oerter, Bob Beamon, Abebe Bikila, Kep Keino and Valery Borzov in athletics were the top ranking stars in sport at this time. Sadly, a tragic shadow was cast over the festivities at Munich by killing of thirteen people. The I.O.C. suspended competitions for a day and organized expiatory ceremonies in honour of the victims. From then on, the gigantic profile of the Games was to expose them to the temptations of violence.

From autumn 1973 onwards a worldwide petroleum shortage made itself felt and criticism grew of the "colossal" costs under which the Games labored. Candidates for their organization became few and far between. For very different reasons the Montreal Games (August-September 1976), the Moscow Games (August- September 1980) and the Los Angeles Games (July-August 1984) suffered boycotts of varying degrees. This did not prevent a crop of prodigious gold medals: Sara Simeoni, Olga Korbut, Irena Szewinska, Cornelia Ender, Daley Thompson, Edwin Moses and many others rendered performances that will long remain in our memories.

While some may hold doubts about the future of the Olympic Games, 139 nations and 7,458 athletes met in Los Angeles to celebrate the XXIIIrd Olympiad. It need hardly be pointed out that this is a record—one among many others which will be set during these Games.

IOC Members assembled for the first Olympic Games: Seated, Coubertin (FRA), Vikelas (GRE), Boutowski (URS),.Standing, Gebhardt (FRG), Guth-Jarovsky (FRG), Kemeny (HUN), Balck (SWE). Photo: Courtesy IOC

Athens 1896: The Olympiad. Photo: Courtesy IOC

Left to Right
Zabala (ARG),
marathon winner,
1932.
Photo: Courtesy IOC

Mildred "Babe"
Didrikson (USA)
1932.
Photo: Courtesy IOC

Jesse Owens and
Helen Stephens
(USA), Berlin, 1936.
Photo: Courtesy IOC

Opening Ceremonies

"…in an afternoon of jostling sunlight were crowds, and banners, wilderness and music." Richard Eberhart

Left to Right
1960 Olympic Decathlon champion Rafer Johnson (USA).
Photo: S. Powell

I.O.C. President H.E. Juan Antonio Samaranch and Los Angeles Mayor Tom Bradley.
Photo: S. Powell

Photo: S. Powell

Photo: T. Duffy

Legendary Los Angeles: Host to the Olympics Again

Myrna Frommer with the assistance of Marilyn Wyatt

T he city has always been magic. It's make believe— movie stars, palm trees, mansions with swimming pools, and beaches that never end. The City of Angels in golden, glorious California. What better place for a fortnight of games, for the coming and going of people from across the globe to partake of an elaborate pageantry of play?

Dressed up in medieval tournament, elegant Beverly Hills boulevards hung pennants and flags from lampposts in colors of sherbet delicious enough to taste. Sites of competition hid the paraphernalia of technology behind rows of shining white tents whose pointed roofs were scalloped-edged. Officials in gold- colored jackets, and volunteers in jumpsuits of apple green took their respites beneath streamered canopies. And over the places of play, great helium balloons hung weightless in the sky. With the props of a fair from the Middle Ages, Los Angeles was ready for processional and parade, rituals of awards, and anthems—all preceded by trumpets and fanfare. In all the fun was the message of tradition, of the need to do some things as they have been and should be done—with all appropriate ceremony.

But not too seriously. After all—these are games. Onto the lot comes the stuff of play—30 foot high jungle-gym, tinker-toy towers of bright vermillion, great shining balls set into their centers, glistening silky sheets of aqua and magenta stretched across their frames. From the cosmopolitan University of Califorina at Los Angeles campus where the gymnasts vaulted and spun and the tennis players served and vollied, to the urban University of Southern California campus where the swimmers powered like motors down the pool's lanes and the divers held themselves motionless in air before turning earthward, to the carnival that was Exposition Park where in the vast Coliseum the Olympics began and ended, at all the diverse sites spread over the greater Los Angeles area the medieval and playful imagery of the Games of the XXIIIrd Olympiad was announced.

This was the set for the 1984 Olympics, the backdrop upon which the drama of the Games was enacted. How it came to be is a story of some people's vision, and the way they made it come true.

Soon after the first Los Angeles Olympics was held in 1932, its success spurred the formation of the Southern California Committee for the Olympic Games (SCCOG), for a return Olympic engagement. Some forty years later, the persistent group finally succeeded in obtaining the 1984 Olympic nomination for Los Angeles.

However, anxious to avoid the same problems Montreal experienced with its 1976 Olympics, when lavish spending on new facilities left the city $1.16 billion in debt, Los Angeles refused to assume financial responsibility for the Games. This radical move alarmed International Olympic Committee (IOC) officials. Games in the past had always been paid for by the host government. The IOC refused to finalize the award of the Games to the City of Los Angeles without a guaranteed method of covering costs.

After months of difficult negotiation with the IOC, Los Angeles' affable mayor, Tom Bradley, appointed a blue ribbon panel in mid 1978 to study the last ditch options. This resourceful group of community leaders came up with a distinctly American solution: the cost of staging the Games would be borne by a private corporation. The Los Angeles agreement was revolutionary. Never before had the Olympic Games been run by a private committee with no ties to the government, operating on funds generated by the private sector.

Announcing its bold agenda for a "Spartan Olympics," the newly formed Los Angeles Olympic Organizing Committee (LAOOC), headed by Chariman Paul Ziffren, President Peter V. Ueberroth, and Executive Vice President, General manager Harry L. Usher, pledged to keep costs to a minimum while honoring the high standards of Olympic competition. The LAOOC's operating budget was estimated at $500 million, to be covered by three primary sources of revenue: sponsorships, television rights, and ticket sales. The amount was amazingly low.

Where but in Southern California could such a plan be visualized? New facilities in Montreal had cost over $1 billion. In Los Angeles, sports facilities were there for the using. How easily the stadiums, arenas, parks, colleges and universities lent themselves to Olympic use. In many cases their identification with the Games was to be accomplished by little more than some application of "Festive Federalism"—the term used to describe the Olympic look—in the environmental graphics of colors, buntings, banners and signs. University dormitories, decorated with Olympic motifs and banked with bright beds of flowers, would be transformed into engaging and hospitable Olympic villages.

This "no frills" Olympics could be envisioned in Los Angeles for the very qualities that critics had derided the city for: its lack of a center and its dependence on the automobile. The greater Los Angeles area is actually a collection of some 94 designated areas, and the Olympic Games were to move out beyond them. The city is the prototype of the metropolis tailored to the demands of the automobile. Because of these qualities, the Olympics could be spread out as never before over some 4,500 miles, connected by 414 miles of freeway. Through the extensive interlocking freeway system

Opposite Page Newly-dedicated statues in front of the Coliseum. Photo: E. Rosenberger

The Olympic
Velodrome
Photo: S. Powell

Festive Federalism
at its colorful best.
Photo: E.
Rosenberger

California is so famous for, all the diverse venues were to be connected in a lace-like pattern. They ranged as far south as San Diego, where in the lush environs of the Fairbanks Ranch and Country Club horses were to be tested for speed and endurance in early equestrian events. They ranged as far north as the Ojai Valley near Santa Barbara in whose Lake Casitas, rowers and canoers were to race. They ranged as far east as San Bernardino County, where a 20-hectare recreational site for shooting competition was constructed especially for the Olympics. And they ranged as far west as the Pacific Ocean where, in Long Beach's parks, marinas and the ultra-modern convention center, matches in volleyball, team handball, archery and yachting would be contested, and further north up the coastline where water polo matches would be contested at Pepperdine University in the hills of Malibu. In the center of all these widely separated venues was the Coliseum where it all began. Refurbished with a new track surface, decorated with an elaborate painting scheme, and replenished with giant computerized scoreboards and videoscreens, the Coliseum in downtown Los Angeles was to serve as the Olympic's hub, a spectacular setting for Opening and Closing Ceremonies and athletic events. The nearby, Los Angeles Sports Arena, familiar to movie goers as the backdrop for the "Rocky" films, would host boxing bouts.

Since the Olympic Swim Stadium used for the 1932 Games was too small for the 1984 Games, Olympic sponsor McDonald's Corporation would underwrite the $4 million dollar cost of a new world-class swimming pool on the University of Southern California campus. A cycling velodrome at the University of California, Dominguez Hills would be built amidst the oil rigs north of Long Beach. The 333.33 meter oval track would be underwritten by the Southland Corporation at a cost of $4 million dollars

A number of events were to be staged at area colleges and universities. California State University would host judo, handball and cycling. Field hockey would take place at the East Los Angeles College. Gymnastics and tennis events were to be held at the University of California Los Angeles. The site for weightlifting would be Loyola Marymount University.

Among the more famous Olympic venues was Dodger Stadium, site of the baseball competition. Perched high above downtown Los Angeles, and accentuated by its familiar collar of palm trees, the home of the Los Angeles Dodgers is one of the most beautiful baseball parks in the world.

The Forum in Inglewood, home of the Los Angeles Lakers, would provide a superb setting for the men's and women's basketball. The spacious Rose Bowl in beautiful Pasadena would host the massive record breaking crowds for football matches. From the vastness of the Rose Bowl to the hushed intimate environs of El Dorado Park site of archery competition, from new up-to-date facilities to those as traditional as the stately Santa Anita Racetrack site of equestrian events, from such fast-paced urban settings as the Forum to the serene, bucolic setting of Coto de Caza in Orange County where modern pentathlon would be staged, there would be the unmistakable look and feel of the 1984 Olympics.

It was to take more than a look and a feel, however, to tie these varied and widely-separated sites together. Whatever was to happen would have to be transmitted to the rest of the world. The image of Pheidippides running from Marathon to Athens with victorious news not only embodied the traditional Olympic spirit, it represented the traditional way humans communicated across distance. The message received first was that carried by the fastest runner. Hardly a way to run an Olympics spread out over hundreds of miles. Communications technology—called by some the "24th event"—was to accomplish the Olympian feat of sending and receiving messages and linking together the far-flung sites. Every venue, every Olympic center was to be provided with a number of computer terminals courtesy of American Telephone and Telegraph that would enable information to move electronically in split second time. Scores and standings would be available to media almost as soon as they happened. Information was to be relayed throughout the world almost instantaneously. A telephone network would be established by AT&T to enable anyone to receive messages from anywhere across the world by seeing his name appear on a screen, going to a phone, dialing a code and hearing the message intended for him. In the preparations for these Games people were able to see that we truly are living in a global village.

As preparations for the games got underway, there was a growing sense of wanting to be a part of it. Eventually there would be 50,000 volunteers attending to the needs of athletes, media people, technicians, and spectators. They were of all ages and backgrounds, and they were to bring with them a kind of good humor and simple human consideration that many thought had been forgotten.

The Los Angeles Games were five years in the making and they culminated many thousands of hours of work by members of the LAOOC staff under the direction of Peter V. Ueberroth. Like a beautiful and elaborate caravan, the 1984 Olympics were a mass of temporary installations, including 47 miles of chain-link fence, 65,000 bleachers, 20,000 signs, 3000 tents and 95 turnstiles which together with the towers, flags, buntings and banners, would be taken down after the Games were over. Vivid murals were to brighten concrete walls and various communities would participate in their own ways through spruce-up campaigns, photography contests, sports fests and neighborhood fairs.

On the last Friday night of July, 1984, a night magical as Southern Californian nights can be, up in the hills above Hollywood, thousands of people assembled to hear the Prelude to the Olympics Concert performed by the Los Angeles Philharmonic Orchestra. The Olympics would begin the next afternoon. Now, in the international language of music, the spirit of common humanity would be evoked, a spirit that would characterize most of the Olympic Games. The concert concluded with the triumphant chorale of Beethoven's Ninth Symphony. And then over the dome of the Hollywood Bowl, into the nighttime sky, dazzling, brilliant fireworks erupted in perfect time to Handel's Music for the Royal Fireworks. The negotiations, the preparations, the transformations were complete. It was time, said the spectacle and sound, for the Games of the XXIIIrd Olympiad to begin.

Colorful flags
decorate Exposition
Park.
Photo: E.
Rosenberger

Los Angeles
skyscrapers.
Photo: G. Takuc

Windsocks in Exposition Park. Photo: E. Rosenberger

National pride runs deep during volleyball competition. Photo: T. Jones

Impressions:
An Olympic Montage

Harvey Frommer

The Games of the XXIIIrd Olympiad of the Modern Era, Los Angeles, California were hype and hoopla, ceremony and celebration, anticipation and achievement. For those who were there as participants or witnesses, the feeling and the images of that summer's fortnight will forever tarry in memory.

The Soviet Union did not show and neither did most of its allies. But the People's Republic of China was there for the first time since 1952. A record number of African nations competed. And tiny countries such as Haiti and Bangladesh were represented by one athlete each. In all, contestants from 139 nations representing all the continents of the globe were in Los Angeles to partake of and take part in the most dazzling, most human of Olympics.

A preamble to the Games was the carrying of the torch from New York City to Los Angeles over the longest route in history. For 82 days over 9100 miles through 33 states, runners night and day ceremoniously transported the torch echoing the run of Pheidippides from Marathon to Athens. Crowds would congregate in front yards or at street intersections to watch runners exchange the symbolic flame. Torch-bearers rounding rural bends in the road after midnight would be greeted by farmers with lanterns and flashlights urging them on. Silent and solitary carriers of the flame were accompanied from time to time by fire engine sirens, church bells, truck horns, occasionally a lonesome bugle.

The torch run seemed to touch all who came into contact with it, causing them to identify with the roots and rituals of the Olympics. And that spirit traveled with the torch into the city of Los Angeles.

Through the early morning fragrance of the eucalyptus trees, through the heat of the California afternoons, to the sweet evenings cooled by the breezes of the Pacific Ocean— the sounds of more than 100 languages accentuated the atmosphere of people mingling with people.

On the beach at Malibu, New Zealand cyclists sat on blankets with California surfers and spoke of their pleasure at being away from the winter back home. At the Coliseum, bare chested American men engaged in friendly repartee with a well dressed contingent from Great Britain. A group of Greek athletes demonstrated their native dance at a disco and soon found themselves giving lessons to others. Volunteer hosts were taught the intricate art of using chopsticks by Chinese coaches.

"U-S-A, U-S-A, U-S-A" became a predominant chorus along with the up-beat tempo of the All American Marching Band's rendition of such American favorites as "In the Mood," "Strike Up the Band," and "Stars and Stripes Forever."

However, the USA was not the only nation to revel in its athletes' accomplishments. At a football (soccer) match at the Rose Bowl, Frenchmen waved their nation's flag and boomed "Viva La France!" Their Yugoslavian adverseries countered by chanting "Yu-Go-Slav-Ia, Yu- Go-Slav-Ia!" Romania was warmly received by predominantly American audiences. Its state television devoted more than eight hours a day to the Olympics showcasing gymnast Ecaterina Szabo, the effusive young woman who won four gold medals, and what they called their "noble weightlifters," the People's Republic of China said it hadn't returned to the Olympics for the first time in 32 years for medals but to once again be part of the Olympic family. Nevertheless, when news of the first gold medal of the Games went to CHN shooter Xu Haifong, firecrackers were set off on the streets of Beijing.

There was delight in the British Virgin Islands, Djibouti, Oman, Rwanda, the Solomon Islands, Western Samoa, and Tonga—all in the Olympics for the first time in their history. Bhutan, beamed too. That nation, so evocative of Shangri-La, located in the heart of the Himalayan Mountains, sent six archers to test their skills in that country's national sport against the best the world had to offer.

Los Angeles, the tinseled city, often criticized for being blase, went through more than a few fresh coats of paint and the draping of pastel banners. It went through a renaissance of spirit that was contagious. On the streets of Westwood, on the beachfront promenades of Santa Monica, on the campus of the University of Southern California, sophisticated Angelinos were drawn to athletes whose computer coded "F" cards hanging from their necks indicated who they were. Citizens and athletes traded pins, small talk, pleasantries.

There was a sweetness of spirit that could be seen in the little girl riding on her father's shoulders, "LA 84" flags clutched in her hands. It was there in the old yellow school buses that ferried journalists from venue to venue, where drivers, harried from contending at times with laborious traffic, still smiled at departing passengers and told them "Have a nice day." It was there in the romances: the American student from University of California at Los Angeles and the handsome Moroccan football goalie, the Egyptian athlete and the volunteer from Venice. It was there in the group of Luxembourg competitors invited to dinner by a Beverly Hills attorney, in the solitary museum visits of Mexican team member Carlos Romo who wanted to be by himself for a while, in the motorcycle escort provided by an Irish policeman for Liam O'Brien, a 3000 meter runner from Ireland who ran through the streets of Los Angeles in early morning workouts. The spirit of the Games had to be in the six Mexican amateur runners who

**Opposite Page
A runner from CIV is embraced.
Photo: T. Duffy**

The Coliseum
Peristyle and the
Olympic statues.
Photo: E.
Rosenberger

Photo: E.
Rosenberger

set off from Guadalajara by foot because they could not afford to fly to Los Angeles. They planned to run from Guadalajara to the Olympics. Three of the six made it. And the spirit found its way into the Thailand women gymnasts who arrived in Los Angeles after dark but earlier than expected. Lodged in North Hollywood for a night, they went out on the streets the next morning only to find themselves in the middle of a Thailand neighborhood. "Only in America," one of them said, "could you walk out on a strange street in a strange country and have the feeling you were in your own neighborhood."

Everywhere there was the body language of triumph, the emotion of long sought goals achieved: Sebastion Coe of Great Britain flinging his arms in the air while emitting a passionate yell after crossing the finish line to win the gold in the 1500 meters race; the Yugoslavian team handball players waving from the high step of the victory stand; American Lou Banach, riding the shoulders of his brother Ed after winning the gold medal in the 100 kg freestyle wrestling; Yashiro Yamashita of Japan being tossed unceremoniously like a ball in the air in celebration by his teammates after being awarded the gold medal in the open judo division competition; Nawal El Moutawkel, the tiny Moroccan woman, first ever from her country ever to win a medal in the Olympics, running childlike with her nation's red and green flag in the Coliseum; and her countryman, Said Aouita, gold medal winner in the steeplechase, being kissed and embraced by men in fezes prior to his victory lap around the track.

Yet winners alone were not the whole story of the 1984 Olympics. One remembers Paul Hoffman, a 73 kg. middleweight, the only weightlifter from Swaziland, a tiny country in Southeast Africa. Hoffman lifted the least weight of all the competitors in all divisions and came in last. But he made history as the first and only weightlifter from Swaziland. "Just to be here to compete," said Hoffman, "I will remember to my dying day." One remembers Francesco Nanni who placed fifth in shooting, but was exultant with his accomplishment. Nanni was part of a sixteen member delegation from San Marino, one of the oldest and smallest republics in the world. There was dancing in the streets of San Marino because native son Francesco Nanni placed higher than any other Olympian in its history.

One remembers Japanese gymnast Maiko Morio, age 17, experiencing her first Olympics. The delicate shy high school student had the misfortune of performing her maneuvers while Mary Lou Retton was earning her double tens. Although Morio's sensitive and highly proficient work was nearly obscured by the tumult caused by America's sweetheart, she carried on flawlessly. And one remembers the raw courage of William Bagonza, a light flyweight from Uganda. Clearly overmatched against USA's gold medal winner to be, Paul Gonzales, Bagonza was battered but stayed on his feet to the end. The decision went to Gonzales, 5-0, but the audience knew bravery was not only a victor's badge.

It was an Olympics of inspirational stories: Greg Barton (USA), born with club feet, undergoing four major surgeries, training at dawn's light in Homer Lake, Michigan, prevailing to win the bronze in men's kayaking; Neroli Fairhall, a paraplegic at age 24 after a motorcycle accident, entering the Coliseum on a wheelchair 15 years later to take part in Opening Ceremonies, primed to compete as a member of New Zealand's archery team; Jim Martinson (USA), once a downhill racer with Olympic aspirations who lost both legs in a land-mine explosion in Vietnam, competing in wheelchair race, one of the events offered for the physically disabled for the first time.

Another human drama was personified by USA cyclist Nelson Vails who won the silver medal. The 24-year-old Vails lived most of his life in the slums of Harlem. He became aware of his talents biking through the streets of Manhattan delivering messages to earn a living. One of the few black cyclists, Vails competed in the Olympics wearing a helmet with the skyline of New York painted on it.

Unique individual confrontations provided high drama. For months the showdown between Mary Decker of the United States and Zola Budd of Great Britain had been ballyhooed. There were those who were critical of the 18-year-old Budd who switched her citizenship from South African to British. Enmity toward the racial policies of South Africa was directed at the 38 kg. athlete.

"Apartheid began before I was born and will probably only be resolved long after I die," said Budd. "In the meantime, I just want to run. I will run and race against anyone, anywhere, of any color, any time. And may the fastest win."

The showdown between Budd and Decker in the 3000 meter never fully materialized. There was a moment of silence in the Coliseum as the two women running stride for stride suddenly became tangled. Decker wound up lying prone in the infield; Budd faltered, and Romanian Maricica Puica, twice Budd's age, blonde hair flying, won the race.

Another publicized match-up was between Dwight Stones (USA) and Zhu Jianhua (CHN) in the high jump, favorites to win this event. Neither was around in the duel for the gold at the end. The 31-year-old Stones blew kisses to the throng at the Coliseum when he was eliminated in the competition and lost a chance at a medal. The high jump event continued with Sweden's Patrik Sjoberg confronting Federal Republic of Germany's Dietmar Moegenburg. The 19-year-old Swedish jumper, his style so reminiscent of Stones, was eliminated. And it was left for Moegenburg to confront himself and the high bar as he set a new Olympic record and won the gold medal.

The luck of the draw matched total opposites against each other. In Greco-Roman wrestling, for example, Frank Andersson (SWE) was pitted against Steven Fraser (USA). Their meeting at the mat also matched different life styles. Andersson, a playboy type, is often featured in Swedish magazines while gold medal winner Fraser, whose wife was expecting, is a deputy sheriff in Ann Arbor, Michigan.

The L.A. Games broke new ground with women confronting women and tradition itself. Seventeen new sports were added—13 for women that included: the marathon, 3000 meter race, 400 meter hurdles, synchronized swimming, three rifle competitions, rhythmic gymnastics, individual road racing in cycling, and kayak fours. These pioneering events for women were part of an Olympic of firsts.

Austria achieved its first gold medal in judo as Peter Seisenbacher defeated Robert Berland (USA), who in losing gave the USA its first silver. New Zealand captured its first equestrian medal while Brazil notched its first football medal, a silver. There was a first-time tie in swimming as Nancy Hogshead and Carrie Steinseifer of the USA swam for the co-gold medal in the 100m freestyle. It was also an Olympics that produced the first woman basketball official, the first woman skipper in yachting, the first diver in history to break 700 on the platform, the first gold medal winner for Canada in women's springboard diving. And Valerie Brisco-Hooks became the first woman to win both the 200 meter and 400 meter races in the same Olympics.

Numbers numbed the mind. More people watched the Games of the XXIIIrd Olympiad on television than any other event in the history of the world. More than six million spectators, another world record, attended the Games. Football at the Rose Bowl attracted over 100,000 for one game surpassing the record for the largest crowd in North American football history. Baseball at Dodger Stadium set new records for attendance. The championship game between the USA and Japan drew just one thousand fans less than the all-time record for a single game achieved by the Los Angeles Dodgers in a World Series game.

Donald Duck turned 50 midway through the Games, and more than 3000 athletes were admitted free as guests of Disneyland. A total of 687 medals were awarded in 229 ceremonies at 16 different venues. The USA had the largest athletic delegation, 614 athletes participated in 24 sports while tiny Andora had but two athletes in just one sport.

Athletes representing approximately 140 nations and 23 sports consumed over 20,000 meals a day prepared by 135 chefs. There were 17,000 security officers.

Despite the staggering statistics of the Los Angeles Games, it is the individual moments that linger. There was 88-year-old Owen Churchill, wistfully watching the yachting race, eyeing the "Angelita"—the same 8 meter craft he sailed to a gold medal in 1932 in the first Olympic Games at Los Angeles. There was Al Joyner, the USA's first triple jump gold medalist since 1904, rooting for his sister Jackie from the infield at the Coliseum. There was "Johnny Mack," out of the Australian bush, the only pinto—painted horse in the Olympics, an oddball among all the sleek steeds in the Equestrian events. There was the young Australian journalist, who understood so well the innate relationship between horse and rider. "They communicate in their own language," she said. "When the horse moves his ears back, he's saying to the rider, 'Tell me what to do, tell me what to do.'"

The myriad moods of the people in Los Angeles also remain in memory: the enthusiastic, clean-cut crowds at Pauley Pavilion relishing gymnastics; the passionate partisan multitudes at the Rose Bowl so totally involved in football; the well-dressed family groups with their neat picnic hampers enjoying a morning's rowing race at Lake Casitas; the boisterous thousands at the Los Angeles Sports Arena savoring the flash and fury of a super heavyweight bout; the young, dynamic urbans at the Forum immersed in run-and-gun basketball; the cosmopolitans gathered in the sun at the Olympic Swim Stadium savoring the breathtaking grace and acrobatic skills of the divers. Composed and raucous, rabid and serene, chauvinistic and international, astute sports fans and those with a nodding aquaintance with athletics, they made up a magnificent montage of people from many countries and walks of life who had assembled to bear witness in the warmth of cameraderie.

Cynics notwithstanding, George Orwell's 1984 never materialized. Neither did the smog, the traffic jam, the security problems. Some said it would be a three ring circus. But the Games of the XXIIIrd Olympiad at Los Angeles turned out to be the greatest show on earth.

Mary Decker (USA)
is consoled by
Richard Stanley.
Photo: T. Duffy

Left to Right

Anderson-Scheiss
(SUI) struggles to
finish women's
marathon.
Photo: T. Duffy

Zola Budd (GBR) in
3000 meters.
Photo: T. Duffy

Olympic Arts Festival:
A Celebration of the Spirit

Richard Stayton

Now all must realize this Festival is like none other seen in this country!

Robert J. Fitzpatrick stood in the aisle of the Pasadena Civic Auditorium and applauded while shouting through the tumult. Exhausted dancers, their soiled costumes dangling in shreds after violent choreography, bowed to the audience and to isolated boos. Under their bare feet lay 160 cubic feet of peat moss, its fertile aroma circulating throughout the 3000-seat theater to hover over the gowns and tuxedos of the gala night audience. The Pina Bausch Wuppertaler Tanztheater from the Federal Republic of Germany had covered the stage with moist earth for their primitive version of Stravinsky's "Rite of Spring," then planned on burying it the next night with real grass, and finally 400 pounds of dried leaves. And so Fitzpatrick had much to celebrate and applaud.

This was June 1, 1984, and after 300,000 miles of air travel, four years negotiating 130 contracts with 18 countries in a myriad of languages, the Olympic Arts Festival (OAF) had at last opened as its director Fitzpatrick planned: to controversy.

"That opening night audience was expecting a pretty dance," Fitzpatrick would comment nine weeks later on the eve of the Festival's final presentation. "And that first night I watched the sense of panic, disbelief, and anger when they first saw Bausch. And yet we only had about 150 people who walked out. But the word went around that this was the most irritating, provocative experience, and people who hated it are haunted by it. We had to open the Festival with a daring, challenging company which crossed all artistic boundaries, merging every one of the arts within one frame. By taking such a risk we sent the audience a message: to expect the unexpected."

Expect the unexpected indeed. Pina Bausch was just the first of ten Festival weeks conceived as a joyful prelude to and celebration of the Games of the XXIIIrd Olympiad, beginning June 1 and ending the last day of competition on August 12. Los Angeles would host over 427 performances by 145 companies in 12 languages, 24 visual exhibitions and seven minifestivals.

All this culture in Los Angeles, a city already speaking 83 languages but with only a single internationally recognized cultural landmark: mammoth letters on a hillside spelling "HOLLYWOOD." Many experts prophesied a San Andreas cultural fault of foreigners babbling in obscure tongues to empty seats.

But in 1980, when the LAOOC search team recommended Fitzpatrick as Festival Director, they were encouraging an unusually ambitious Festival for America.

Fitzpatrick insisted the Festival reflect the ideals of the fifth century B.C. Olympics, immortalized by Pindar, when all political conflicts were suspended. Despite Rule 34 of the Olympic Charter mandating an Arts Festival conducted in a spirit of international cooperation, Fitzpatrick recalled the 1936 Berlin games when art became a tool of Nazi propaganda. LAOOC President Peter Ueberroth guaranteed Fitzpatrick complete independence except for one command: "Make it good." A $5 million grant by the Times-Mirror Company allowed Fitzpatrick freedom to take risks in programming.

The Music Centre, the Mark Taper Forum in theater, Bella Lewitzky's The Dance Gallery, and the Los Angeles County Museum of Art assisted in co-production and selection. The Los Angeles International Film Exposition (Filmex), a preexisting festival, moved back its normal scheduling dates in order to be an official Olympic participant. Fitzpatrick wanted the People's Republic of China represented in the Festival because 1984 would be the first Chinese Olympic appearance since 1952. He flew to China and traveled by train between freezing theaters, at last signing the Chengdu Acrobatic Troupe and the Central Ensemble of National Music, two companies tracing their art back over 2000 years. During the delicate signing stage, a Chinese ambassador to the United States invited Fitzpatrick back in the year 2005, when both would be 65, to sit on the Great Wall together and discuss where each country's development had led.

But politics between the two countries, often volatile, did not infringe. When a Chinese tennis professional left her team to request political asylum, the OAF feared that China would veto its Arts Festival participation. But then they received a call from a Chinese official: "These threats to pull out of the Olympics do not apply to our being in your Festival." Such an international spirit of cooperation characterized the majority of contractual negotiations.

During intermission at Covent Garden, Fitzpatrick met up with Sir John Tooley, General Director of the Royal Opera. Tooley suggested the Royal Opera be a Festival participant. The world famous opera company not only came to the United States for the first time, it premiered a new production of "Turandot"—the first Royal Opera premiere ever outside London.

Luck assisted in bringing to the Los Angeles County Museum of Art the major Festival exhibition "A Day in the Country: Impressionism and the French Landscape." Discovering that the Louvre was constructing a new museum in Paris to house its 19th century collection, the OAF reasoned that the new museum would not realize its projected opening date in 1984 and succeeded in obtaining Impressionist paintings which had never before been exhibited outside of France.

**Opposite Page
Theatre du Soleil,
Shakespearean
drama spoken in
French.
Photo: Courtesy OAF**

An actor entertains
in the Festival of
Masks.
Photo: Courtesy OAF

Freeway walls
became decorative
murals.
Photo: Courtesy OAF

Previous Olympic Arts Festivals had either been only during the games and therefore were eclipsed and forgotten by the Games, or stretched over a year. In either case, the Festival impact was negligible. OAF decided to compress the Festival into an intense ten weeks, with the first seven showcasing international companies and art for primarily local audience, and the last three focusing on American art for the expected crush of international visitors. All theater, requiring more traffic for prop and company movement, would cease a week prior to the Opening Ceremonies. In addition, theater's style and energy competed with a game atmosphere, whereas dance complemented the physical grace of athletics, and so the final two weeks would offer only dance events plus some exhibition openings.

To overcome the vast distances that separated Festival sites in Los Angeles, the strategists came up with clever tricks. A series of mural paintings were commissioned for the freeways, and rainbows of color haunted the retinae of passing motorists, psychologically reminding them that they were in the midst of a Festival. At each event site one discovered identical symbols and colors: "festive federalism," it was called. It was visible in the form of hues on huge stars, pillars, confetti and flags. And there was the ticket brochure, designed like a lush Williams-Sonoma catalogue, inviting the public to purchase tickets as beautiful gifts. Who could resist?

The catalogue cover depicted the Festival's official image: an actor's mirror reflection as he applied make-up to his already whitened face. His gesture implied that soon the Festival would help the United States of America find a new way to see itself. France's Le Theatre du Soleil, the first Festival entry performing completely in a foreign language, evoked this implication. Staging foreign language theater without simultaneous translation had been called by OAF's critics "the ultimate suicidal gesture," especially when they are Kabuki-style Shakespearean productions, as were Le Theatre du Soleil's. The company's artistic director, Ariane Mnouchkine, required her ensemble to literally sprint on-and-off a 48.5 meter long stage while shouting lines. In true Olympic tradition, the company spent half its rehearsal time in Paris doing physical training. But Mnouchkine's versions of Shakespeare's "Richard II," "Twelfth Night," and "Henry IV, Part 1" lasted over four hours each! Americans would sit still for this?

"I just couldn't sit still during the first performance," remembers Fitzpatrick of Le Theatre du Soleil's American premiere at the Festival. Every time I heard a creak in the bleacher seats, I thought five or six-hundred people were simultaneously rising to walk out. I kept trying to figure out how I was going to explain this to Mnouchkine and to my family and the press."

But no one left the theater. During intermission, the actors were visible in their dressing rooms just beyond structural frames. The public gazed at the actors gazing at themselves in the dressing-room mirrors—just like the official Festival poster predicted. When the opening night performance was over, Fitzpatrick rushed to congratulate Mnouchkine.

"I thought he was lying," Mnouchkine later admitted. "I thought Fitzpatrick was just being kind and we were a miserable failure." Mnouchkine and her players were used to the Europeans' rhythmic style of applause to display approval and assumed the American whistles were derisive.

Le Theatre du Soleil became the Festival's "must see" production, while across town on the University of California at Los Angeles campus, the Royal Shakespeare Company's more traditional interpretation of "Much Ado About Nothing" also created sold-out audiences and frantic efforts to find tickets. For the final Sunday of "Twelfth Night," hopeful attendees began lining up at the theater box office at 4 a.m., trying to get any cancellations.

Suddenly the Festival euphoria was contagious. The standing ovations given Le Theatre du Soleil and the Royal Shakespeare Company spread. Applause at the dance events

so disturbed Fitzpatrick that he considered making an announcement before performances requesting that the audience not applaud until a movement was concluded. But renowned dancer and choreographer Merce Cunningham said to him, "Relax and do nothing. I think it's wonderful. You're getting people here who don't know 'when' or 'how' it's appropriate to applaud. You're getting first timers. People who have never seen live dance before are coming out!"

The Festival literally taught the "laid back" audiences of California how to give standing ovations, and it reminded the sophisticated visitors how exciting fresh, spontaneous viewing can be. In parties all over Los Angeles, it wasn't the latest Hollywood gossip which fueled conversations, it was—unbelievably—Shakespeare. The Bard was back, and his texts lay open on laps as audiences carefully followed the foreign company's performances.

The OAF advisors decided that if one were to enlist foreign language productions, then the key to understanding for Americans would be familiar stories. Shakespeare appeared more than once, and Italy's Piccolo Tiatro di Milano's "The Tempest" stole the hearts and breaths of thousands while Ariel floated high above the Royce Hall stage on a thin wire.

Another source of familiar stories, the ancient Greek tragedies, brought more than audiences together. At one point at UCLA, two adjacent theaters simultaneously offered Greek classics. Japan's Waseda Sho-Gekijo presented a Noh version of Euripedes' "The Trojan Women" while L.A. Theatre Works performed an all-black version of Aeschylus' "Agamemnon." During intermissions, the two companies shared the same dressing area where blacks and Orientals discovered each other in the true Olympic spirit of brotherhood.

Australia's wild big top punk music crew named "Circus Oz" created such a sensation with their acrobatics that an independent producer invited them to perform after the Festival in Los Angeles. Three-thousand miles from home, they unexpectedly searched for temporary housing, and members of the Festival staff provided them with places to stay. Suddenly, they watched as Circus Oz acrobats with punk haircuts floated in a pool, discoursing with a Royal Opera diva lying on a divan.

The Festival turned all of Los Angeles into a stage. A team of medieval flag-wavers from Italy would appear and disappear at various locations demonstrating their colorful Renaissance art of baton twirling—only with flags. Japan's Sankaijuku lowered themselves upside down by ropes from the Dorothy Chandler Pavilion before an open-mouthed noon hour crowd. Their bodies nude except for a loincloth and their heads shaved, powdered white with ash, they dropped to the public plaza and wriggled back inside the Pavilion and disappeared.

But an exchange relationship also was established. Pina Bausch performers marvelled at late night television, a luxury unavailable in the Federal Republic of Germany, and became expert mimics of car salesmen. All visiting companies attended Disneyland. Of course, some also took tours of the movie stars' homes . . . including Pina Bausch herself.

By the eve of the competitive Games, the Festival had achieved its goal: "To be a celebration of the spirit, making us realize that I have eyes to see and ears to hear."

Nowhere was that message delivered with more poetry than at the Hollywood Bowl before over 18,000 with "Prelude to the Olympics: A Gala Concert." While the Los Angeles Philharmonic Orchestra played Aaron Copland's Symphony No. 3—composed during World War Two's darkest days as a promise of peace—architect Frank Gehry's choreographed searchlights danced their beams over the night's sky. Their movement, in tune with Copland's soaring music, intentionally recalled the searchlights of World War Two to provide a message for our own era of peace.

The Festival began easing its schedule during the games, yet remained a potent companion reflecting the Olympics. Dance events continued to sell out. The American Tap show

at the Japan American Theatre brought together surviving dancers from a purely American art, tap dancing. And the Pasadena Civic Auditorium, where the Festival began with Pina Bausch, played host to sell-out audiences of over 3000 a night, to witness Twyla Tharp's final public dance, "Fait Accompli." The 41-year- old experimental choreographer publicly announced that her body could not endure the strain of pure dance any longer and composed "Fait Accompli" as an artistic farewell. Her athletic choreography led muscular men and lithe women dancing through clouds of thick steam. When she stepped out of the mists, her choreography required an exhibition of doubt and declining strength. To the sold-out audience witnessing her final live performance, many remembered that morning's women's marathon, the first ever. Joan Benoit had won, but the more memorable image remained that of Gabriela Andersen-Schiess lurching out of the tunnel and onto the Coliseum's track, only to collapse at at the finish line. The two events merged into one—that ancient race, the marathon, named after a great Greek victory from the fifth century B.C.—and the dancer's struggle to say goodbye to her art. In both it was the human drama which captured the imagination.

Members of the
Korean National
Dance Company.
Photo: Courtesy OAF

Performers in the
Theatre Sans
Fils in a puppet
presentation.
Photo. Courtesy OAF

The Games

"...they shall dive, and they shall run...and hurl their lances in the sun." Alfred Noyes

Archery: The Quiet Sport

Richard Sapp

It is the quiet sport of the Olympic games. At its venue, there are hushed conversations rather than cheering crowds. Athletes, spectators, and coaches lean across the railings and peer from beneath colorful umbrella stands to watch participants who are deep in an inner well of concentration, focusing their minds and mastering their bodies. Here are the finest athletes in the world, yet they are known only within their sport. They neither seek nor expect wealth, fame, or a lasting memorial to their having competed at all. They compete only to see a name, a country, and a final score set in small type at the bottom of a long list in a volume of Olympic records. This is the fate even of gold medalists who live in relative obscurity until the next Olympic trials. The sport is archery—the quiet sport of the Olympic Games.

World class archery competition is often described as if it were a meditative rather than an athletic event. The uninformed or disinterested compare it to watching grass grow or paint dry. The mechanics are deceptive for they appear to be simple. But it is the unseen, the mind training, the alert relaxation, the effortless control of breathing, the emptying of the mind, the awareness of the heartbeat—it is a wholly self-imposed discipline that makes one man and one woman the very best in the world. American archer Rick McKinney has described this state of mind as "not even being in this world."

At the Games of the XXIIIrd Olympiad, the best in the world were Darrell Pace (USA) and Hyang-Soon Seo (KOR). Hyang-Soon Seo represented a strong archery team from one of a number of outstanding Asian national contingents competing in Los Angeles. For years, KOR has developed its archery training program, and its women have emerged as the top female team in the world. Archery was one event which the Soviet Union and their boycotting allies would not have significantly influenced.

Pre-Olympic publicity highlighted the race for the men's gold medal between Pace—a seven time USA men's champion, two time world champion and 1976 Olympic gold medalist—and fellow American Rick McKinney—a six time USA men's champion and two-time world champion. It was expected they would duel to the last arrow as they had in the 1983 World Championship Games, where McKinney defeated Pace by one point on the final arrow. But for the Olympics, it was not to be.

Pace, who McKinney has described as a "shooting machine" turned in an unbelievable second round after tying McKinney for the lead in the first 36 arrows. By the end of the first day, Pace led McKinney by 13 points and was never headed. Before the competition was concluded, he led by 50

points and had set a new Olympic record of 2616 points breaking his previous mark set in 1976 in Montreal.

Pace's outstanding performance overshadowed the struggle between McKinney and Hiroshi Yamamoto of Japan for the silver medal. Into the final 36 arrow set at 30 meters, Yamamoto maintained a slim advantage. Perhaps McKinney, a resident of Glendale, Arizona, better understood the sultry heat of Southern California, because in the final set of arrows Yamamoto lost his concentration and settled for the bronze medal not far ahead of his countryman, Takayoshi Matsushita.

For Pace, the victory was bittersweet. "There's no money to be made in archery," he said. An electronics technician by profession, this quiet champion has trained for the past two years, while his wife, Beth Ann, has supported the family working as a hair dresser. And Pace has already announced that he expects to be the favorite in Seoul, Korea, in 1988, at the Games of the XXIVth Olympiad.

Months before Pace won his second gold, former USA Olympic Archery Coach Al Henderson predicted a KOR victory in the women's event. The favorite at that time, was Jin-Ho Kim who eventually took the bronze. The gold went to her teammate Hyang-Soon Seo; the silver to Li Lingjuan of the People's Republic of China.

Although it received scant publicity in the USA and Europe, the women's competition was intense. The standings seemed to shuffle during each round. After a near disastrous opening round, Li was mired in 15th place; but she soon fought her way to the top and held on. After three days, it appeared she was headed for the top—then the Koreans punched gold and Li settled for silver.

But in the Olympics and certainly in the quiet sport, it is not only the medalists who are victors. The archer competes intensely with himself. His art transcends technique and arises from the archer's unconscious. If this is true for the able bodied athlete, it is more so for the handicapped archer. Although she finished well down the lists, Neroli Fairhall of Christchurch, New Zealand scored a great victory for all archers, all athletes. Fairhall, a paraplegic, had been confined to a wheelchair for 15 years since a motorcycle accident ended her career as an equestrian. Fairhall, using the same equipment as other archers on the line, was as much an Olympic champion as Pace or any other gold medal winner. Perhaps she knew Olympic gold was beyond her reach, but to her credit she never showed it. From the opening ceremonies when she wheeled into the Coliseum in her blue New Zealand blazer and white slacks, through the final arrow and the last fireworks of the Closing Ceremonies, she was a champion.

Under the auspices of the Federation International de Tir

**Opposite Page
Pace (USA) on the way to his second Olympic gold medal.
Photo: D. Cannon**

a l'Arc (FITA), Olympic archery competition is a grueling 20-hour test of stamina, concentration and control—or "muscle memory." Each day for four days, competitors shoot 72 arrows. On the first and third days, men shoot sets of 36 arrows at 90 and at 70 meters; women shoot at 70 and 60 meters. On days two and four, men and women shoot 36 arrows each at 50 and 30 meters.

It is, of course, the longer distances which separate the Olympic and world class competitors from those who are only "very good." At 90 meters, the target looks about the size of a half dollar and the bullseye, 11.4 cm in diameter at that range is only a pinpoint which the archer's pin sight covers.

FITA rules also govern equipment allowed on the shooting line. Archers draw recurve bows, men pulling 18-20 kilograms and women 13-15 kilograms. The modern recurve design is based on an ancient form used by the Turks for shooting from horseback. Up to four stabilizing rods may project from the handle of the bow; these fiberglass, graphite, or aluminum rods absorb vibration and reduce bow torque upon arrow release. The maze of gleaming rods, limbs, sights and arrows at the equipment and shooting lines resembles nothing so much as a pipe fitter's dream.

Virtually all arrows used in world class competition today are metallic anodized, precision drawn aluminum shafts. Shot from a 18.675 kilograms, such an arrow travels at an average speed of 202-217 km per hour.

To control a single shot, archers perform seven distinct, rhythmic functions: they take a comfortable stance; they grip the bow firmly but without tension; they fit the arrow to the string; they clear their minds of all thought and feeling. They then draw the bow and anchor beneath their chin. Making the final aiming point adjustment through their forward mounted peep sight, they concentrate on the sight pin. Finally, they loosen their three-finger grip on the Kevlar synthetic string and the arrow releases. A smooth, simultaneous release is crucial. The bow hand must be steady and in the follow-through position; the archer must remain momentarily in the status quo while the bow rocks forward. Gold medalist Pace calls this concentrated effort, "lashing the body to the bow."

Jim Easton, LAOOC Commissioner of Archery, was keenly aware of the intricate relationship between the Olympics and world archery competition. "Archery would probably be one-tenth the size it is today without the Olympic games," he said. In Los Angeles, 35 nations, 109 archers were represented at the shooting line. Included in the original Games of the Modern Era, dropped in 1920, and later reinstated, archery is today a permanent Olympic fixture.

The "double FITA" round shot by the world's Olympic

archers is the marathon event of the sport. Still, there was only applause for the medalists, no victory laps with a national flag before a hundred-thousand cheering spectators and no storm of reporters and photographers. The athletes in El Dorado Park knew, nevertheless, they were all winners, all champions, all the finest in the world.

Dr. Helen Bolnick, co-director of the USA National Archery Association's college division perhaps said it best: "Go to the Olympics and you see the very best, the very best in the world. It's absolutely breathtaking." And it was.

Athletics: Bound For Glory

Mark D. Levine

To the hundreds of thousands who were lucky enough to be in the Los Angeles Memorial Coliseum for ten days in August 1984 when athletic events were being contested, and to the millions who watched on television, the men's running competition was filled with all the drama and excitement one would expect when the best from around the world gather to compete against each other.

There was the expected and the unexpected. Names of heroes of the Games—those who achieved the ultimate success captured the cherished gold medals—became household words. By now who hasn't heard of Carl Lewis or Edwin Moses? Sebastian Coe of Great Britain, and fellow countryman Steve Cram, gold and silver medal winners of the 1500 meter race, proved beyond a doubt that Great Britain still dominates that distance. Once again, Europeans demonstrated that the distance events—the 10,000 meters and the marathon—are not controlled by USA runners. Conversely, Carl Lewis in both the 100 meter and the 200 meter events, Alonzo Babers in the 400 meter race, and the USA in the 4x400 meter relays proved that the sprints are wholly American. The list of heroes is as long as the roster of gold medal winners in the 13 men's running events.

Where there are winners, however, there are losers. To the many who never made it to the victory stand, there is a special agony. Alberto Salazar of the USA and Rob de Castella of AUS were both considered favorites in the marathon. Yet, seemingly out of nowhere, a 37-year-old Portuguese runner, Carlos Lopes, won in an Olympic record time. Fernando Mamedo, also of POR, expected to do well in the 10,000 meter, did not finish. Henry Marsh of the USA, thought to be a potential gold medalist in the steeplechase, collapsed in fourth place at the finish line, and Steve Ovett of GBR, a favorite in the 800 meter and 1500 meter races, went home with nothing.

No chronicle of the Games of the XXIIIrd Olympiad would be complete without giving full credit to the phenomenal performance of Carl Lewis. He achieved his goal of securing four gold medals—equaling Jesse Owens' accomplishment in the 1936 Berlin Games. And although most journeys begin with a small step, Carl Lewis' began with a giant stride the day after the start of track and field.

The sun was strong as the crowd waited patiently for the first of the Lewis spectaculars. Even the unfamiliar knew of the 23-year-old legend. He had been featured on the cover of major international magazines, and his accomplishments had been hailed by politicians and sportsmen alike. With upwards of 90,000 spectators in the stands of the Los Angeles Coliseum, Lewis had to perform. He had promised the world he was going after Jesse Owens' record. Should Lewis not

grab the gold in the 100 meter dash—so early in athletics competition—there would be no reason to spotlight him through the following eight days.

While Lewis was mentally and physically prepared for the final event, it was not necessarily a cinch that he would win. After all, there was talented competition in the finals, not the least of which was his teammate Sam Graddy. After his heats in which he qualified for the finals in the dash, Graddy said, "I am going to do everything I can do to stop Carl from getting four gold medals. I think my name is written on the medal as much as his."

As the 100 meter men walked onto track, the crowd was in a frenzy. Throughout the stadium, only two chants could be heard: "U-S-A, U-S-A" and "Lewis, Lewis, Lewis." Other contenders received warm applause: Graddy, Ron Brown (USA), and Ben Johnson (CAN) who would prove to be a formidable foe. Within 9.99 seconds it was clear that no one would grab the gold from Lewis. Graddy, in the lead for the first 50 meters, made an admirable attempt. The second 50 meters was a different story. Lewis blew past Graddy, who was able to maintain his second place for a silver medal.

"This is by far the toughest event for me because so much can happen. I get so emotional when I win the 100 because it is the most difficult of the four in which I am competing," Lewis said after his race. "One down and three to go!" Lewis' exuberance— clearly demonstrated when he snatched a large USA flag from a spectator in the stands and took a victory lap—was understandable, not only in terms of his own goals, but because the 9.99 seconds provided the largest margin of victory in this event in Olympic history. When he stepped onto the awards platform in the number one position for the awarding of the gold medal, Carl Lewis was clearly in control.

His fans didn't have to wait too long for the second feat in his quadruple quest. Two days after his 100 meter victory, Lewis achieved another gold in the long jump with an impressive 8.54 meter leap.

After the long jump competition, Lewis promised that the next day's 200 meter final would be the best race of his life. He kept his promise by achieving an Olympic record of 19.80 seconds, and beat teammates Kirk Baptiste who won the silver and Thomas Jefferson who earned the bronze. With three down, one to go, Lewis was confident. He had a few days in-between until the last of the four—the 4x100 meter relays—time to take a much needed rest. Lewis' coach, Tom Tellez, had urged the runner to take a breather. "He looked a little bit tired and sluggish in the 200 meters," Tellez said. "Kirk (Baptiste) was coming after him at the end. It could have been the fatigue he felt coming on the long jump."

**Opposite Page
Lewis (USA) won
four gold medals.
Photo: S. Powell**

The crowd was waiting impatiently for the final of the Lewis streak. When the relay event finally took place, and Lewis, along with team members Ron Brown, Sam Graddy, and Calvin Smith, achieved the gold, the crowd was ecstatic, especially because a new world record time of 37.83 was set. Lewis stood proudly on victory platform number one while "The Star Spangled Banner" was played. Three times earlier in the week, he had been there. This time, however, he was standing not only for himself and his country, but for history as well.

Was there ever any doubt that Edwin Moses would take the gold in the 400 meter hurdles? The senior statesman of men's track and field events hadn't lost a race since 1977, and by the 1984 Olympic Games had recorded 104 victories.

The 90,000 persons in the stands roared their approval as Moses moved toward the blocks. A few months earlier at the USA Olympic trials, the noise of the crowd and "whirr" of the cameras caused the runner to have a false start. In international competition, two false starts means disqualification. Now, once again photographers' cameras began their customary "whirr", and Moses reacted by jumping the gun. Unlike the Olympic trials, however, the judges refused to charge him with a false start, blaming the noise from the cameras instead. When the gun went off again, the Moses reaction was the same as it had been in the 104 previous races he had won.

Running and hurdling next to him on the track were some of the best in the world, including 20-year-old Danny Harris (USA) and the Federal Republic of Germany's Harald Schmid, the only hurdler to have beaten Moses since 1976. They could have been formidable competition. What actually happened, though, was a repeat of eight years of 400 meter hurdle history. Moses easily finished first. The real battle in this race was for the silver. Harris clocked a fast 48.13, and Schmid picked up the bronze in 48.19, but not before protesting that Harris had bumped him several times before the finish. The protest was disallowed. Moses admitted afterwards that he was very nervous before the event. Why, he was asked, would an athlete who has won 104 straight races be nervous? "Because," he said, "number 105 was for the gold."

For years, Greg Foster was considered to be the only choice for the gold in the 110-meter hurdles. Track fans around the world knew it. His family knew it. He knew it. But dreams can die as well as come true in Olympic Games. And Foster's dream died when he came in second to teammate Roger Kingdom.

Still, it was grace, never a Foster trademark, that characterized his behavior when the gold medal eluded him. "As long as it was another American, it was fine with me," he said after his race. Was the loss hard to take? "It would have been a little easier had I won the gold," he admitted. An upset always leads to retrospection. Foster blamed his loss on what he considered at the time to be a false start by Finland's Arto Bryggare, the eventual bronze medal winner. However no false start was called by the judges. Foster's hesitation may have very well cost him the gold, especially since he finished a mere three hundredths of a second behind Kingdom (13.20 vs. 13.23 seconds).

As for Kingdom, he was as surprised as Foster with his victory. He did not even realize he had won until the playback screen in the Coliseum told the real story. "The win lets me know I am a world class hurdler," Kingdom said after the race. Coming from the mouth of a gold medalist, this should rank as the understatement of the 1984 Games.

One of the up-and-coming names in the international athletics arena is that of Joaquim Cruz of Brazil. There was anticipation that he might excel in either the 800 meter or 1500 meter race. As it turned out, a virus required him to scratch from the list of runners in the 1500, but not before he had demonstrated his prowess by winning the gold in the 800 meter against strong opposition.

"Cruz is a supreme champion," said Sebastian Coe who won the silver medal. The champion, in fact, had run the 800 meter in a shattering 1:43, breaking an Olympic record by half a second. Considering his early training was on the football (soccer) field—as is the case with many Brazilian athletes—his accomplishment is all the more incredible. Cruz discovered track almost by accident. He demonstrated promising skill in the 800 meter and 1500 meter despite the relative unpopularity of these events in Brazil. After emigration to the USA, he managed to pass an English examination that allowed him to enter the University of Oregon. Regardless of where he lives, as a Brazilian citizen he is allowed to compete for his country—and compete he did.

Despite the fact that Cruz had won all his preliminary rounds in this event, nothing was taken for granted. Certainly Coe and the USA's Earl Jones would offer substantial competition, and there was a possibility he would be challenged by Ed Koech of Kenya. When the gun sounded, however, it didn't take long to see who was the master of this event.

Great Britain continued its tradition of domination in the 1500 meter race with a gold by Coe and a silver by Cram. The other potential winner, mile record holder Steve Ovett, was ill and did not finish. "It was an extremely satisfying victory," Coe said. "The whole year has been as much a mental battle as a physical one. To make a comeback is one thing. To do it in an Olympic year, with all the jitters . . . I'm elated I finished up this way."

The comeback to which he referred was particularly impressive after a long series of back-of-the-pack races. Knowing that he is, as a British Broadcasting Company newsman called him after he won the 1500, a "racing machine," Coe entered the hospital for tests. They revealed a case of toxoplasmosis, a disease similar to mononucleosis but of greater severity. After a recuperation period of seven months, Coe resumed running. Coe's running battles were not only with other track stars but with the British media with whom he had enjoyed a love-hate relationship over the years. His bowing gesture in his moment of triumph, directed at the British media, was an ironic bit of body language.

Some of the legendary runners of all time, have came from Africa (Abebe Bikila, Kip Keino and Ben Jipcho). But the running events of the 1984 Olympics revealed a substantial change in that trend. Kenya could not afford to purchase television broadcasting rights for the Games and, as a result, the only video coverage seen in that country was provided gratis by the BBC, which amounted to about an hour a night. However, there was one major exception to the dearth of top African distance runners. That occurred in the 3000 meter steeplechase, a race that rendered a major upset to the United

Opposite Page
Cruz (BRA) won a gold medal in the 800M.
Photo: T. Duffy

Cruz (BRA) takes a victory lap.
Photo: T. Duffy

States of America. The expected favorite, Henry Marsh, did not even win a medal, whereas Kenyan Julius Korir demonstrated that Africans still are a major international track force. Hardly an unknown, Korir exploded onto the international racing scene when he won the Commonwealth Games in Brisbane, Australia in 1982. He earned his victory at these Games the hardway: with an electrifying 58 second sprint for 417 meters of his last lap. He came off the final water jump a step ahead of Marsh and high- stepped for the final straightaway. His final time of 8:11.80 was half a second under Marsh's American record.

The Kenyan gold medal was followed by a silver for Joseph Mamoud of France, and a bronze for Brian Diemer of the USA. The big story, though—Henry Marsh—was an illustration of how anything can happen in a meet. In the world championships in Helsinki in 1983, Marsh tripped over the final hurdle and lost what would have undoubtedly been a medal. In 1980, of course, he shared the same fate as other American athletes, and in 1979 he missed the world cup because of a bout with mononucleosis. In these Games, too, he fell victim to a virus that had been hopping from family member to family member in his household. Marsh collapsed at the finish line at the end of the final race and was taken away by ambulance attendants; his condition was diagnosed as extreme fatigue triggered by a virus.

The distance events, in general, disrupted what seemed like a preponderance of an American sweep of running events. First there was the steeplechase. Then came the victory in the 5000 meters by Said Aouita of Morocco, the first gold medal in men's athletics for that North African nation. The victory must have made Morocco's King Hassan feel the gift of $30,000 he gave to each of the athletes prior to the Games was a good investment. The money was allocated to the athletes to support themselves while training. It paid off in the case of Aouita, whose 13:05.59 set an Olympic record for 5000 meters. The gold medal offered an opportunity for the Moroccan to proudly display his national flag while taking a victory lap. Shortly thereafter, he received a phone call from his king. "I am dedicating the victory to the African continent, the Arabian countries, and especially to my country, which will not sleep tonight waiting for the news," he proclaimed.

Celebration was rampant in other parts of the globe during the big ten days. In Italy, there was dancing in the streets when Alberto Cova won the second longest race in the Games, the 10,000 meter. His victory climaxed athletics' triple crown: the 1982 European championship and the 1983 world championships and, now, the Olympic Games. His gold medal wasn't a big surprise to veteran athletics watchers who have seen how he manages to run strong, tactical races. What was a surprise is that another favorite in the 10,000, Fernando Mamede of Portugal, who only a few weeks earlier had set a world record in the 10,000 meters, dropped out of the race after only 11 laps. Asked what happened, he pointed to his head and shook it slightly.

Another POR runner, however, didn't have such bad luck. Carlos Lopes, 37, in one of the premiere events of the Olympics— which also happened to be the final event of the Games—walked, or rather ran, off with the gold medal in the men's marathon in an outstanding Olympic record time of 2:09:21. If there was any race in the Olympic Games in which all of the "favorites" did not achieve according to their track records, this was it. The roster of runners who finished after Lopes reads like a Who's Who in Marathoning: Rob de Castella of Australia, who hadn't lost a marthon since 1980, finished fifth; Alberto Salazar of the USA, who holds the world record in the marathon, came in fifteenth, two spots behind his chief American rival, Peter Pfitzinger; Toshihiko Seko of Japan, who hadn't lost a marathon since 1979, was the fourteenth man across the finish line. There is no doubt that all the runners felt that a finish under 2:10 was impossible considering the Los Angeles conditions. All the runners, that is, except

The indomitable Moses (USA) winner, 400M hurdles. Photo: T. Duffy

Left to Right
Lopes (POR) the
champion Olympic
marathoner.
Photo: T. Duffy

MEX dominance in
the 20km walk is
upheld by Canto.
Photo: T. Jones

Start of 4x400M
relay USA, GBR,
CAN, CIV.
Photo: T. Duffy

Cova (ITA) exults
after 10,000M
victory.
Photo: S. Powell

Photo: T. Duffy

Games of the XXIIIrd Olympiad Los Angeles 1984 **57**

Lewis (USA),
McFarlane (GBR)
and Sharpe (CAN) in
100M heat.
Photo: T. Duffy

Carlos Lopes.

Lopes' victory, timed to coincide with the Closing Ceremonies of the XXIIIrd Olympics, was a fitting tribute to the spirit of the Games. An athlete who most did not expect to win, came in to the Coliseum to take an energetic last lap and looked stronger than most marathoners do at the end of the 26 mile, 385 yard race. While the people of the world celebrated the end of the Games, Lopes proudly stood before his country's flag proclaiming the glory of sport to the thousands in the stands, and the estimated two billion who watched the Closing Ceremonies on television.

Among the most popular sports around the globe, men's running events were actually the first competitions in the ancient Olympic Games. A sort of 200 meter sprint was the first event won in 776 B.C. by Coroebus of Ellis. The sport has come a long way since Coroebus used stone slabs as starting blocks. The technology has changed and so has the roster of runners.

Yet, there is a thread that connects Carl Lewis, Edwin Moses, Sebastian Coe, Alberto Salazar, Carlos Lopes, Said Aouita to Abebe Bikila, Kip Keino and further back to Emil Zatopek, Jesse Owens and others.

The thread ties all the winged footed runners of yesterday and today to tomorrow.

Opposite Page
Coe (GBR), 359,
leads in the
1500M.
Photo: T. Duffy

Athletics: Best In The Field

David Woods

The decathlon, that 10-event test of strength, speed and endurance, determines the greatest all-around athlete of each Olympics. Decathletes who labor in obscurity are suddenly thrust into the world's spotlight every four years. To become the Olympic decathlon champion is perhaps the greatest plateau an athlete can achieve. It is a hard-earned honor, one that takes years of physical and psychological preparation yet only two days of pressurized competition. It was an honor that awaited either Daley Thompson or Juergen Hingsen, for these were the two highest-scoring decathletes in the history of the Olympic Games.

In a contest of man against man, these Olympics offered the ultimate confrontation: Thompson vs. Hingsen, little man vs. big man, Olympic champion vs. world record-holder. The outcome was most closely watched in the homelands of Thompson (Great Britain) and Hingsen (Federal Republic of Germany).

Before the Olympics, Hingsen had also acquired a reputation for failing to meet Thompson's challenge. Although he had broken the world record three times, Hingsen had lost to Thompson in all six of their previous meetings. When he fell behind by 122 points after only one event, the 100-meter dash, critics were quick to exclaim: "It's over already." Thompson's lead grew even greater after the second event, when he long jumped 8.01 meters. Hingsen, 2.00 meters tall and weighing 97 kilograms, figured to cut the margin against Thompson in the shot put. He did, by nine points. But in the next event, the high jump, Hingsen was limping and obviously in distress. "Now it's really over," the critics repeated.

Hingsen's talent had never been questioned, and now neither will his courage. After receiving medical treatment on his patella, he proceeded to jump 2.12 meters and pick up 77 points on Thompson, whose 2.03 was not among his best. Thompson completed the first day by running 400 meters in 46.97 seconds, giving him 4633 points, the most ever for the first five events. Hingsen had 4519, just 17 behind his own world-record pace.

After beginning the second day by winning the 110-meter hurdles, Hingsen began to believe that, despite Thompson's big lead, he was in a position to win this decathlon. He temporarily went ahead in the next event, the discus, with a personal best of 50.82 meters, while Thompson could manage only 37.90 and 41.24 through two rounds. Going into his last discus throw, Thompson trailed Hingsen by 68 points. However, it was the Briton's turn to come through, and his throw of 46.56 was his best ever in a decathlon. He still led, but by only 33 points. "I was pretty sure I would get him in the pole vault and javelin," Hingsen said afterward. "Then in

the 1500, I would have blown him way. I was pretty sure I would get him."

Instead, something got to Hingsen. He became ill, retired to the Coliseum tunnel and vomited. For the second time in the competition, he required medical attention. Dizzy and disoriented, he passed in the pole vault until the bar reached 4.50 meters. One miss. Then, a second. One more would mean zero points in the vault, effectively eliminating him from the decathlon. Hingsen did clear the bar, but could go no higher. And when Thompson went on to clear 5.00, the lead grew to an insurmountable 152 points.

Focus now shifted to Thompson's drive toward Hingsen's world record. After the javelin, Thompson needed to run 4:34.8 in the 1500 meters to break the record. He crossed the finish line in 4:35.00—incredibly, missing the world record of 8798 by exactly one point. More significantly, Thompson became only the second man ever to win two Olympic gold medals in the decathlon. "All I wanted to do was win," Thompson said. "I thought I could break the world record in any other decathlon. Here, the most important thing was to win."

Hingsen's countryman Siegfried Wentz won the bronze medal followed by Guido Kratschmer, completing a sweep of second, third and fourth places by FRG.

As expected, the pole vault competition developed into a duel between American and French vaulters. That was not supposed to bode well for the French, because the Americans had the advantage of jumping in the same Coliseum where they had jumped in the U.S. Olympic trials, and they had the decided advantage of enthusiastic crowd support. Mike Tully was the most formidable of the Americans. He won world cup titles in 1977 and 1979 and qualified for the 1980 Olympic team that did not go to Moscow. Tully set an American record of 5.81 meters at the U.S. trials. Before the Games, he raised that to 5.82. Pierre Quinon (FRA) had set a world record of 5.82 in 1983 before his countryman Thierry Vigneron broke it with a vault of 5.83. But Quinon's competitive record was more erratic than Vigneron's. When he needed two attempts to clear 5.45 at Los Angeles and then missed his first attempt at 5.65, it appeared that Quinon was in trouble. Only 10 days before he had injured his thigh, and he massaged his pained leg throughout the competition. "I have been suffering the last few days, but I knew I had to put it out of my head when I came here," he said later. That he did. In the cat-and-mouse game of passing and vaulting among Quinon, Vigneron, Tully, and Earl Bell (USA), it was difficult to sort out the current leader. Quinon, vaulting in the order ahead of Tully, passed his second and third attempts at 5.65 and thus had only two attempts at 5.70. Tully had taken the lead by clearing 5.65 on

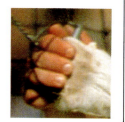

Opposite Page
Tiainen (FIN) grabs the gold in the hammer throw.
Photo: T. Duffy

his third and final attempt. Quinon gained the lead at 5.70, clearing the bar on his first attempt. Since Tully could do no more than stay even with Quinon, he passed 5.70. Vigneron and Bell, each of whom had last cleared 5.60, missed three times and shared the bronze medal. "It's nice to have a medal, nice to have a souvenir," said Bell.

So it came down to Quinon and Tully. And once more Tully could only watch as Quinon cleared 5.75 on his first attempt. Again Tully passed. Finally, at 5.80, Quinon missed. He never got off his pole on any of his attempts at 5.80. But Tully couldn't make it, either, failing to get off his pole on his second try and merely running through the uprights on his third. The gold medal belonged to Pierre Quinon.

All the vaulters complained of a headwind, but Quinon managed to adjust better than the rest. He switched to a stiffer pole midway through the competition. "It was a test of tactics, and the decisions of Quinon and Vigneron were intelligent ones," said French vault coach Jean Claude Perrin. "Quinon took some risks, and they paid off."

Dietmar Moegenburg of the Federal Republic of Germany took no risks in the high jump. He cleared every height he attempted until the bar reached the world-record measurement of 2.40 meters. He missed three times, but it was of little consolation to the People's Republic of China's Zhu Jianhua that his world record of 2.39 was secure. The most popular athlete in the world's most populous nation had to settle for the bronze medal, partly because of circumstances beyond his control. The jumpers knew to be ready for the interruption of medal ceremonies, but they couldn't have been ready for Britain's Steve Ovett to quit the 1500-meter final directly behind the high jump pit. Doctors surrounded Ovett

just as it was Zhu's turn to jump. It was to have been his second attempt at 2.33, but when officials insisted that he wait, Zhu passed. His concentration broken, the 21-year-old Zhu missed his only two attempts at 2.35. Patrik Sjoeberg of Sweden cleared 2.33 on his second attempt and slipped in to grab the silver medal. Zhu took the bronze, the first medal ever won by CHN in athletics. "I said to him afterward that at least he has four years," said 31-year-old American Dwight Stones, fourth at 2.31, the same height cleared by Zhu. Like Zhu, Moegenburg was a prodigy of the high jump, ranking first in the world in 1979 at age 18. He was the European champion in 1982 and fourth at Helsinki in 1983.

Carl Lewis was more than anyone could contend with in the long jump. Having already won the 100 meters, the American was going for the second of his four gold medals. Earlier that day, he had run the first and second rounds of the 200 meters, so it was generally assumed that he would not take all six of his allotted attempts in the long jump. But when he jumped 8.54 meters on his first attempt, fouled his second and passed all the rest, he was roundly booed. Lewis wanted a gold medal; the crowd wanted a world record. "This was probably the most difficult competition I've ever been in," he said. "Not because this is the Olympics, but because we got a late start after the hammer throw. It got very cold very quickly. I was a little sore after the second jump, and I didn't want to risk any chances. If somebody would have jumped farther, I wouldn't have come back." Unruffled as always, Lewis said he took the boos as a compliment. To him, that meant the crowd wanted only to see him perform.

Even Gary Honey of Australia and Giovanni Evangelisti of Italy, the silver and bronze medalists, conceded that the con

Left to Right
Joyner (USA) in the
triple jump.
Photo: D. Cannon

Moegenburg (FRG),
high jump gold
medalist.
Photo: D. Cannon

Wilkins (USA), silver
medal in discus.
Photo: D. Cannon

Yoshida (JPN), 5th in
javelin.
Photo: D. Cannon

Photo: T. Duffy

Left to Right
Thompson's biggest
hurdle: a second
decathlon gold.
Photo: S. Powell

Thompson clears
the pole-vault bar
at 500cm.
Photo: T. Duffy

Thompson (GBR) in
decathlon shot put
competition.
Photo: S. Powell

contest for the gold was over after Lewis' first jump. But the two other medals weren't decided until the final two rounds. American Larry Myricks struggled, but when he went 8.16 meters on his fifth attempt, he moved into third place. The very next jumper, Evangelisti, went 8.24 on what was his final attempt, pushing Honey to third and Myricks to fourth. Honey followed Evangelisti in the order, and had an identical jump of 8.24. Since Honey had a better second jump, he moved into the silver spot and Evangelisti into bronze. Myricks, the last jumper of the competition, was off again on his approach to the board and could only step through the sand.

Honey had injured his back in the qualifying round and was happy just to be competing. In becoming only the second Australian to win a medal in the long jump, he continued his record of excelling in big meets. Evangelisti, whose record in big meets had not been so good, became the first Italian ever to win a medal in the long jump.

Another American, Al Joyner, won the triple jump on his first attempt. Before the Olympics, Joyner was barely known outside his hometown of East St. Louis, Illinois. Americans Mike Conley and Willie Banks were favored in this event. Lack of attention didn't bother Joyner. Instead, it motivated him. "I decided if they didn't know who I was, I would make sure they knew." He proceeded to jump 17.26 meters, the best of his career.

Some had predicted medal sweeps by Americans in both the shot put and discus, but Alessandro Andrei of Italy and Rolf Danneberg of the Federal Republic of Germany paid no attention. They not only prevented sweeps, together they swept the gold medals. Andrei held his form in an event in which athletes frequently throw far below personal bests. He won the shot put with a distance of 21.26, close to his best of 21.39, and became the first Italian to win a medal in the event. Americans Michael Carter, Dave Laut and Augie Wolf finished 2-3-4. Laut and Wolf observed that the interruptions for medal ceremonies were distracting, just as they were for the high jump. Andrei just managed the distractions better than the rest, and turned in the longest put, four out of the six rounds.

Danneberg was an even greater surprise than Andrei. The bearded, bespectacled discus thrower, an unemployed school teacher, had done little to suggest he was capable of winning a gold medal, having placed third in his national championships in 1984. What separated him from the rest in Los Angeles was his ability to throw close to his best distance, just as Andrei did. With no wind, the distraction of a large crowd watching other events, and the pressure of an Olympic Games Dannenberg still managed to throw 66.60 meters on his fourth attempt to wrest the lead from Wilkins. Danneberg's personal best, 67.40, was achieved under much more favorable conditions. Americans Wilkins and John Powell, rivals for years, were forced to settle for the silver and bronze medals. The third American, Art Burns, finished fifth.

Finnish throwers Arto Haerkoenen and Juha Tiainen won the javelin and hammer, respectively. Of special cause for celebration was Haerkoenen's victory in the javelin, an event that has long served as a source of national pride for Finland. The gold medal was that country's sixth in the javelin, more than any other nation, but its first since 1964. "After working for 15 years, always thinking you would get it (the gold), and finally getting it, is a great feeling. I'm very happy," said Haerkoenen. Another surprise in this most unpredictable of events was Britain's David Ottley, a stevedore's son, who celebrated his 29th birthday on the day of the javelin final. His throw of 85.74 in the first round led the field through three rounds, until Haerkoenen threw 86.76 in the fourth. The silver still represented a first for Britain, which had never before won any medal in the javelin. The bronze won by Kenth Eldebrink was the first medal for Sweden in the javelin since 1928. Unfavorable wind conditions prevented all of the throwers from reaching their best distances.

Finland's other gold medalist, hammer thrower Tiainen, recorded two poor throws in the finals. His third throw of 78.08 was more Tiainen-like. Karl-Hans Riehm of the Federal Republic of Germany, the last thrower in the order and directly behind Tiainen, immediately followed with 77.98. Although he couldn't catch Tiainen, Riehm was ecstatic about his silver medal. "I had been waiting for 18 years for this," he said. His countryman Klaus Ploghaus, won the bronze medal.

Although he didn't even advance past the qualifying round, the man who probably enjoyed these Olympic Games more than anyone was 44-year-old American hammer thrower Ed Burke. When he finished seventh in the Olympics in 1964 and 12th in 1968, Burke retired from competition, and didn't pick a hammer up again until 1979. His daughters were watching the Soviet Litvinov throw in the televised world cup meet, and his wife explained to them that their father used to do that. The family then went for a drive to San Jose State University, where Burke threw a rusty old hammer taken from the garage. "I threw it," he said, "and I knew I had a quest."

That quest brought him to another Olympics, 20 years after his first. He was flag bearer for the USA team at the opening ceremonies. And though he didn't make another hammer final, he fulfilled his quest. "It was a thrill just to walk into the stadium and see so many people and to hear so many cheering," he said. "I think that maybe I said more for middle-aged people by not advancing here today. I showed them it's possible to feel satisfaction in just competing, not in the winning."

Which is exactly what Pierre de Coubertin had in mind in the first place.

Athletics: Great Leap Forward

Cliff Temple

Until the 1960 Games, women were apparently thought physically incapable of racing distances as long even as 800 meters in the Olympics. Yet the Los Angeles Games will be remembered for opening a whole new dimension in women's running. Each of the three new categories—the 3000 meters, the 400 meter hurdles and the marathon—provided its own historic and dramatic chapter to the history of the Games.

The sight of the diminutive marathoner Joan Benoit running into Olympic immortality will surely help to inspire women the world over to take up running themselves. Benoit, a shy but determined 27-year-old from Maine, was the world record holder for the distance with her 2:22:43 set at Boston in 1983. On paper, this made her two minutes faster than anyone else in the field. But with so many differing courses, those persons knowledgeable about running realized such comparisons were meaningless.

So Benoit went into the race shouldering enormous pressure from an American public which practically demanded success. Yet inside herself she knew that the two Norwegians, Ingrid Kristiansen and Grete Waitz, would be formidable rivals. Kristiansen had run the world's second fastest marathon three months earlier; Waitz, the 1983 World Champion, had long dominated women's distance running and sought an Olympic gold medal as the missing jewel in her crown. Additionally, Benoit had just scraped into the USA team, winning the trial marathon in May after having undergone emergency arthroscopic surgery on her knee just 17 days before that race. And 26 miles of hammering concrete roads and absorbing shock from 30,000 strides is not usually prescribed for such a condition.

Then there was the fear of the heat and the smog. The 8 a.m. start at Santa Monica City College was held beneath low gray clouds with even a chill in the air. And as the 50 women lapped the track two and a half times before heading off along their hard route to the Coliseum, conditions were practically perfect.

After only three miles, Benoit, in a white peaked cap to ward off the effects of the sun, was leaving the pack behind. Waitz, Kristiansen, and the others let her go, confident that her impatience would be her undoing. But as they watched the silver-gray clad Benoit pull further ahead, they were also dropping their gold medal chances down the nearest drain.

"I didn't want to take the lead that early, but I promised myself I would run my own race," said Benoit, "and that's exactly what I did."

"Joan took a chance, and I didn't," said Grete Waitz afterwards. The chance paid off, as Benoit, flicking the peak of

her cap up and down according to the position of the sun, never saw another runner, only thousands and thousands of spectators watching her heroic run into Olympic history. By the time the Norwegians realized that it was time to chase her, she had vanished. Waitz, expecting to be able to watch the leading vehicle and its pace clock all the way, had not even bothered to wear a digital wristwatch and found herself too far behind to even read it.

In the Coliseum, the spectators could see Benoit's progress on the huge visual scoreboards. And when the little figure entered the arena through the traditional tunnel and ran into the sunlight, it was like a TV character bursting forth from the screen. She won in 2:24:52, some 500 meters ahead of Waitz, who overcame back problems to finish. "Today I could not have beaten Joan anyway," said Waitz. Rosa Mota, the European champion from Portugal, took the bronze and was the only runner among the 44 finishers who complained it was too cool.

But capturing the imagination of millions of TV viewers and the stadium crowd was a 39-year-old Swiss runner, Gabriela Andersen-Scheiss. As she came into the stadium after 30 runners who had already finished, she was in trouble. The sun was now hot, and she had been on the road 20 minutes longer than Benoit. She lurched and reeled in almost drunken gait, suffering from heat exhaustion, leaving officials with an agonizing choice: should they pull her off the track and save her the efforts of the last 500 meters or let her carry on, and possibly worsen her condition? It was like the 1908 Marathon, where officials helped the Italian Dorando Pietri across the line and then had to disqualify him from the gold medal place for receiving assistance. As the crowd of 70,000 urged her on, medical officers approached, but Gabriela veered away, clearly aware of her situation and determined to finish in an agonizingly protracted walk-run. It took her five minutes to complete the circuit of the stadium, but when she finally crossed the line and collapsed into the arms of doctors, the ovation she received was louder even than that for Benoit. She soon recovered, and history will show she was 37th in 2:48:42. "The last two kilometers are mainly black," explained the Swiss runner. "It always seemed longer to the finish than I thought".

The painful sight of the dehydrated, struggling woman depicted on Swiss television triggered many phone calls. Many Swiss callers thought Gabriela Anderson-Scheiss should have been taken off the track and been given medical attention: but her effort in retrospect showed courage and determination which justified the addition of the event to the program.

If there was controversy over whether Andersen-Scheiss

should have been stopped, it faded by comparison to the "did she fall or was she pushed?" incident in the women's 3000 meter final. Mary Decker, 1983 world champion, but deprived of ever being able to compete in the Games because of injury or boycott, would be running in front of the fans in her native state of California.

She had even decided to concentrate on just the one event, despite also qualifying in the 1500 meters at the USA trials, because she felt that the schedule of heats and finals might be too much for her fragile legs. Her main opposition was expected to come from the Romanian Maricica Puica, the 1984 World cross-country champion, although far more media attention was to focus on a waif-like barefooted runner named Zola Budd.

Budd, born in South Africa which is suspended from membership in the International Olympic Committee, had posted phenomenal times for an 18-year-old prior to the Games. In April 1984 she was granted British citizenship stemming from her British-born grandfather. She had bettered Decker's world 5000 meter best while in South Africa the previous January. Just before the Games, Decker had bettered Budd's world 2000 meter best.

While Puica loomed as the main threat in the Decker camp, the match-up with Budd caught the public's imagination. So when the final found them side by side in the early stages, leading the field, the tension was growing. Just after completing the fourth of the seven and a half laps, Budd made a move to get away from Decker. At the 1750 meter point they collided. The stadium froze. Suddenly Decker was flat on the infield, unable to get up or continue. A chorus of boos broke out, unsettling the inexperienced Budd who faded to finish a disappointing seventh. Puica, the Romanian Decker feared most, won the gold medal in 8:35.96.

What happened to Decker? Examination of video tape showed that she appeared to catch Budd's heel with her foot about six strides before she fell, causing Budd to almost stumble and Decker to fall over Budd's splayed left leg. After the race Budd was disqualified. She was reinstated following a British appeal, when the Jury examined tapes from six different angles and declared that Budd had not intentionally impeded Decker. The incident was a tragedy for both women and for the Games, which was robbed of what would have been a classic finale to the race. The regrettable outburst by Decker afterwards, holding Budd responsible, made the incident even less palatable as was Decker's refusal to shake hands with the young runner who had always idolized her. As the videotape seemed to indicate, if anyone was to blame for the fall, it appears to have been Decker herself. Now it may not

be until the 1987 World Championships or 1988 Olympic Games in Seoul that the pair will meet again with so much at stake.

The least known women's champion must have been Nawal El Moutawakel who earned Morocco's first-ever Olympic gold medal in winning the 400 meter hurdles, the third new event on the program. A student at Iowa State University, the 22-year-old El Moutawakel had been supported by the financial help of the King of Morocco in her preparations. "All I wanted to do was to make the final," she said afterwards.

If the boycott by the Soviet bloc affected the results of the women's events more than the men's, the results were not all negative. The 400 meter hurdles would probably have been dominated by the Soviet and East German athletes. For smaller nations to enjoy success, even in their absence, is to spread the enthusiasm and example for many thousands of young people.

If the host nation had a stranglehold in any area, it was the sprints, as American athletes took the gold and silver medals in the 100 meter, 200 meter, and 400 meter as well as both relays. Evelyn Ashford was an outstanding 100 meter champion in 10.97 seconds, an Olympic record, which wiped out the memory of the 1980 Olympic boycott and her own misfortune in the final of the 100 meter at the 1983 World Championships. In that race, Ashford was overshadowed by her own teammate Valerie Brisco-Hooks, who earned three gold medals.

Brisco-Hooks served as an inspiration to those who feel that motherhood means an end to a track career. After her son was born, in 1982, Valerie had an urge to get back into shape through a return to sprinting. "I know for a fact that motherhood meant I had extra strength, and my recovery from training seemed to be much quicker," she said. Her coach, Bobby Kersee, persuaded her to look towards the 400 meters as her future, although she resisted—even disliked—the event. In June 1984 she became the first American woman to run under 50 seconds in the 400 meters. She lost the USA trials 400 meters to Chandra Cheeseborough, but won the 200. On the basis of that victory, Ashford decided to tackle both events in the Olympic Games. In the 400 final she turned the tables on Cheeseborough, posting a new Olympic and USA record of 48.83 seconds. "We're right there with the Europeans now," she said. And although her victory was achieved in the absence of the Czechoslovakian world record holder Jarmila Kratochvilova (at 47.99), the gap which existed between the USA and the rest of the world had closed.

The situation was similar in the 200 meter, where Brisco-Hooks completed a difficult double in another Olympic record

Ashford (USA) sails to victory in the 100M.
Photo: S. Powell

Ashford (USA) women's 100M gold medalist.
Photo: S. Powell

of 21.81. She overtook fast-starting teammate Florence Griffith at halfway and opened up a two meter lead by the finish. Along with a third gold medal in the 4 x 400 meter, her 49.23 leg contributed to another Olympic record of 3:18:29. Her time was a full 3 seconds better than challengers CAN and FRG. She came not that far from equalling Carl Lewis' much more publicized feats. But Brisco-Hooks had another motivation for excelling. In 1974, her brother Robert was killed while training on a high school track in Los Angeles when he was struck by stray bullets from a gang fight.

Gabriella Dorio, a 27-year-old physical education student from Padova in Italy, knew what it was like to be an also-ran. In 1980, she and Mary Decker were the only non-Eastern bloc runners to break four minutes for 1500 meters. But so often she would set a fierce pace in a race, only to be swept aside at the kick. It had even happened to her earlier that week. In the 800 meter final, she led at a fast lick before losing out in the sprint for the line to Doina Melinte (ROM), Kim Gallagher (USA), and Fita Lovin (ROM).

When Dorio lined up for the 1500 meters, her third successive Olympic final at the event, there seemed little hope for victory. The very slow early pace seemed to be playing into the hands of the sprinters again. And with Melinte in the field, the results seemed predictable. But at 900 meters Dorio

picked up the pace dramatically, stretching out a bunched field. Melinte, a tall, rangy girl with long legs, seemed content to track the Italian until, with 250 meters left, Melinte moved past her into the lead, and it appeared over. But this time Dorio, the girl who could not sprint, who had never won an Olympic medal, came back with a vengeance. With the Italians in the crowd beside themselves with joy, she steamed past Melinte in the final 100 meters to win in 4:03:25. The overall time was slow, but the manner of victory by a girl who refused to give up was the stuff of which history is made.

Ulrike Meyfarth (FRG) was, until several years ago, almost consigned to history. She was the 16-year-old schoolgirl who, at the 1972 Munich Olympics, won the high jump gold medal in front of her home crowd with a world record leap. Even at the time, it was hard to imagine how one so young could adapt to live the rest of her life with such a monumental success behind her. She admits she had problems coping with the demands of being a celebrity and a normal teenager. She failed her university exams, and came nowhere near retaining her Olympic title in 1976. In 1980 FRG boycotted the Moscow Games. So when Meyfarth stood on the high jump fan in Los Angeles, twelve years had passed since she had won in Munich. It had been a long time, but now an adult of 28, it was a chance to turn back the clock in a way most of

us could only imagine. By clearing 202cm, an Olympic record, she not only defeated the 1980 champion Sara Simeoni (ITA), but re-established herself as the world's number one woman high jumper. There have been comeback stories in the Games before, of course, but few spanning so many years.

In the long jump, world record holder Anisoara Cusmir-Stanciu (ROM), (first with 6.96 meters) and Vali Ionescu (second with 6.81 meters) contributed to their nation's tally of medals in women's track and field, which served as a reminder from time to time of who had decided not to come. Even then, Carol Lewis, the sister of the much-bemedalled Carl and a pre-Olympic favorite, shocked United States fans by inexplicably failing to qualify for the final rounds of the long jump.

The javelin, however, was scarcely affected by the boycott. In 1980 at Moscow, Great Britain's Tessa Sanderson had been one of the medal favorites but could not manage to qualify for the final. In Los Angeles, she not only took the gold medal, she defeated 1983 World gold and silver medalists Tiina Lillak (FIN) and Fatima Whitbread of Great Britain, in the process. Sanderson became the first individual GBR gold medalist in women's events since 1972. "I hope my Moscow experience is well and truly buried now," she said. "But its taken an awfully long time for me to come back from an experience like that." Lillak, whose dramatic last throw in Helsinki had won her World title in 1983, was not wanting for support in Los Angeles. But the effects of a stress fracture in her ankle early in the season had taken its toll. The surprise of the competition came later, when the 1982 European champion, Anna Verouli of Greece, was disqualified after failing a routine drug test. Ironically, she had not even qualified for the final stages of the competition in Los Angeles.

The shot put was one women's field event that was greatly affected by the boycott. The gold and silver medalists, Claudia Losch (FRG) and Mihaela Loghin (ROM) were the only two throwers of the 1983 World top 25 who were not missing from the 1984 Games. Their duel also provided one of the closest results of entire Olympics.

Losch led the competition in the early going with her second round throw of 20.31 meters. Then Loghin went ahead in the fourth round with 20.47 meters, only to see Losch, who has only been competing seriously for three years, retaliate with a final throw of 20.48 meters, the difference being the width of a small fingernail. The pair finished about a meter and a half clear of bronze medalist Gael Martin of Australia. The discus throw was a similarly close affair with the Netherlands gaining their only track and field medal through Ria Stalman's half-meter win over Leslie Deniz of the USA.

In the heptathlon, expanded from the five-event pentathlon

The first-ever women's marathon. Photo: T. Duffy

of previous Games, it was one of the new events—the 800 meters— that provided the pulsating finish. Jackie Joyner (USA) was the pre-event favorite. Even after overcoming a disastrous long jump she still led marginally before the 800. In the long jump, Joyner had fouled her first two efforts and needed to take off way behind the board, losing a lot of distance, in order to ensure some points. Her 6.11 meter effort was well below her best, but kept her in the contest. All of this was despite the effects of a hamstring injury which was heavily bandaged.

In the 800 meters, which traditionally finishes off the competition, Joyner needed to stay within two seconds of the Australian Glynis Nunn and seven seconds of the West German Sabine Everts to secure the gold. Everts won the event in 2:09.05, but the Australian managed to drag herself 2.5 seconds clear of Joyner to earn the 36 points necessary to turn a 31-point deficit into a narrow five point win, 6390 to 6385.

Joyner at least had the satisfaction of seeing her brother, Al, win the triple jump gold at the same time. Al was lucky not to have had his sister disqualified when, in his excitement, he ran alongside her on the infield during the 800 meters, an action technically constituting assistance.

With easy victories in both the 4 x 100 meter and 4 x 400 meter relays on the final day of track events, the USA had, as expected, won a fair share of medals.

With standards rising so quickly, it will take improvement over 1984 achievements to win medals in Seoul in 1988. As an example, performances which won medals for men, not so many Olympiads back, are now needed by women to place. Still, women have come a long way since 1928, when the 800 meters was added— then dropped—from the Olympic program because of the scenes of exhaustion after the final. In Seoul, the women's track 10,000 meters will be contested for the first time. If successful, it will remain part of the Olympic program.

Physiology may dictate that women may never compete with men on equal terms, but natural justice acknowledges that at least they will now have the same opportunities.

Melinte (ROM) 315, Benning (GBR), 1500M. Photo: T. Duffy

Left to Right
Losch (FRG) in a winning shot put toss.
Photo: IOPP

Staniciu (ROM) wins the long jump gold.
Photo: IOPP

Meyfarth (FRG) high jump.
Photo: IOPP

Sanderson (GBR) winning the javelin gold medal.
Photo: T. Duffy

Puica (ROM) wins in
the 3000M.
Photo: S. Powell

Decker (USA) paces
Budd (GBR) in the
3000M final.
Photo: T. Duffy

Opposite Page
Benoit (USA) in the
first Olympic
women's marathon.
Photo: T. Duffy

Brisco-Hooks (USA),
in the blocks, 200M.
Photo: T. Duffy

Basketball: Fury at the Forum

Harvey Frommer with Al Browning

Coach Bob Knight of the USA and Coach Antonio Diaz-Miguel of Spain have spent some time together during the last decade. While visiting each other in their respective nations, the famous coaches have engaged in a strategic table game known in their society as "basketball checkers."

They have met for about two weeks every year to move coin-like "players", up and down a hand-held board, symbolic of the court over which they rule. No jumping is allowed, just a teaming of unusual mental skills. It has become a popular game worldwide. In the People's Republic of China, coaches take part in that type of "checkers" the same way Knight and Diaz-Miguel do. In Yugoslavia, the home of the 1980 Olympic Games gold medalists, coaches have mastered the game. In India, coaches are still trying to get the hang of it.

Interestingly, these unselfish hombre-to-hombre encounters between Knight and Diaz-Miguel have been staged to enhance the comprehension and refinement of man-to-man defense, motion offense and other key ingredients that make basketball so tasty for fans.

The two men from distant countries are more than ships passing during the night, rather "the best of friends," according to Knight. Their warm relationship understood, they were in Los Angeles meeting on the highest of international levels, as adversaries clashing in the finals of the Olympic Games tournament. The Americans prevailed in crushing fashion, 96-65.

With its domination of the tournament, a sweep of seven games, and a 32.1 points average margin of victory, the USA served notice to the world that one loss long ago does not signal the crumbling of a dynasty.

"The United States of America is at least 50 years ahead of the rest of the basketball world," Diaz-Miguel said after the gold medal game. The statement echoed in The Forum, the home of the Los Angeles Lakers of the National Basketball Association and the host arena for Olympic basketball competitions. And it reverberated when USA women swept their way to a championship. They defeated KOR, 85-55, in the gold medal game.

USA men have a 77-1 record in the Olympic Games. That spans nine gold medals. No other nation in Olympic history has so totally dominated a single sport as have the American men, though the championship that got away still remains the subject of controversy. In 1972 at Munich, the Soviet Union burst the bubble, winning 51-50 with or without help from game officials who provided an extra three seconds for a final shot after time had apparently expired.

"Munich was the scare that has made the United States of America put added emphasis on the Olympic Games," said Canadian coach Jack Donohue, whose team lost to Yugoslavia, 88-82, in the bronze medal game. "That loss forced the USA to become more professional about the way it selects its team and prepares for the tournament," he continued. "Nobody will catch up with the USA as long as it stays serious about this."

There are probably those in Moscow, Kiev and Leningrad who would disagree with that statement, which brings up the most asked basketball question at the Olympic Games in Los Angeles: Could the USA have beaten the Soviet Union in 1984?

"We felt we had the best team ever put together, and we wanted to prove that," said Michael Jordan, a forward whose 20 points led the United States of America over Spain in the final game. "By winning the gold medal, I think we accomplished that."

But the Soviet Union was not in Los Angeles, which, coupled with less-than-overwhelming performances by Yugoslavia and Italy, made the tournament one of the least competitive in history.

Nevertheless, the gold medal is not tarnished, according to USA players. "This was a once-in-a-lifetime deal for us," said forward Sam Perkins, who played with Michael Jordan on a national championship team at the University of North Carolina. "In college," continued Perkins, "you have four years to realize the ultimate goal. In the Olympic Games, you only have one." There is no comparison. A piece of gold is something to treasure. With or without the Soviet Union, this is the highlight of my life." Wayman Tisdale, a USA center, his gold medal hanging from his neck, agreed with Perkins. "This is the happiest moment of my life."

Knight chose to make a final and somewhat exciting dunk during his last statement to the news media. "I want to dispel one thing," said Knight, the temperamental, at times self-glamorizing, coach from the University of Indiana. "We could beat the Soviet Union any time they want to play us."

With or without the URS, everybody seemed to exit Los Angeles pleased to have taken part in the rigorous basketball competition, all of them convinced the best team won the tournament. Many of them were proud of their stature at the international level.

The United States of America was first. Spain was second. Yugoslavia was third. Canada was fourth. Italy was fifth, winning its final game 111-102 over Uruguay, which was sixth. Australia was seventh, winning its final game, 83-78, over eighth place FRG which handed the USA its toughest game, 78-67. Brazil was ninth, winning its final game, 86-76.

There were several individual stars. Michael Jordan,

**Opposite Page
Alford (USA) jumps
against Margall
(ESP).
Photo: A. Chung**

The USA's strength: the depth of the bench. Photo: A. Chung

Donovan (USA) snares a rebound. Photo: A. Chung

University of North Carolina, averaged 16.5 points per game, thrilled a pro-USA crowd with his crafty passes and fluid moves toward the basket, and drew rave reviews from other coaches. "He is like an airplane," said Diaz-Miguel. "Jordan is like a rubber band," said Jean Luent, the France coach. Another one of the USA players who torqued the potent team was Leon Wood. A local hero just five years out of Santa Monica High School in Southern California, Wood played point guard. And he piloted the USA team setting up the scoring of Jordan, Tisdale, Patrick Ewing, and others.

The leading scorer in the tournament, however, was not an American but Mohamed Soliman of Egypt. He averaged 25.6 points per game playing for a team that last winter had a hapless tour of several small colleges in the USA. But the Egyptians recovered and, with Soliman leading them, surprisingly fought their way into the Olympic Games by winning the African qualifying tournament.

Uruguay was also a surprise entry in the Olympic Games tournament which provided an opportunity for dazzling shooter Horacio Lopez, to strut his stuff. He didn't disappoint anyone as he averaged 24.9 points a game for his team that gave no quarter and refused to back down from a scuffle or two. Commentary that preceded and followed an early round 104-68 USA triumph over Uruguay reflected the character of the losing team.

Uraguay's Ramon Ethcameddi, an overmatched head coach, told his players before the game: "Have respect for the fans, try to demonstrate the best of your abilities, and try to do your best although you may end up losing."

The Uraguayans, stifled, out-shot, out-rebounded, followed their coach's suggestions. And in defeat, they earned the affection and the respect of the crowd at the Forum. "We knew the USA was best in all aspects of the game," explained Uraguayan star Horacio Lopez, "but we could not allow the USA to put more heart into the game, so we had to try as hard as we could."

The Games were characterized by outstanding performances by other athletes. Oscar Schmidt of Brazil finished third in scoring with an average of slightly over 24.1 points a game, while the new Italian superstar, Antonello Riva, compiled 23.4 points a game. Riva's club team acquired contract rights to the 22-year-old from a smaller club for a $3000 bus and half a dozen basketballs. As it turned out, Riva was quite a bargain.

Yugoslavia's team arrived in Los Angeles with a highly rated status. A major part of the high esteem afforded Yugoslavia was the presence of 32-year-old forward Drazen "Dolly" Dalipagic. Living up to his advance billing, Dolly averaged 22.7 points per game and saved his best show for last by scoring 37 points in the bronze medal game.

Dalipagic has a mustache and a hook nose which attract fan interest. He plays in Italy where the money is, during the summer. Twice he attempted to earn a position with National Basketball Association teams in the USA, the Boston Celtics in 1976 and the New York Knicks in 1980. Dolly returned home both times unable to convince his wife that life in the USA would be better.

In 1976, Spain did not qualify for the Olympic Games. Four years later in the Olympics, it wound up fourth behind Yugoslavia, Italy, and the Soviet Union. Their fourth place showing in 1980 indicated that the run and shoot philosophy of their coach, Antonio Diaz-Miguel, would eventually bring dividends.

The payoff came in Los Angeles when Spain defeated Yugoslavia 74-61 in the semifinals to earn a pointless second shot at the USA. "I am proud of this team," Diaz-Miguel said. "I wonder if Bobby Knight wants to trade two players for the final game?" he quipped.

Canadian coach Donohue observed the gold medal game matchup and commented wryly, "only a terrorist attack" could keep the USA from claiming the spoils. He was correct—leaving a Knight to bask in shining armor.

It was in 1982 that Knight accepted the responsibility of leading the USA in its drive for an Olympic gold medal. After getting into the effort, his boxing gloves deposited at home, he expressed his sentiments: "I have spent most of my life fishing and doing nothing of real importance. Now, I have the chance to contribute to something more worthwhile."

It was, of course, pure understatement. Accepting the USA Olympic basketball team coaching position put the native Ohioan in line to become only the third coach in USA history to win an National Collegiate Athletic Association (NCAA) title, a National Invitational Tournament (NIT) title and an Olympic gold medal.

USA collegians were scouted extensively. Seventy-two were invited to a tryout camp. The roster was eventually trimmed to 16, four over the limit, and the coaching staff visited each athlete to analyze the roles each potential player would be expected to perform. "I think that helped," Knight said. "Everybody knew what would be expected of them."

The final cut of four was made and a series of exhibition games against professional players from the National Basketball Association polished individual skills and made the American team tougher and more unified. By the time the squad arrived in Los Angeles, about the only question was whether its controversial coach could behave well enough to avoid causing an international incident.

American women achieved equality with their male counterparts in excellence on the court. Led by Cheryl Miller, heralded as the best woman player in history, by a deep supporting cast, and directed by Coach Pat Summitt Head, who was driving a tractor at age seven while living on a farm in Tennessee, the talented Americans romped through the tournament with ease.

Miller, who averaged 16.5 points per game and had 42 rebounds and 19 steals in six games, mused about sitting in a rocking chair as a small girl living at home and dreaming about having a gold medal draped around her neck.

The exciting Miller did something about her dreams. In high school she once scored one hundred points in a single game. She has led the University of Southern California to two consecutive NCAA championships. Now she has added her dream, Olympic gold,, to her stellar achievements.

"I wish I could play like her," said Jung A-Sung, a star from KOR. "Until now, I have never seen a woman play like a man," said Seung-Youn Cho, the KOR coach.

Lea Henry, a former standout at Tennessee under Coach Summitt, is a study in contrast to Miller. She is a small guard who plays a fundamentally sound game. She is a winner, not a flash, and she engineered an explosive USA offense that threw some powerful numbers at the opposition: 83-55 over Yugoslavia, 91-55 over the People's Republic of China, 81-47 over Australia, 92-61 over Canada, 84-47 and 85-55 over KOR.

In 1976, Henry was a 16-year-old girl living in South Georgia. She and her father, W. T. Henry, were watching the opening ceremonies of the 1976 Olympic Games on television. She turned to him and said, "Dad, will you come watch me play when I make our Olympic Games team?"

She did—and he was there. He saw her become pale while trying to restrain tears as "The Star-Spangled Banner" was played after the presentation of gold medals.

There were also individual stars from other nations. Forward Hwa-Soon Kim (KOR) led all scorers with 16.8 points per game. Her poise and rainbow-like shots dazzled fans. Bev Smith of Canada, 14.2 points per game, and Jasmina Perazic of Yugoslavia, 13.0 points per games, were eye-catchers, too.

One of the more intriguing contests was the People's Republic of China against Korea. It was a confrontation of Asian women's basketball teams with tremendously contrasting styles. The team from the People's Republic of China featured seven players over 183 cms including gigantic center Chen Yuefang at 205 cms. The KOR team was a club that provided a throwback to the way basketball was played in the 1950s. Their offense was based on a weave that created the oppor-

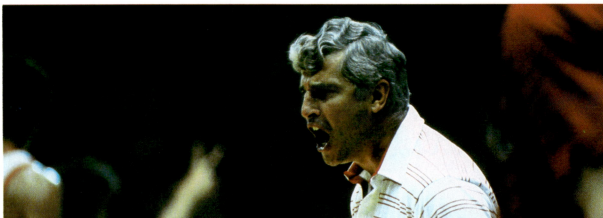

Who's the fieriest of them all? Bobby Knight (USA). Photo: A. Chung

Alford (USA) defenses Jose Luis Llorente (ESP). Photo: A. Chung

Miller (USA) relaxes
on the bench.
Photo: A. Chung

Boswell (USA) races
for a loose ball with
Hyung (KOR).
Photo: A. Chung

tunity for long set shots. Another feature of their game was the fast break. The main weakness of KOR was their small size compared to most of the other teams—a defect they compensated for with quickness.

KOR defeated CHN 69-56 in a battle of quickness and guile versus size and strength. "The goal was to be in the Olympics not to beat the People's Republic of China," said coach Seung Youn Cho, obviously pleased with KOR's win. "Our defensive strategy worked, which was to prevent their larger players from getting to the basket, stop them in midfield. Our offensive game was a slow break—waiting for them to tire and then taking a chance at a quick shot."

One of the most exciting of all the women's basketball games was an early round clash between Canada and Yugoslavia. Outside the Forum the heat of the afternoon California sun was at its peak. On the polished floor of the arena that has hosted many National Basketball Association play-off games, Canada and Yugoslavia played frenzied basketball.

The lead kept see-sawing back and forth. Players were shuttled in and out from both benches. The game came down to its final minutes—just a few points separating the teams. It was such a physical contest that both squads lost three players each on fouls. When the final buzzer sounded, Yugoslavia won the game by a single point, holding off a last frantic rush by the Canadians.

The final standings in the women's basketball tourney saw the USA women finish by defeating KOR. In the semi-final game, the People's Republic of China defeated Canada 73-57 to take the bronze. Australia and Yugoslavia were tied for fifth.

The Soviet Union was not around to challenge the women's teams either, and the question moved to, 'how well they would have done against the USA women'.

Coach Pat Head Summitt took a long time to answer the question: "This team finished the same way it started—on a winning note, but also playing as a team. We had great contributions from our starting five and also from our bench. One of the great things about this team was it played as a team—unselfishly and together.

"I think it's the best women's basketball team ever assembled in the United States. When people think about women's basketball in the future, they will think about this team. I think this will be a great incentive for young players. "I can only compare this particular team with the teams here. The question that everyone asks, of course, is 'Could this team beat the Soviet Union?'"

The Soviet Union notwithstanding, basketball invented in the USA in 1891 by Dr. James Naismith in Springfield, Massachusetts, imbedded in the fabric of USA sports with its quick tempo coming out of city schoolyards, basketball at the Forum in the LA Games produced double gold winners for the United States of America.

And in this most exciting of sports, the only native American game that is popular throughout the world—other nations, too, distinguished themselves: the running Spanish men; the fiery Uruguayans, the spunky KOR women, the impassioned Yugoslavian women . . . and the others who made basketball at the XXIIIrd Olympics a dazzling success.

Boxing: Lords of the Ring

John Crumpacker

When Paul Gonzales says, "Where I come from, you have to fight to get respect," he's not talking figuratively. Where he comes from, you either join a gang or get beat up by a gang. Sometimes you do both. "You have to gain respect," he said. "Most of the time, to gain respect, you have to fight."

By the age of 15, Gonzales had gained a deep appreciation for his own life because he saw how quickly it could end. At 12, he was riding in a 1964 Chevy Impala with some friends, and they ventured into a small patch of East Los Angeles claimed by a rival gang. "The car stalled in a dangerous park," Gonzales recalls. "I got shot in the back of the head with some shotgun pellets. At 12 years old, I saw my life passing in front of me." The injury proved not to be serious.

"I was running with gangs at the time, trying to find myself," he said. "You either joined a gang to be part of the crowd or you joined a gang for protection. I learned from my mistakes by following people. I should have been a leader, like I am now."

Paul Gonzales is certainly a leader. He returned to his home in Alisos Village to his mother, Anita, and his four brothers and three sisters an Olympic boxing champion, a gold medal hanging from his slender neck. Perhaps symbolizing his life as a 20-year-old compared to what it was as a 14-year-old, Gonzales did not even have to fight a final time to earn the most lustrous of all Olympic medals. On the evening of August 11, Gonzales stepped into the blue canvas ring in the Los Angeles Sports Arena fully expecting to fight Salvatore Todisco of Italy. But in his semifinal fight the night before, Todisco sustained a broken thumb, and fighters do not fight with broken thumbs, just as football players do not play with broken feet. Gonzales won in a walkover to win the gold medal in the lightest Olympic category, 48 kilograms. For one whose formative years were a nightmare, Gonzales is now permitted to dream.

Gonzales, who talks of studying to be an architect states, "I want to build a gym. I want to do something to let kids know that no matter what you do, academics or sports, you can have a dream. I have a saying—if you have a dream, live it, because if you let that dream die, you die with it."

Sharing in Gonzales' dream is a frantic, fast-talking Los Angeles City policeman named Al Stankie. Gonzales has developed a father-son relationship with Stankie over the years. His face breaks into a wide smile and his brown eyes twinkle noticeably when he tells how this big-city cop plucked a tall, skinny barrio child out of a gang skirmish and dropped him between the ropes of the boxing ring at the Hollenbeck Youth Center, in the basement of the police station where Stankie works. "He's what you call a ghetto-cop. He started recruiting kids off the street to box," Gonzales said. "We were having a gang dispute. We didn't use gloves. We used our fists. I was a tall, skinny kid fighting for respect. He walked in there with a uniform and said, 'If you guys want to box, why don't you go to the police station and box for our team?'" The police station is the last place an East Los Angeles gang member would go voluntarily, but the idea of putting on gloves and fighting according to rules struck a responsive nerve in Gonzales. At less than 45.5 kg, he wasn't going to win too many free-for-alls.

"Two weeks later, I snuck into the gym and put the gloves on. It felt good," he said. "In my first fight I knocked my opponent out in the first round. My coach (Stankie) said, 'Son, if you stick with me, I'll make you world champion.'" Gonzales' storybook rise from gang member to gold medalist was not as simple as that, however. Stankie, assigned to community relations by the Los Angeles Police Department, would have to drag Gonzales out of the park a few more times until the conversion was complete.

Gonzales maintains gang life made him what he is today. "Where I live, there are 13 major gangs. Everyone is trying to take over. I got out of the gang when I was 14. I'm still considered a homeboy. The only difference is I know what I want. I learned from my mistakes. I've always been a competitor. My attitude is either to eat or be eaten."

At 48 kg, Gonzales by necessity is not much of an eater, but he clearly has emerged from the barrio with a toothpick and a belch of satisfaction.

Gonzales was a stylish and popular boxer throughout the massive Olympic Games program. With only a single day of rest, there were 359 boxers going at one another in 345 fights. Out of those 359 boxers from every pocket of the globe, excepting Cuba and the Soviet Union, Gonzales was judged to be the best. In somewhat of a surprise, he was awarded the Val Barker Cup, signifying the best boxer of the tournament, "I deserve it. I beat the best," he said simply.

The record shows that he did just that. Gonzales' toughest opponent was also his first opponent, Kwang-Sun Kim (KOR). Going into the fight, Kim was rated second in the world, the International Amateur Boxing Federation (AIBA), and Gonzales was rated third. After nine minutes of boxing, Gonzales showed how sound rankings really are. He took Kim apart. With thunderous applause and booming chants of "U-S-A! U-S-A! U-S-A!" greeting each punch, Gonzales scored a unanimous 5-0 decision over Kim. He jabbed and danced through his next three opponents as well—5-0 over William Bagonza (UGA), 5-0 over Jose Marcelino Bolivar (VEN), and 4-1 over John Lyon (GBR)—to get to the final where he did not have to break a sweat or throw a punch to earn the gold

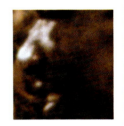

Opposite Page Dewitt (CAN) embraces Mohamed Bouchiche (ALG). Photo: A. Chung

medal. Having conquered the amateurs, Gonzales will soon turn professional in a division, light flyweight, that does not get much exposure or big-money fights. But if anyone can create interest in the "mini-moscas," as the division is called in Spanish, it is the charismatic Gonzales.

"My first big paycheck I get, I'm going to buy my mother a house. We've lived in the ghetto too long," Gonzales said. Don't bet against him. "No matter where I go, I'll go back to Alisos. Those are my roots. The ghetto can make you or break you. It made me what I am."

As expected, the Olympic tournament was dominated by the Americans, the result of the overall strength of amateur boxing in the USA combined with the Eastern bloc boycott of the Games. The Soviet Union and Cuba were missed, and the presence of those countries would have done much to quell voices of instant patriots who screamed insanely for anyone filling out a USA team uniform. Yugoslavia's Redzep Redzeporski, who won the silver medal in the 51 kg, or flyweight, class, noted: "As long as an American is standing on his feet for three rounds, it's hard to get a decision."

Dong-kil Kim of (KOR) would have to agree. He was fighting American Jerry Page in a quarterfinal bout in light welterweight division. It was an extremely close fight, the kind that could have gone either way, and Page was given a 4-1 decision. The large number of flag-waving Korean-Americans who made the short hop from Los Angeles' Koreatown to see their ancestral sons do battle rained a chorus of boos down from their balcony seats. The Korean Boxing Federation immediately filed a protest. Soo- In Oh, Vice President of the Korean Boxing Federation, in a fit of pique, said, "We are now seriously considering pulling out." His boss, Seung-Youn Kim, was more reasonable. "I think not, and I will make the decision." The decision was to stay, and their patience was rewarded when middleweight Joon-Sup Shin took a rare close decision, 3-2, over Virgil Hill, an American from North Dakota. Hill was the only American to lose a gold-medal fight. In victory and defeat, the KOR followed a tournament-long policy of refusing interviews. Hill, the first Olympian from North Dakota in 20 years, was anything but loquacious after the fight. "I feel terrible, rotten," he said. "I worked 12 years for this moment. Who remembers second place?" Hill does have a distinction, however. He is the only American boxer to earn a silver medal in the 1984 Olympics. And since Atlanta's Evander Holyfield took the bronze medal in the light heavyweight division, that can only mean one thing: the USA won a ton of gold. American boxers won nine gold medals, an Olympic record by three.

USA coach Pat Nappi was fat and happy after the tourna-ment, despite stinging criticism of his coaching methods from his own boxers. "I hoped for 12 gold medals, but the kids did a hell of a job, all I care about are the results. I believe the people here were calling them the way they saw them. There is one judge from each continent and I don't see how they can be more fair than that."

In fact, some of the decisions were anything but fair. In a light middleweight semifinal match, for example, Christophe Tiozzo of France drew Shawn O'Sullivan of Canada. O'Sullivan has the face of a classic Irish fighter, and in fact he is quite skilled. But after three fights to get to the semifinals and one big one to go for the gold medal, O'Sullivan was clearly lacking on this day. Close through two rounds, the fight turned dramatically in Tiozzo's favor in the third. The fighter from France repeatedly hammered away at O'Sullivan's head and seemed on the verge of dropping the Canadian. The fight ended with O'Sullivan still on his feet, and minutes later, he was given a 4-1 jury decision over the exasperated Tiozzo. Justice, poetic or otherwise, was served in the final, when Frank Tate of the USA scored a 5-0 decision over O'Sullivan for the gold medal. "The referees and judges have been intimidated by the American audience," O'Sullivan claimed. "Maybe not intimidated, but they've been kind of bending over backwards for the Americans."

Don't tell that to Evander Holyfield. His was the most unfortunate story of the Olympic tournament. Holyfield, a hard-punching, soft-spoken 21-year-old, was well on his way to being named the most outstanding boxer of the tournament. He stopped Taju Akay of Ghana and Ismail Salman of Iraq before the allotted time and hammered Syivaus Okello of Kenya so fiercely and so quickly that the Kenyan dropped to the canvas with three seconds left in the first round, there to stay. That put Holyfield into the semifinals against New Zealand's Kevin Barry, whose upper arms bore a tattoo each. His face was getting tattooed as well, by Holyfield's gloves. The two fighters clinched toward the end of the second round, and referee Gligorije Novicic of Yugoslavia twice said "Stop" to Holyfield and Barry. A split second after Novicic uttered his second "Stop," Holyfield found Barry's unguarded jaw with a heavy left hook, and the black-clad New Zealander crashed to the floor. That set off a chain reaction that affected all three medals in the light-heavyweight class. Because Barry was knocked down and out with a blow to the head, he is automatically prohibited from fighting for 28 days. Barry would have fought Yugoslavia's Anton Josipovic for the gold medal because Holyfield was disqualified for his tardy punch. Josipovic thus won the gold medal in a walkover, Barry got a silver medal that he really did not deserve and Holyfield, unquestionably

Lopez (MEX) and Stecca (ITA) in bantamweight finals. Photo: IOPP

Page (USA) after a blow from Dong Kil Kim (KOR). Photo: IOPP

the best fighter in the division, was awarded the bronze. On the whole, very unsatisfying.

When the Holyfield disqualification was announced, the small delegation from placid New Zealand discovered how abusive an angry, pro-American crowd can be. Nearly all of the 11,729 fans in the Sports Arena booed with gusto and quite a few of them flung garbage in disgust. "We're getting out of Los Angeles fairly soon," a shaken Barry Sr. said. At least they did not leave empty-handed. Young Barry has a silver medal to match the silver leaf logo on his New Zealand uniform. "I knew one of us would eventually get a raw deal to satisfy the complainers," Holyfield said. "I never thought it would be me." And with good reason. The way Holyfield was fighting, there was no way a decision could have gone against him. Ironically, Holyfield said after the Okello fight, "I go out and take care of business. I don't try to do anything to get attention. I just go in to win. I try to keep my composure and let the other guy see how relaxed I am." Like all USA fighters, Holyfield would not even consider any medal other than the gold. "I think a bronze medal is a losing medal. I'd rather get the gold." He has the bronze instead, and Holyfield must take solace in the simple fact he was the best light-heavyweight in the Games.

Josipovic, the Yugoslav who won the gold medal without throwing a punch, was gracious and expansive at the medal ceremony. After receiving his gold medal, he extended his hand to the American and pulled him up to the top of the victory platform. "This is the greatest honor I have had. I believe Holyfield is a great fighter as his matches have proved," Josipovic said. "I would have liked to have fought Holyfield, but the crowd does not realize that. We have no power over the judges' decisions, but I am prepared to box Holyfield. I believe the Olympics are the spirit of friendliness and goodwill. I took the opportunity to have Holyfield join me at the top step. Holyfield is a very good, very experienced fighter. I would have liked to fight him, to show what I'm capable of doing and win the medal that way." Spoken like a true student of literature.

While Americans were winning their record nine gold medals (Paul Gonzales, 106; Steve McCrory, 112; Meldrick Taylor, 125; Pernell Whitaker, 132; Jerry Page, 139; Mark Breland, 147; Frank Tate, 157; Henry Tillman, 201; and Tyrell Biggs, over 201), boxers from other ports of call were providing a lush and diverse landscape for the tournament.

Welterweight Rudel Obreja was part of the Romanian delegation that received an enthusiastic welcome from 90,000 spectators at the Opening Ceremonies in the Coliseum on July 28. Obreja had to fight on the first day of the boxing program against Michael Hughes of Great Britain, so he was not able to take part in the ceremonies. He did watch on television, however, and was moved. "The American public is superb. I was more affected than if I had seen them in person," Obreja said. "All the (Romanian) athletes that were in the ceremonies had a very good impression. I regret that I did not go." Obreja's teammate, light-middleweight Gheorghe Simion, wasted little time in catching the proper Olympic spirit. After being eliminated in the first round by Dal-ho Ahn (KOR), Simion spent the rest of the tournament selling—not trading—Romanian team pins. He was asking three dollars each and had no trouble finding takers. As the only true Eastern bloc country participating in the Los Angeles Games, Romanian pins were coveted. As for Obreja, he joined his teammate on the sidelines when he was beaten by eventual gold medalist Mark Breland in the second round.

One of the better stories of the tournament was told by Pedro Van Raamsdonk of The Netherlands. Pedro, in Holland? "Spain and Holland were in the 80 years' war back in the 1600s. That's where it came from, I think," Van Raamsdonk said. "My father's name is Pedro too. My middle name is Johannes—is that Dutch enough for you?" That will do just fine, Pedro. Van Raamsdonk entered the tournament ranked third in the world, but he did not survive the quarterfinals.

Tillman (USA) connects with a right to Muscone (ITA).
Photo: IOPP

Page (USA) versus Dong Kil Kim (KOR).
Photo: IOPP

He was beaten by Aristides Gonzales of Puerto Rico. While he was active in the ring, Van Raamsdonk cut an odd figure in his blue shorts and yellow singlet. He is impossibly tall at 1.9m, yet has no trouble making the 75 kg weight limit. He looks like he would be more at home on a surfboard or roller skates, yet he is serious enough about his boxing to spend several months of the year training at the Questar Gym in Hollywood.

Then there was the touching story of 26-year-old Mahamadrajab Halibi of Lebanon. He drew the unfortunate assignment of fighting eventual silver medalist Shawn O'Sullivan of Canada in the second round after a first round bye. O'Sullivan floored Halibi at 1:17 of the second round and stunned him with a straight right punch 15 seconds later, and the bout was wisely stopped. Halibi, it develops, entered the tournament at a considerable disadvantage. Because of the war raging throughout his country, Halibi had to do train in an underground bomb shelter in Beruit. "It is very difficult," he said. "The sound of bombardment was clear, but I was away from it."

Even without the Eastern European countries and Cuba, this tournament showed what a grand spectacle Olympic boxing can be. Where else would you see someone from Romania fighting someone from the Central African Republic; someone from Sweden doing battle with someone from Uganda; someone from the tiny island nation of Tonga fighting someone from Yugoslavia? Celebrities such as Farrah Fawcett, Ryan O'Neal, David Keith, Mohammad Ali, Sugar Ray Robinson, Thomas Hearns and John Madden thought enough of the concept to take a look-see. In the words of Yugoslavian boxer, Anton Josipovic, "I believe the Olympics are the spirit of friendliness and goodwill." Now, if they could only do something about the judging.

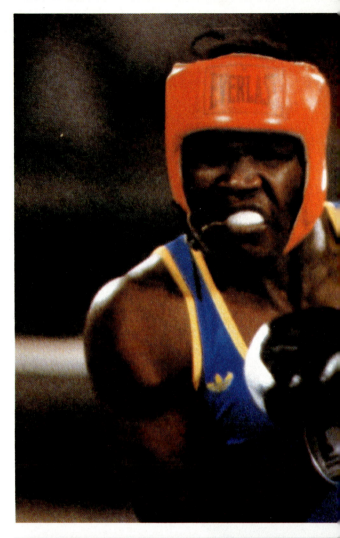

Ortez (PUR) spars with Chil (KOR) in lightweight competition.
Photo: A. Chung

Canoeing:
Flat Water Fever

Eric Evans

New Zealand's Ian Ferguson shattered the belief that Olympic canoeing champions arise only from countries boasting long traditions in the sport and thousands of paddlers from which to choose, when he won three Olympic gold medals in kayaking on Lake Casitas. Here was a country at the far end of the world, as far as one could get from the center of world canoesport, with a mere 17 kayakers from which to select an Olympic team. Yet New Zealand captured four of the five golds in men's kayaking events. Here was its best paddler, a 32-year-old accountant from Auckland who retired after the 1980 Olympics where he barely made the finals in two events—returning to the sport and besting the world's elite in every event he entered.

Lake Casitas saw other surprises as well. In front of the largest crowds in USA canoeing history, and with the absence of the perennially strong canoeing nations from eastern Europe, Romania with more Olympic medals than any other country was expected to dominate the competition. Although Romania placed more boats in the 12 finals than any other country, it shared honors with Canada in the canoeing events, while Swedish paddlers proved to be the swiftest in the women's kayak classes.

On a windless Friday morning with the sun just breaking through the 8 a.m. mist, perfect conditions for canoeing, Romania's Vasile Diba bolted from the start line. Pursuing his third straight Olympic medal in the K-1 500, Diba led at 250 meters, but thereafter it was Ferguson's race. Ferguson's victory marked New Zealand's first gold medal in canoeing competition. It would not be the last.

Sweden's Lars-Erik Moberg, took the silver medal. Bernard Bregeon of France, like Ferguson a short stocky man in a sport ruled by tall athletes, won the bronze medal, while Diba faded to fourth.

A duel was anticipated in the C-1 500 between world champion Costica Olaru (ROM), 24, and Larry Cain (CAN), 21. Olaru is known as the hottest canoeist in the world, particularly in rough waters. But Casitas' surface was like glass, and Olaru was not only thoroughly beaten by Cain (giving Canada its first canoeing gold since 1936), but also outstroked at the finish by Denmark's sole canoeing entry, Henning Jakobsen.

Sweden's King Carl Gustav and Queen Sylvia had scarcely taken their seats at Lake Casitas when they were quickly brought to their feet by the open-water victory in the K-1W 500 of subject Agneta Andersson over Barbara Schuttpelz (FRG) and Holland's Annemiek Derckx. Andersson's win was Sweden's first-ever women's Olympic canoeing medal and especially poignant in that her career had nearly ended in 1983 with a heart infection. She was to earn her second gold medal

of this Olympics with an overpowering victory in the K-2W 500.

Less than an hour after receiving their medals for K-1 500, Ferguson and Moberg readied themselves for the always fast and furious K-2 500. Ferguson and teammate Paul MacDonald swept to a convincing victory over Moberg and partner Per-Inge Bengtsson. In a photo finish, Canada's Hugh Fisher and Alwyn Morris passed Italians Daniele Scarpa and Francesco Uberti, and the Romanian duo Nicole Fedosei and Angelin Velea in the last few meters for the bronze.

In the C-2 500, all eyes were on Romania's Ivan Potzaichin and Toma Simionov alongside Yugoslavia's Matija Ljubek and Mirko Nisovic. Potzaichin, 35, was competing in his fifth straight Olympics and had won five medals, three of them gold. Ljubek had won a gold in the C-1 1000 in 1976. The grand old men of canoeing, winners of innumerable World Championships, were meeting in perhaps their final Olympics. The Romanians shot into the lead, but in the final hundred meters however, Ljubek and Nisovic powered past. Potzaichin could only watch in frustration. Spain finished in third place marking the first trip to the podium for Spanish canoeists.

Alan Thompson continued New Zealand's strong performances in men's kayaking by leading from start to finish in the K-1 1000. Thompson, 25, a plumber by trade, had, like all of New Zealand's kayakers, started his career paddling surf skis.

Yugoslavia's Milan Janic rebounded from his ninth place in the K-1 500 to take the silver. But the biggest cheers from the predominantly American audience were for Michigan's Greg Barton, 24, captain of the American Olympic canoeing team who won third place. Barton, raised on a 2,000-acre pig farm, summa cum laude graduate of the University of Michigan, was born with a deformed foot and paddles with a special foot brace in his kayak. Barton's Olympic medal was the first in USA men's kayaking since 1936.

FRG's Ulrich Eicke looks like a lion, a large powerful man with a thick mane of curly hair. He paddled like one as well with a startlingly clear victory over Canada's gold medalist Cain. It was a fitting finish for Eicke, 32, who said that the C-1 1000 would be his final race. Denmark's Jakobsen won an additional medal—the bronze.

The K-4 500 was a new event on the Olympic program. But a team of old hands from Romania, Agafia Constantin, Nastasia Ionescu, Tecla Marinescu, and Maria Stefan, lifted some of the gloom from their camp with Romania's first gold medal of the day. Sweden took the silver. Andersson's third medal of the Games made her the first woman to win three medals in a single Olympics. Canada bested the USA and FRG for the bronze, making this their second women's medal in

**Opposite Page
Canadian 21000
meter final, strokes
against MEX.
Photo: IOPP**

kayaking. Earlier Alexandra Barre and Sue Holloway won the silver in the K2W-500.

A measure of the competitiveness of K-2 1000 is evident in the winning time posted by Hugh Fisher and Alwyn Morris (CAN), a full-blooded Mohawk Indian. Together they posted a time that was over 2.5 seconds faster than the best previously recorded in Olympic K-2 1000 competition. Morris waved a feather during the awards ceremony. Bregeon (FRA) won the silver at the helm of his K-2 with partner Patrick LeFoulon. Barry Kelly and Grant Kenny won the bronze, Australia's first Olympic canoeing medal.

Potzaichin and Simionov (ROM) had their revenge on Ljubek and Nisovic for the Yugoslavians' earlier victory. Starting quickly, the Romanians shot out to a fantastic 2.158 second lead at the 250-meter mark. The Yugoslavians, closed after 500 meters, but Potzaichin watched them over his right shoulder with each paddle stroke all the way to the finish. In third, almost seven seconds behind, were Didier Hoyer and Eric Renaud (FRA), who had lost the bronze in the C-2 500 by the thinnest of margins.

The men's K-4, the final canoeing competition, was perhaps a microcosm of the overall event. New Zealand led the pack, with Sweden a solid second, and the Romanians on the outside looking in as another western country, this time France, nudged them into fourth.

For Ian Ferguson (NZL) it was his third gold medal, only the second time in Olympic history that a paddler has won three golds in canoeing in a single Games. "Perhaps," said Alan Thompson (NZL), who won his second gold, "our results prove the spirit to train hard and the spirit of togetherness we have in New Zealand amongst our team, means more than money, fancy equipment, and a large pool of athletes."

Baron Pierre de Coubertin couldn't have said it better.

FRG pulls ahead of
ESP in 21000
meter Canadian
competition.
Photo: IOPP

The finish of a
Canadian single
event, Lake Casitas.
Photo: S. Powell

Cycling: Wheels Of Fire

Tim Blumenthal

The balance of power in international bicycle racing is shifting. Continental Europeans have dominated the sport since the first world championships in 1893 and the inaugural Olympic cycling events three years later. But the last dozen years have been marked by the emergence of world champions from Japan, Australia and most recently, the USA. Furthermore, track and road riders from Canada, Mexico, South America, and the British Isles have risen from the bottom rank to become top contenders.

These dramatic changes in cycling were proclaimed by results of the eight Olympic bicycle races in Los Angeles. Consider: the USA, a nation that hadn't produced a cycling medalist since 1912, won four gold and a record nine medals in all; Canada, which last won an Olympic medal in 1908, won two silvers; and Mexico and Japan earned their first-ever Olympic cycling medals. In contrast, France, Italy, and Belgium, three of the leading nations in Olympic cycling history, won but one medal each.

The Olympic cycling program opened with two individual road races. They were held in the inland Orange County community of Mission Viejo, about 50 miles south of Los Angeles. The 79-kilometer morning event was the first Olympic women's bicycle race. A crowd estimated at 250,000 lined the 15.85-kilometer circuit. Forty-four women finished, but Colorado's Connie Carpenter, outsprinted the lead group of five riders for victory to become the first woman to win an Olympic bicycle race, and the first USA rider to win the Olympic road race. Accomplishing this, the 27-year-old Carpenter announced her retirement in a post-race press conference. Rebecca Twigg of Seattle added to the USA celebration by taking second, just a wheel's width behind Carpenter. The one-two USA finish set the tone for the seven events to come.

The 190-kilometer men's road race boiled down to a contest between a lead group of seven that formed on the eighth of 12 laps. It included Steve Bauer of Canada, Norwegians Dag Otto Lauritzen and Morten Saether, Colombian Nestor Mora, and three USA riders: Alexi Grewal, Davis Phinney and Thurlow Rogers. Grewal, attacked alone near the end of lap 11 and took a 28-second lead into the final 15.6 km circuit. With one lap remaining, this 23-year-old had a chance to become the first USA man ever to win the Olympic road race. That possibility held special meaning because Grewal nearly didn't get to compete in the event for his training methods and independence often put him at odds with the USA coaching staff. Additionally, just two weeks prior to the Games during the Coors Classic in Colorado, Grewal's post-race urine sample apparently showed the presence of an illegal substance. Grewal admitted swallowing a herbal tablet before a race, but said he had no idea the tablet contained anything illegal. International rules dictate an automatic 30-day suspension if a rider is found to have an illegal substance in his bloodstream. A second test showed the same result and Grewal was suspended. It appeared he would miss the Olympics. The matter took a bizarre twist when it was learned that Grewal takes a legal asthma medicine. Grewal challenged the suspension by claiming the test result could have been triggered by the asthma medicine, not by anything in the herbal tablet. A five-member jury ruled in his favor. However, between his sour relations with the coaches and his near-suspension, Grewal had a tough time just getting to the Olympic Games.

And there he was, 176 km into the race, holding the lead. Suddenly, Bauer counterattacked. The Canadian caught Grewal on the steep Vista Del Lago climb with about eight miles remaining. The other five in the front group dropped well behind. A worldwide television audience looked on as Grewal appeared to lose all his energy. For a moment, as Bauer passed, Grewal seemed almost incapable of continuing, let alone battling Bauer for the gold. But somehow he kept going, staying in the wake of the Canadian to the top of the climb, then recovering on the 4.8 km downhill respite that followed. The duo approached the finish line still together, and almost a minute ahead of all other riders. Bauer, known as one of the best amateur road sprinters in the world, appeared to have the edge. A general axiom of road sprinting is try not to make the first move. The duo rolled slowly down Marguerite Parkway eyeing each other down. The pace got slower and slower. Bauer finally initiated the sprint about 90 m before the line. Grewal remained calm and kept his bike right behind Bauer's. With about 50 meters to go, he came flying by to win by almost a bike length.

The five track events were held on the two-year-old Olympic Velodrome on the campus of California State University, Dominguez Hills in Carson. Even though its more than 8000 seating capacity was one of the largest in Olympic history, there were still 30,000 more requests for tickets than seats available.

Track cycling was one of the Olympic sports most affected by the Soviet-led boycott. But one event where the Soviets and East Germans wouldn't have been favored was the 4000-meter team pursuit, in which FRG won the '83 world championship and set the outdoor world record.

However, in the L.A. Games the FRG team never showed good form and they were caught in the semifinals by the USA whose previous Olympics best was 10th place.

The final pitted the USA against Australia. USA rider

**Opposite Page
Photo: T. Jones**

Dave Grylls pulled his left foot out of his toe-strap at the start, so the USA had to compete with three riders against the Aussie's four. Steve Hegg, the American rider who had earlier won the individual pursuit gold, put in an extra effort. But it was not enough and the smooth Australians won by three seconds.

The use of revolutionary aerodynamic equipment was an interesting sidelight at track events. Frames, components, clothing, shoes, helmets and tires—all equipment, in fact—were modified to reduce weight and decrease wind resistance. About six of the 30 nations that competed in the Olympic track events used solid, spokeless disc wheels constructed of kevlar or carbon fiber which cost at least $1,000. Proponents of solid wheels claim they create less turbulence (and therefore increase a rider's speed) than spoked wheels. Critics say they are heavy and unstable in anything but calm conditions. Some riders say solid wheels offer nothing but a psychological boost—and that is reason enough to use them.

The new bicycle technology is beyond the financial means of many nations. Some foreign coaches called for a return to standardized equipment. "The rider, not his equipment, should determine the result," said one coach.

In the 1000-meter time trial, all three medal winners including gold medalist Freddy Schmidtke (FRG) used standard bicycles that barely differed from machines ridden 20 years ago. Meanwhile Rory O'Reilly (USA) appeared to struggle for control of his "funny bike" equipped with a solid rear wheel and a solid chainring. He finished eighth. Individual pursuit winner Hegg wore a skin-tight rubber suit and rode a radical 5.85 kg bike. After beating Rolf Golz (FRG) in the final, he said, "If I feel good about my equipment, I ride well."

Hegg and Golz not only engaged in a cycling duel but also jousted verbally. "You wouldn't have beaten me in Germany," Golz snapped at Hegg. "I thought that was kind of rude," responded Hegg. "I would've beat him in Germany. I would've beat him anywhere."

USA sprinter Mark Gorski of Costa Mesa, California, didn't lose a ride in his march to the gold. He beat his countryman, Nelson Vails of New York City, in the final. In heat one versus Vails, Gorski covered the final 200 meters in 10.49—the second- fastest time in Olympic history.

The final event of the Olympic cycling program was the 100- kilometer team time trial, held on the Artesia Freeway near the velodrome. Using solid front and back disc wheels, the Italian foursome rode the fastest 100-kilometer time in Olympic history, 1:58:28. Switzerland, which used solid rear wheels, won the silver and was 8 seconds faster than the USA bronze medalists. The team time trial bronze was the ninth USA cycling medal of the '84 Games. Prior to this, there were only three USA Olympic cycling medals.

By the close of the 1984 Olympics, some people complained that the drama of the Games had been sapped by USA domination. But to just about anyone familiar with the dark history of USA cycling in Olympic competition, the American bicycle racing successes of the Los Angeles Games were a refreshing change. For other nations, it is a change to be learned from—a change to be countered four years down the road at the '88 Games in Seoul, Korea.

Australia's gold
medal-winning
4000m pursuit
team.
Photo: S. Powell

Hegg (USA) raises
his arm in victory.
Photo: S. Powell

Left to Right
Ropret (YUG) in the
road race.
Photo: D. Cannon

Nakatake (JPN) collides with Lee (TPE).
Photo: D. Cannon

Nitz (USA) on one of
the new "super"
cycles.
Photo: S. Powell

Phinney (USA) is
drafted by Maurer
(SUI).
Photo: S. Powell

Men's individual
road race pulls away
from the start.
Photo: S. Powell

Equestrian: Grace and Stamina

Bill Cutting

Unique in all Olympic competition, equestrian events measure the training and conditioning of not one, but two superb athletes. Each athlete—horse and rider—must continuously depend upon the skill and experience of the other. To be successful, they must communicate through a mysterious set of signals: a tap of the hand, a prod with the knee or a whispered command. It's part of the subtle beauty that makes equestrian events so thrilling to watch.

The site for the equestrian events, 50-year-old Santa Anita Park in suburban Arcadia, is one of the world's most splendid horse racing venues. Manicured pathways and promenades surround the park and spill over into the infield, graciously ushering visitors to and from the various seating areas. Though its customary patrons are more attuned to thoroughbred perfectas than to equestrian perfection, Santa Anita was temporarily converted into an equestrian facility for the 1984 Olympics because it provided ample room for competitors, horses, trainers, and spectators. In fact, with a total seating capacity for 31,000 along with space for an additional 50,000 at Fairbanks Ranch in San Diego (site of the endurance phases of the 3-day event), the 1984 Games permitted more spectators to marvel at the grace and stamina of more horse and rider teams, than at any other site in modern Olympic history.

In every sense today's equestrian program commemorates a modern European military tradition. The schedule consists of three disciplines: dressage—a minutely precise series of compulsory maneuvers; show-jumping—a real crowd-pleaser in which horse and rider must successfully clear a variety of obstacles; and the three-day event—an exhausting competition that combines dressage and jumping along with a demanding day-long endurance test that is itself divided into four phases.

In the three-day event, partisan crowds in record numbers and temperatures in the high 80s with 65 percent humidity combined to keep the heat on both horse and rider. With the dressage portion of the event already completed, Hansueli Schmutz (SUI) riding Oran enjoyed a comfortable lead, with Bruce Davidson (USA) on J.J. Babu, and Karen Stives (USA) on Ben Arthur hard on his heels. The endurance competition was held at San Diego's Fairbanks Ranch and Country Club. The cross-country phase, one of four for the day, was pure Americana, with jumps resembling a western town, a California mission, and a Z-shaped obstacle named for the movie "The Mark of Zorro" which starred silent movie actor Douglas Fairbanks, original owner of the ranch. In spite of its imaginative design and colorful obstacles, the 7.25 kilometer Fairbanks Ranch course was in reality a punishing test for every competitor.

Lucinda Green (GBR), the pre-competition favorite in the three-day event, commented at the start, "I don't think a dressage score is going to amount to a whole, whole heap, because that cross-country out there is tough." Green's comment proved prophetic. Diana Clapham, Green's teammate, was one of a handful of riders who were unceremoniously dumped in the drink at the course's most imposing water obstacle. By sundown, it was Stives and her sleek gray gelding Ben Arthur, who held the lead, having negotiated all four phases of the tough Rancho Santa Fe endurance course flawlessly, including the 33-obstacle cross-country. Stives' score allowed the USA to maintain a comfortable lead over nearest rival Great Britain in team competition, as well.

After a one-day hiatus to allow for travel and rest, the three-day event resumed at Santa Anita Park for the fourth and final competition: jumping. The stage was set for an airborne duel between Stives, Virginia Holgate (GBR), and a 27-year-old dairy farmer from New Zealand, Mark Todd, aboard a dark brown gelding named Charisma. As he had at Rancho Santa Fe, Todd cleared every obstacle and finished the day without a penalty point. Stives needed a similarly perfect round to take the gold, but a single errant rail proved her undoing. Todd took the gold, Stives the silver and Great Britain's Virginia Holgate aboard Priceless, the bronze. Team three-day medals are tallied by adding the scores of the three best riders from each country. In team scoring, USA riders, on the wings of a perfect jumping round by Torrance Fleischmann and a strong performance by six-time Olympian J. Michael Plumb along with Stives, managed to win the gold from a determined team from Great Britain, while the Federal Republic of Germany was awarded the bronze.

Next up was team jumping where a horse and rider must, in two rounds, clear a variety of fences in a prescribed amount of time. The Santa Anita Park jumping course was judged by all competitors to be technically difficult, one that could, at a given moment, expose any weakness a horse and rider might possess. Joe Fargis (USA) and his 11-year-old mare Touch of Class jumped their first two rounds without a single fault. Teammate Leslie Burr on Albany jumped her two rounds with just one knockdown, setting up a huge American lead that the other 14 teams could scarcely hope to overcome. It was only the middle of the second and final round when Conrad Homfeld (USA), aboard the magnificent gray stallion Abdullah, cleared each of his 15 jumps without a mishap, assuring the USA of the gold medal. The early lead was so convincing that USA team member Melanie Smith was able to pass on her final round. Once again, Great Britain took the silver, and the

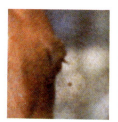

Opposite Page Sloothak (FRG) on Farmer in team jumping. Photo: IOPP

USA show jumping team: left to right Fargis, Burr, Homfeld and Smith. Photo: A. Chung

Federal Republic of Germany the bronze.

Just as the free-wheeling jumping competition seems well-suited to the casual American temperament, so it would seem that dressage with its emphasis on tradition and precision should appeal to riders from the European nations. Dressage, a French word that means, "training", is most similar to compulsory school exercises in figure skating, in that horse and rider must perform a series of difficult maneuvers and change of gaits in a prearranged order. Team dressage also known as the Grand Prix Test is distinguished from individual dressage or Grand Prix Special Test.

At the end of the first day of competition, the team from Switzerland held the lead over a field of 19 on the strength of superb rides from Otto Hofer on Limandus and 1976 Olympic gold medal winner Christine Stueckelberger riding Tansanit. Still to come was world and Olympic team dressage champion Dr. Reiner Klimke (FRG) riding Ahlerich. Herr Doktor Klimke, a lawyer from Munster, Westphalia, totally dominated the second day of competition with an exacting performance. As it turned out, Dr. Klimke's second day score, the highest posted during the entire team dressage event, was clearly needed to bolster weak performances by teammates Uwe Sauer aboard Montevideo and Herbert Krug on Muscadeur. "I was supposed to go for 'sure' and 'quiet' to help preserve for the individual dressage event", Klimke noted later. "But I had to come forward because the marks of the others were not high enough." Thanks to Klimke's nearly flawless ride, the team from the Federal Republic of Germany sailed to its fourth Olympic gold medal in this discipline. Much further down the line, the team from Switzerland took the silver, edging out the team from Sweden, which captured the bronze.

The following day's individual dressage event told a similar story of grace, style and precise horsemanship by Klimke. Traditionally the Grand Prix Special Test of individual dressage is even more demanding than the team competition. However, Dr. Klimke and Ahlerich, as they had the day before, turned in a performance sufficiently brilliant to take home their second gold medal in dressage. In winning the event, Klimke not only proved he was the finest dressage rider in the world, he also captured his first individual Olympic gold medal, an honor which had thus far eluded him, despite a 1982 world championship in individual dressage. "It is what I have lived for", Klimke beamed. At the close of competition, Anne Grethe Jensen (DEN) found herself with a silver medal. Otto Hofer (SUI) took the bronze.

Sunday morning, the final day of the Games, dawned brilliantly. The San Gabriels were, for once, unobscured by the bedevilling smog that had kept them shrouded for most of the two weeks of competition. One final event would have to be decided before the equestrian competition ended: individual show jumping. In the day's first light, USA's equestrian chef d'equipe Frank Chapot warned the press not to expect a repeat of the team jumping results. "No one is that much better than everyone else," Chapot cautioned. There is no standout." The USA riders—Fargis, Homfeld, Melanie Smith and Leslie Burr—were strong, as their team gold had justifiably shown. But also on the program were Paul Schockemohle (FRG) on Deister, winner of the prestigious Grand Prix of Aachen earlier in the year, Mario Deslauriers (CAN) riding Aramis, along with an imposing field of some 50 other riders. After two rounds of competition, USA teammates Joe Fargis and Conrad Homfeld were locked in a struggle for the gold medal. Of the pre-event favorites, only Deslauriers, and Heidi Robbiani (SUI) on an American mare Jessica, were left to determine third place. Deslauriers was edged out for the bronze in a jump-off by Robbiani, who put together a superb, clean round. In so doing, she became the first woman in Olympic equestrian history to take an individual jumping medal. In the end, the gold medal belonged to the USA.

But to which competitor?

Homfeld and Fargis had each finished the first two rounds with identical scores. Each was the owner of a single gold medal. And each could claim the other not only as a friend, but as a partner in a Virginia breeding stable. After the course was cleared, and with H.R.H. Prince Philip (GBR), President of the Federation International Equestres, looking on, Homfeld and his 14-year-old stallion Abdullah, took the arena. Six fences. Seven jumping efforts. When his ride was over, Homfeld had knocked down two barriers. Fargis, by virtue of his first two rides could safely knock down one barrier and still take the gold. That cushion was clearly unnecessary for Fargis, who skimmed the entire course without a fault. For his part, Touch of Class finished the round with nary a hair on his tail out of place.

Later that evening, a capacity crowd gathered in the Los Angeles Memorial Coliseum to celebrate the Final Event: Closing Ceremonies. But before the songs could be sung, the rockets could be fired, and the Olympic flame extinguished, there remained some unfinished business. In the long evening light, three horse and rider teams pranced stride for stride into the Coliseum. To the delight of crowd, each stepped forward to receive their medal. But as Fargis, Homfeld and Robbiani stood on the victory platform and took in the applause, they knew there were three other athletes in the Coliseum, who deserved the award just as much as they.

Persson (SWE)
aboard Joel at
Fairbanks Ranch.
Photo: T. Jones

Todd (NZL) emerges
from the water on
Charisma.
Photo: T. Jones

Klimke (FRG) on Ahlerich, gold medal winner in dressage. Photo: T. Jones

Candrian (SUI) on Slygof in team jumping.
Photo: T. Jones

Griggs (CAN) on Jack The Lad at Fairbanks Ranch.
Photo: T. Jones

Team and individual jumping winner Fargis (USA) on Touch of Class. Photo: T. Jones

Fencing: A Flurry of Style

Richard Cohen

With a fanfare of trumpets, the curtains parted, and there at the Long Beach Terrace Theater sat two rows of officials of the Federation International d'Escrime, elegantly clad in dinner jackets. Even the TV cameramen wore tuxedos. Fencing events have been hosted in theaters before, but rarely with such style, or in front of a 3000-seat auditorium.

Sadly, the fencing was not of a standard to match its surroundings. The individual foil and sabre finals were exciting, but only the epee looked world class.

All the fencing up to the final was held in the Long Beach Convention Center. Rising to the occasion, the Italians made a fine time of it. They ended the competition with three golds, a silver and three bronzes—over 24 percent of their total Games tally. France, who in 1980 took four golds and a bronze, showed that this was no fluke, collecting two golds, two silvers and three bronzes. Federal Republic of Germany had two golds and three silvers. Only five medals went elsewhere.

In the opening event, the men's individual foil, all three Italian fencers, two from FRG, and two from FRA, reached the eight-man final. The opening bout featured the remaining finalist Thierry Soumagne (BEL) against Matthias Behr (FRG). It was Behr who, two years ago, had his foil break and kill the reigning Olympic and world champion Vladimir Smirnov (URS). There was a frightening moment in the bout when Soumagne was hit and doubled up, but he was soon himself again—although Behr triumphed 10-5.

The favorite, Andrea Borella (ITA), the winner of this year's world cup, was outfenced in the second bout of the final by the 30-year-old Fredric Pietruszka (FRA), and lost 10-6. Third was Stefano Cerioni (ITA), 1984 under-20 champion.

The final was mainly memorable for the remarkable escapes of Mauro Numa (ITA). In his opening bout he came back from 6-8 down against Phillippe Omnes (FRA) with only a minute to go to win 10-8. In the semi-final he was led by Cerioni 6-1 and 7-3, but won 11-9. And in the final he was 7-1 down against Behr, but with a flurry of hits won on the very last touch 12-11. Cerioni beat Pietruszka 10-5 for the bronze.

The women's foil saw the first-ever fencing gold for the People's Republic of China. Jujie Luan had been at the top of her sport for some time with both silver and bronze medals in world championships. Here, in her fight for the gold, she beat Cornelia Hanisch (FRG), world champion of 1979 and 1981, 8-5. Third was Dorina Vaccaroni (ITA), who beat the impressive young Romanian Elizabeta Guzganu, also 8-5. Vaccaroni was the pre-competition favorite, with victories this year in Budapest, Como and Paris. Judging from her later poor performance in the women's team event, she reached Los Angeles far from her best.

Sabre had the smallest entry—35—and provided the least impressive competition. Not one of the finalists had won an event in this year's world cup. The top seed, Franco Della Barba (ITA), lost to the 32-year-old American, Peter Westbrook, 11-9 in their fight for the final, and then in the repechage to the moustachioed Romanian, Marin Mustata, by the same score. The other two Italians Giovanni Scalzo and Marco Marin duly reached the last eight, and found themselves drawn against each other. Marin normally defeats his older teammate, and so it was this time, 11-9.

Though just 21 years old, Marin despatched his French opponent, Herve Granger-Veyron, with ease, 10-5, in their semi-final bout, and faced Jean Francoise Lamour (FRA), for the gold medal. Lamour took an early lead but Marin put in a late spurt for the score to reach 11-all. Lamour, with the priority of attack in his favor, forced Marin back toward his two-meter line and attacked. Marin counter-attacked, and the decision could have gone either way. The director, Tamas Kovacs of Hungary, who had been excellent throughout, favored the attack.

Westbrook took a bronze, America's first Olympic fencing medal since 1960, their first sabre medal since 1904.

The epee was at least a quieter affair. With the largest entry of all—65—it saw three competitors from FRG reach the final. In one of the most attractive bouts of the final, Philippe Riboud (FRA), world champion 1979, second in 1978 and 1982, pipped Alexander Pusch (FRG), champion of 1975, 1976 and 1978, 12-11. Riboud had been ill throughout 1983 and at times seemed to be running out of breath, but Gilbert Lefin, the outstanding French epee coach, had told him to come on guard with his hand well raised, and so offset Pusch's regular attempts to flick his blade on to Riboud's wrist. The advice cost him the bout.

Possibly the bout exhausted Riboud, for in the first semi-final he lost to his countryman, Philippe Boisse, 12-11. The second saw Bjorne Vaggo of Sweden—a surprise finalist, who had not reached an A category final all season—despatch Stefano Bellone (ITA) 10-8. The Swede had good distance and an effective counter-attack. More important still, he had earlier in the year moved to Paris to concentrate on training. He was no match for Boisse in the final, getting only five hits. Riboud beat Bellone for the bronze.

After the individual events France had two golds and a bronze, and indeed in the epee had outclassed the other nations. However, it is worth recording that in Moscow, besides the French medals, Sweden and Italy may both have won golds but the remaining sixteen medals all went to countries not

Opposite Page Omnes (FRA) lunges an opponent in individual foil. Photo: D. Cannon

participating in Los Angeles. Even had Cuba and the East Europeans been present, however, it is hard to imagine any team other than Italy's as a favorite in the team foil. They duly made the final, though with a close 9-7 victory over France, Angelo Scuri gaining an excellent four victories. In the other semi-final FRG won 9-3 over AUT. In the final, Mauro Numa equalled Scuri's performance, winning his bouts 5-0, 5-0, 5-3, 5- 2, and giving his team the victory at 8-7. France defeated Austria 9-3 to take the bronze.

Only three nations had a realistic chance of a sabre team medal—Italy, France and Romania. ITA beat FRG 9-3 in one semi- final and FRA triumphed over ROM 9-4 in the other. FRG then rallied well, to lose to the Romanians only 7-8. The Romanian No. 4 Alexandru Chiculita, won all his fights, 5-1, 5-4, 5-0, 5- 1, to secure his team the bronze.

The opening fight of the final marked the low point of the entire competition. Granger Veyron faced Dino Meglio, a highly unorthodox opponent, and for the first three and a half minutes of the six minute bout not a single attack was attempted. They simply chased each other off the end of the piste. Four seconds short of five minutes both fencers received a special warning for 'offending against the spirit of the sport'— for which a repetition can mean expulsion. There was a quick exchange of hits, then another lull, during which a wag in the audience shouted: 'Let's get some Hungarian fencers in here!' Whether fired by this or by the thought of time expiring at 5.18, Meglio launched an attack, lost the hit, and in a flurry of last minute actions found himself the loser, 5-4. The rest was an anticlimax.

Ten teams competed in the women's foil event, which was marked by several close matches. USA beat GBR on the last hit of the last fight. ITA defeated CHN 9-7 to reach the semifinals, ROM beat FRA 8-7 and FRG overcame ITA 8-8 on hits to reach the final. FRA beat ITA 9-7 to secure the bronze. Only the final itself was decisive, Weber and Hanisch gaining three wins each in a 9-5 victory, FRG's first-ever gold medal at this event in either world championships or Olympics.

The men's team epee saw CHN gain sixth place. KOR also did well to place seventh, defeating SWE 7-3, and eliminating SUI in their first round pool.

In the semi-finals FRG defeated CAN, FRA and ITA. In the final FRG was always a fight or more ahead, and won 8-5. Italy took the bronze over a much-improved CAN.

Football:
The International Pastime

Harvey Frommer with Tim Schum

Olympic football is better for the changes it introduced in 1984, and the United States of America can stand a little taller in world football circles for its unexpected, even extraordinary, support of the football matches.

An examination of several aspects of play underscores the fact that Olympic football (the most highly attended sport at the '84 Games) is in a stronger position in the Olympic movement than ever before. It has a realistic chance, with continued change, to take its rightful place among the world's most important FIFA-staged football events by 1988.

Historically, Olympic football has never generated the world-wide frenzy of other events sponsored by the Federation Internationale de Football Association (FIFA), principally because of the lack of balance in the competition itself. With team rosters dominated by the same players who would compete as World Cup representatives of their countries, the inequality of the Olympic football competition due to roster disparity, in large measure was thought responsible for the less-than-enthusiastic response by the football world to the quadrennial Olympic football competition. The redefinition by FIFA of player eligibility standards which allowed professionals to engage in the competition, while controversial, seemingly had a good impact on the 16th Olympic football tournament.

Under the FIFA edict, amateurs maintained eligibility, but for the first time, professionals were deemed eligible for football competition with the exception of countries from Europe and South America. Teams from those continents could not use professionals who had competed in World Cup competition.

This, coupled with the late withdrawal of the three medal winners from the 1980 Moscow Olympics (TCH, GDR and URS) stamped the Los Angeles football tournament as unique even before kickoff. It was not only the first to legitimize the use of professionals, but the first since 1952 not to have any of the previous medal-winning teams back to defend places.

With first round play scattered at four venues: Cambridge, Massachusetts; Annapolis, Maryland; Palo Alto and Pasadena, California—3000 miles distant from each other, east coast to west—the 1984 tournament exposed the competition to a wide audience, and the response of the 800,000-plus spectators in attendance for the first phase of play was well-noted by FIFA officials present.

Whether it was the substitution of Italy, Norway and the Federal Republic of Germany for the withdrawn countries or parity brought about by the new eligibility standards, final round play in all groupings saw very equalized competition.

The Chile-Norway (Group A), Cameroon-Canada-Iraq (Group B) and Egypt-United States (Group D) matchups meant seven teams were battling for three final round spots at Palo Alto and Pasadena during the final two nights of play.

"It made it very difficult trying to keep one ear on the scoreline in Annapolis while trying to coach the team on the field," said Canadian coach Tony Waiters in a post-game interview in Boston, following his team's 3-1 conquest of Cameroon.

The victory by Canada unraveled a myriad of possibilities in Group B play going into the August 3 kickoffs at Cambridge and Annapolis. Simply put, Yugoslavia had clinched first place in the competition while Cameroon, Canada and Iraq all had the potential to move on. Iraq, a decided underdog, led Yugoslavia at half-time by 2-0 in its bid to clinch a West Coast place.

It was this shocker that Waiters referred to in his comments. If maintained, with Iraq in the lead and with Canada not able to widen its 1-0 halftime advantage over Cameroon, surprising Iraq would have emerged a winner on goal advantage. "We tried to keep the Iraq score from the boys at the half, but it must have crept in the room somehow," smiled Waiters in recounting the Canadian locker room scene at game's mid-time pause. "We told the team—keep pressing for more goals."

With the public address announcer keeping the Harvard Stadium crowd informed of Annapolis action, Waiters saw his team extend its lead to 2-0, only to have Cameroon narrow the margin to 2-1. Needing only a tie for advancement, the African team went all out for the equalizer, but in doing so it stretched its defense to the limit. Further weakened by the loss of two players to red cards, Cameroon gave Canada the opportunity it needed to score the game's decisive fourth goal. Just about the same time as Canada grabbed its 3-1 lead, it was reported that the Yugoslavian offense had erupted for four second-half goals to short circuit the bid of Iraq, 4-2.

"This is the greatest moment in the history of Canadian football," was Waiters' summation of his team's victory over Cameroon. Waiters, however, was red-carded in the match and was forced to the sideline for his team's quarter-final match with Brazil. "My first red card in 27 years of football", he noted, perhaps indicating the frenzy of the moment for himself and the Canadian team.

The USA team had a chance to make history in Group D action at Palo Alto. After defeating Costa Rica 3-0, before a crowd of 78,265 for the first USA victory in Olympic play in 60 years, the USA team was defeated in its second game by Italy, 1-0. A USA victory over EGY was needed to move the

**Opposite Page
An early round
match between ITA
and USA.
Photo: D. Cannon**

FRA and BRA in
finals action at the
Rose Bowl.
Photo: IOPP

Gymnastics: Moments of Magic

Phil Jackman

Cut and dried. That's how experts saw the results of the team and individual competition of men's gymnastics as the Games of the XXIIIrd Olympiad opened in Los Angeles.

But something happened between the slicing and the curing. The vaunted world champions from the People's Republic of China fell behind on the first day and never fully recovered. More unexpectedly perhaps, Li Ning, the 20-year-old who despite his youth is already dominant in the individual events throughout the world, faltered to an alarming third in the all-arounds.

It was the luck of the draw that got the self-assured American team off and winging and, with an exceptional performance in the compulsories, gave the USA a lead in the team competition they never relinquished.

CHN and JPN were scheduled into the early session of compulsories just a short snooze after the rip-roaringest Opening Ceremonies of the modern era. CHN's coach Zhang Jian complained mildly about the scoring following the opening morning session, but in gymnastics this is normal. Scores often build up as the day and the competition progresses. Still, CHN stacked up a dozen scores of 10 with Li getting a pair.

The USA knew what to do with the much-desired evening starting times. CHN and JPN were already in with their scores of 294.25 and 292.40, respectively. "When you see a lot of 10s in the morning, you know you have to get 10s just to catch up," USA coach Abie Grossfeld stewed. "It's a little scary, but I knew our guys had it in them and I knew we could do the same." One of the reasons I felt we could be successful is the ability of our fourth, fifth and sixth place guys; they're definitely better than the People's Republic of China."

The USA never did get around to matching 10s. However, it forged ahead to a 295.30 score with a bunch of 9.8 to 9.7 advantages among the little guys. Nobody would notice what was happening until it was all over.

"Shocking is not a strong enough word to describe an American men's team leading the Olympics after the compulsories," gasped Frank Allen, coach of the University of Nebraska team which had two of its former athletes on the six-man squad. "It is simply the ultimate for American gymnastics. The team finally made the country sit up and take notice."

It was in mid-euphoria after a break in the action that coach Grossfeld noted, "There's a lot of meet left." Bart Conner, a wizened veteran of 10 years and competing on his third Olympic team, added, "I still don't think the pressure has been turned onto us. We still have nothing to lose. The People's Republic of China are the world champions. They still are feel-

ing the heat to get past us. CHN and JPN will be pressing to catch up. And when you're pressing, you have a greater chance of losing."

With things very definitely going their way, the Americans fell back and regrouped. Besides Conner, who had made a brilliant comeback after double surgery on his left arm, the USA six included University of California at Los Angeles' tough trio of Peter Vidmar, Mitch Gaylord and Tim Daggett, the top scorers in the USA Olympic trials, and Jim Hartung and Scott Johnson of Nebraska. Jim Mikus, also of Nebraska, served as the alternate.

The night of the optionals was magical. Pauley Pavilion, where Vidmar, Gaylord, and Daggett had spent more than half their waking hours since graduating from high school, was a disrupted beehive hours before the competition.

The USA started with the floor exercise, then fell behind CHN for the side horse, rings, vault, parallel and horizontal bars. The Americans were away from the gate impressively. They increased their team lead by .25 to 1/30, but CHN wasn't about to give in easily. At the rings, Li and his worthy backup Tong Fei tossed consecutive 10s. Not 50 meters away, the USA was finishing up on the side horse. The pressure was on. Daggett flew across the apparatus in spectacular fashion to a strong dismount. The seemingly conservative 9.9 set it up for Vidmar to post a matching tally and, the damage, a loss of .65, was substantial but not devastating.

The CHN got another 10 on the next apparatus, the vault, by Lou Yun. This was matched by Gaylord on the rings as the scores shot up toward the rafters, then through the roof. Conner posted a 10 on the parallel bar; Dagget scored a 10 on the horizontal. They were needed as Tong Li, and Li Xiaoping made a habit of scoring 9.95s.

After the rosin had cleared and the boisterous sellout crowd of 9,356 had dispersed into the night, Conner quipped, "You know, these days all a 9.9 will get you is a certificate of participation."

USA leaders knew that short of the Earth leaving its axis and crashing into the sun they had the team title cinched with one rotation remaining. They nursed their lead confidently and finished with a .60 advantage over CHN. The all-but-forgotten Japanese were well back, but they would be heard from after a slight pause while the Americans went beserk.

Conner looked like the geyser 'Old Faithful' as he stood on the top step of the victory stand with his mates during the medals presentation. Almost on call and every minute or so, tears would well in his eyes.

Born in 1958 in Chicago, Conner teamed with Kurt Thomas during the late 1970s to make the USA one of the leading

Opposite Page
Daggett (USA) on
the vaulting horse.
Photo: S. Powell

powers in gymnastics. He won a world championship gold in 1979, but this hardly compared to the thrill of his first Olympic gold.

"It has to be the biggest moment for all of us," he said. "Now we've proved we're on a level with People's Republic of China and the Soviet Union."

Grossfeld, with considerable time in grade on Conner, said simply, "I never thought this would happen in my lifetime. No one who knows gymnastics would ever have thought we could pull this off against the People's Republic of China." He likened the victory to that of the USA's hockey team's "Miracle on Ice" victory over the Soviet Union during the 1980 Winter Olympics at Lake Placid.

This was Grossfeld's fourth coaching appearance in the Olympic Games. A veteran of 35 years in gymnastics, he had been an outstanding athlete in his own right, representing the USA for 15 straight years on 26 different international teams. In 1956 and 1960 he was a member of the USA Olympic team. Thus the New York City-born Grossfeld, who had seen it all, was hardly engaging in idle banter as he gave the coach's perspective.

Scott Johnson spoke for his mates: "We thought the CHN team was untouchable. The object was to beat the Japanese. After we won the compulsories, though, the objective chang-ed. Everything had to go perfect . . . and it did."

The fact that the USA was not only able to hang on but come away winning impressively did not surprise Vidmar, the solidest performer on the American team. "The fact that we were still the underdogs in spite of our lead relaxed us," he said. "The nothing-to-lose attitude and being able to keep focused in on the necessity to keep doing our routines to the best of our abilities were very important."

Daggett admitted, "While we weren't sure before the compulsories we could pull off an upset, maybe we didn't really believe it; afterwards, we said, 'Yeah, we can do it.' The confidence gave us the extra measure we needed."

Conner summed up the feeling of the evening for the Americans: "We've all had individual successes. But they can't match the success of a team. Here we're talking about six times the emotion."

With about 60 million people watching in the USA and perhaps another two billion around the world, the Americans were instant celebrities. It wasn't until last call in a bar across the street from the Olympic Village that they were able to congregate for a celebratory beer. Their hearts still pounding and their brains still turning over at a feverish rate, Gaylord announced grimly, "Uh, guys, don't forget, the all-arounds are tomorrow."

For three days, the focus had been on the USA and CHN: Peter Vidmar and Li Ning, Tong Fei and Bart Conner. Koji Gushiken was poised and ready to do something about it.

Entering the all-around competition, the rock-steady Vidmar held a microscopic .05 advantage over the spectacular Li. As an 18-year-old, Li had won six of seven individual gold medals at the 1982 world cup. Tong was close in third position. Conner was fourth, followed by Gushiken, Xu Zhiqiang, and Gaylord.

The evening started with the front-running Vidmar tossing a 10 at the field with a routine on the horizontal bar considerably jazzed up from the routine he did during the team competition.

"It was different," he explained, "because in the teams it was important to do the things you were sure of. Now it was a let-it-all-hang-out situation." Besides, nothing but the spectacular figured to hold Li and yes, Gushiken, back.

While another sellout crowd sat mesmerized watching Vidmar and Gaylord performing together a rotation behind Li, Conner, and Xu, Gushiken was off in a corner smacking out routine after routine to near perfection. He did a 9.95 on the rings, followed by a 10 on the vault, then a 9.9 on the parallel bars and another 9.95 on the horizontal bars. Suddenly, no longer was it a Vidmar vs. Li competition because Li went

9.8 on the parallel, and Vidmar "slumped" similarly in his floor exercise. Gushiken, sensing his advantage, barged through the opening like a wolf exiting an unlocked cage.

On the next to last stop of the competition, Gushiken took over from Vidmar. While Li was crashing on the parallel bar—"I was too careful in the move I was attempting and made a mistake," he explained later, Vidmar stamped out a 9.9 on the vault. Gushiken's 9.95 on the horizontal bar grabbed the lead for good. He held Vidmar off with a 9.9 floor exercise.

The Japanese star indicated there was never any doubt in his mind he would recover from the fifth spot starting the evening and make it to the top. "I knew if I did things at my pace success would come to me."

Gushiken had had his share of success in the past. A world champion medalist who had helped put Japan on the world gymnastic map, this 28-year-old gymnast had earned his first Olympic medal—the gold.

Vidmar, expressing surprise that he gained the second step on the victory stand to become the first American ever to win a medal in the all-around competition, wasn't even phased by being overhauled by Gushiken. "This is great," said Vidmar who had celebrated his 23rd birthday by winning the USA Olympic trials, "but I wouldn't trade anything for that gold team medal that we won. And as for Gushiken, he's great.

Gaylord (USA) on parallel bars. Photo: T. Jones

Vidmar (USA) grasps
high bar during
individual
competition.
Photo: T. Jones

Li (CHN) on the
vaulting horse,
individual
competition.
Photo: T. Jones

Left to Right
Tong (CHN) on
parallel bars.
Photo: T. Jones

Li (CHN) on pommel
horse.
Photo: S. Powell

Gushiken (JPN), winner of the all-around
competition.
Photo: IOPP

You not only have to admire his ability, but also his timing."

Li Ning, who finished third, said he was surprised Gushiken pulled it out. But the victor said it was his intention all along to win two gold medals, "to make up for the Olympics missed in 1980." Gushiken, a 27-year-old instructor at the Nippon Physical Education College in Tokyo couldn't see toward the end of the competition. "Tears were coming down," he said, "I could not watch anyone." About midway through his 16-year gymnastic career, Gushiken had suffered an Achilles' tendon injury that required surgery. This came shortly after he broke an ankle. "The doctors gave up on me coming back," he said, but Gushiken never gave up on himself.

Meanwhile, Li bore up well under the pressure of being expected to win, only to miss the top two spots. "I wouldn't say I feel disappointed," he said, "but I feel a little regret." Disappointment or regret, it didn't matter. Li didn't allow the feeling to linger. Dead ahead were the individual apparatus contests concluding a week of intense competition.

The veteran Conner was slightly aghast at the way things went. "It took a 10 to win every event," said Conner. "Li Ning was just unbelievable. He nailed everything." It was as if Li swooped down from another planet to take part. He won golds in his first two events, finally putting consistency together with his well known strength. "Before, in his tumbling," noted Conner, "he didn't seem to stick a single dismount. There was always a little hop. There wasn't one tonight."

In the third event, the rings, Li was golden once more, sharing the medal with his nemesis, Gushiken. The only reason Li was pushed back to a silver on the vault is that teammate Lou Nun capped his exceptional week on the apparatus by doing back-to-back 10s.

It was only after the entire competition was finished and the mats and paraphernalia stored that the absence of the URS came up for extended discussion. Conner was convinced "the USA could have beaten anybody." And Abie Grossfeld was quick to point out, "The Soviet Union gymnasts may be sitting home saying our win is a fluke, but who cares? They wouldn't have come in here as the world champions, anyway."

As for the head-to-head competition, the USA coach indicated that even if Soviet world champion Dmitri Bilozerchev had competed, the edge would have rested with Li. "Li does a double-twisting, double back somersault on the floor with a slow run. It's unreal. It's like long-jumping 29 feet with a slow run. And he lands lightly."

"I'm sure he could break the high jump record if he could somersault over the bar. He can do a somersault over 10 feet— and land on his feet. He wouldn't even need a pit."

Gracious after a fall to the bronze medal in the all-arounds, Li had second thoughts following the individuals. "I felt I should have received the gold in the all-arounds if the judging had been fair. Before I came here I predicted I should get four or five gold medals. But, in the compulsory exercises, the judging was not fair. This pressured me in the later competitions."

As opposed to the women's portion of the gymnastics competition, where complaints of the judging were constant if not deafening, the grousing over marks was minor among the men. It wasn't so much the scoring, said CHN coach Zhang Jian, but the crowd response. "The enthusiastic crowd reaction to the American team hindered our athletes' performances. But the enthusiasm was to be expected here."

Thinking back over his 30 year involvement in the sport, Grossfeld said, "We used to guess at just about everything. The whole world has improved in this sport and now we've caught up. From now on, all major competitions will be like golf tournaments. It will not be a certainty who is going to win. It will depend on the day."

"When we won the bronze at the Worlds," recalled Conner, "we thought we had the breakthrough we needed to really elevate gymnastics in the USA. It didn't turn out that way and the flow was hurt by the '80 boycott.

"But I think since '81 we've had the feeling we were right there and ready to emerge. That's how long the six of us have been together. We weren't received well in Moscow at the '81 championships and maybe that affected us. But the six of us have been together for a few years now and all along we've had the talent to do well. At last we finally did it."

"Having been around for 10 years, I've seen us have some success," observed Conner "but we never really jelled until now. We knew we were good coming out of the trials—but we didn't know how good. It's like Vidmar said, 'We know we're going to get a medal in the Olympics. The only question is: what color?'"

These 1984 accomplishments echoed those of the 1932 Games in Los Angeles when American men gymnasts won five golds including victories in rope climbing, Indian clubs, and tumbling. The sport had changed radically since those Depression days. Achievements echoed the report card of the earlier team.

Conner could not help taking satisfaction. "Typically, in the past guys have bailed out, and a whole new group would have to come in and start from scratch. We've all pretty well agreed that we're going to stick around for a year or two and that will solidify the program. What happened here is a wonderful motivation for younger athletes."

And Conner should know. He runs a gymnastics school in Tempe, Arizona. No sooner had the sight of six young Americans receiving the team gold registered with millions of TV viewers when the telephone began ringing off the wall in Arizona.

"I'll never forget when I injured myself in competition last December 1983 in Japan," Conner concluded. "The great Soviet Union gold medalist Nicolai Adrianov was standing nearby and seeing the extent of my injury, he said, 'It's all over for you, Conner. You're too old, now you're injured. You've had it' 'I'll have to remember to give Nicolai a call.'"

Gushiken (JPN) and Li (CHN) co winners on individual rings. Photo: T. Jones

Left to Right
The USA wins team gold medal.
Photo: S. Powell

Vidmar (USA) accepts congratulations from bronze medalist Li (CHN).
Photo: S. Powell

Men's individual vault Lou (CHN). Morisue (JPN), Gaylord (USA), Li (CHN) and Gushiken (JPN).
Photo: S. Powell

Gaylord and Daggett (USA) after Daggett's side horse performance.
Photo: S. Powell

Tong (CHN) in a highbar flyaway dismount.
Photo: S. Powell

Gymnastics: A Touch of Softness

Murray Olderman

As the silver medal dangled from her neck on the victory podium at Pauley Pavilion, Kathy Johnson recalled, "I felt like a kid eyeing a lollipop." Forgotten for the moment were the 15 years of intense physical and emotional strain that preceded the ceremony. So the question asked a few minutes later by a journalist was not as innocuous or naive as it sounded. "What," he wanted to know, "does it take to be an Olympic gymnast?" Kathy, who called herself "The Old Lady" because she was shy by a month of her 25th birthday, volunteered to answer for the five American gymnasts, all of them teenagers, seated with her.

"Guts," she said thoughtfully, "and nerves of steel." She paused. "And a touch of softness."

These were the qualities that suffused the top level of competition in the 1984 Games. They manifested themselves in Mary Lou Retton, a 16-year-old sprite from Fairmont, West Virginia, who had only minimal international experience before bouncing ebulliently across millions of television screens throughout the world. They were certainly present in Ecaterina Szabo, an 88-pound bundle of choreographed motion from the Transylvania region of Romania. She took four medallions of gold and one of silver home to Brasov, where her father works for the railroad.

But while Ecaterina captured the medals, Mary Lou captured the hearts. In the process, she epitomized the spirit of the Olympics. The chunky, tiny dynamo—1.4 meters tall, won only one gold. But it was the coveted medal for the individual all-around competition, the gymnastic equivalent of the decathlon. Mary Lou also took home two silver and two bronze medals.

Their exploits amounted to pure, athletic theater, and reinforced the thesis that women's gymnastics has become the glamor event of the Olympic Games and the favorite sport of the quadrennial fiesta. One USA survey posed the question, "If you were limited to watching one event, and one event only, in the Olympics, which event would that be?"

Male respondents picked women's gymnastics by a slight margin over other events, but 80.6 percent of the women polled voted for the sport, giving it an overall plurality of 47.2 percent. That's why a ticket to Pauley Pavilion during the first ten days of the Games quickly became the most cherished ticket in Los Angeles.

Women's gymnastic competition in its current form has only been on the Olympic agenda since the 1952 games in Helsinki. Its popularity really dates from 1972, when Olga Korbut (URS), the "Elf from Grovno," electrified audiences in Munich and on worldwide television with daring back somersaults and startling balance beam maneuvers. In 1976, Nadia Comaneci

brought perfection to the sport with an unheard of collection of "10's" on the uneven bars and balance beam, then continued her supremacy in 1980 at the Moscow Games.

Even before the Los Angeles spectacle, Mary Lou Retton was singled out as the potential darling of the 1984 Games, to be rivalled perhaps only by Romania's Szabo, who finished third in the all around and first in the floor exercises at the world championships in Budapest in 1983. Romania, second only to the Soviet Union, produced as expected in the Olympics, but the significant development in Los Angeles was the achievement of the American women, who had never won a medal of any kind under the present format.

In colorful Pauley Pavilion on the campus of the University of California at Los Angeles (UCLA), the USA made a spectacular breakthrough as a world gymnastic power by finishing second in the team competition to the Romanians. This feat was followed by Retton's all-around gold and an additional two silvers and three bronze medals in the individual events on the final day. And remember, this was by a country that had always been shut out. Kathy Johnson provided one of the most dramatic moments in the entire Games. In her final exercise as a competing athlete, she performed a graceful, nearly flawless routine on the balance beam, scoring a 9.85, good for a bronze medal (many thought she merited a higher score). At the medal ceremonies all of her pent-up emotions, her years of work, of struggle and of sacrifice saw fit to release themselves. And so she wept.

Gymnastic performances are evaluated by a team of four judges who vote after each routine. The maximum score they can award is 10. They are guided by the ROV factor: Risk, Originality, Virtuosity. Gymnastics has its own language—layouts, tuck somersaults, back somersaults, Tsukaharas, Barinas, Thomas flairs, Cuervos—many of them named for legendary gymnasts who perfected the maneuvers. The sport has a theatrical veneer that helps explain its current popularity—high visibility, proximity to the crowd—and courage.

The various national teams marched onto the floor of the 9000 seat Pavilion, to the strains of John Philip Sousa. The martial music punctuated their rotations after each event, and as they traveled to the different exercise areas. Then the gymnasts simultaneously catapulted into vaults, revolved around uneven bars, somersaulted precariously on the beam, and bounded through floor exercises in a pseudo four-ring-circus of continuous action.

First-round compulsories in the team competition immediately produced an uproar of controversy. USA coach Don Peters vigorously protested four times the scores of a

Opposite Page Retton (USA) receives the adulation of the crowd. Photo: S. Powell

ever won by an American woman.

While computers were clicking out the final score—79.175 for Retton, 79.125 for Szabo, a bare .05 margin of victory—and the arena still resounded from the clamor after that vault, Mary Lou nailed a superfluous second vault for another 10.

Except for Romi Kessler, an elegant Swiss gymnast who finished ninth in the all-around, the top 10 spots were dominated by the ROM, USA and CHN. And they were to capture all the medals in the individual events championships.

There was an expectation the Mary Lou Retton-Ecaterina Szabo show might continue, but the final Sunday belonged to the little Romanian champ. She won three gold medals in the vault, the floor exercises and the beam, her cumulative scores in the first two setting new Olympic records.

There was another dispute over the scores, with the Americans claiming that Szabo had not performed the required two different vaults. "I was shocked," said Retton bluntly. "I go higher, and I go farther, and I stuck mine; she did not. She threw one Cuervo tuck and one Cuervo pike. You're supposed to throw two different vaults."

The judges did not agree with her, and under Olympic rules the USA could not protest the score for a competitor from another country.

Mary Lou settled for a silver in the vault and bronze medals on the uenven bars and in the floor exercises, where she lost a point for stepping out of bounds on her first tumbling pass.

Wu (CHN) on the balance beam. Photo: S. Powell

The lone individual American gold went to Julianne McNamara on the uneven bars, where she tied with the graceful Ma Yanhong of CHN, the 1979 world champion. Another tie, with Szabo on the balance beam, also enabled Romania's Simona Pauca to collect a gold.

McNamara had a chance for second gold in the floor exercises, in which her preliminary score going in was only .025 below Szabo's. The lights abruptly went out in Pauley Pavilion after her routine, while Szabo was standing by to perform. When electricity was finally restored, a 10 went up for Julianne. Unfazed by the delay or the score of her opponent, Szabo launched her program to the medley of American ethnic music. The result: a 10, giving her a third gold of the night, a fitting and symbolic conclusion to the women's gymnastic competition.

Altogether, there were 17 perfect scores of 10 in the 1984 Games, surpassing the total number of perfect scores recorded in all previous Olympics. Szabo was called back to the podium by the full house for a curtain call. Was she surprised? "Not surprised," she answered through a translator. "Delighted." And she announced her plans for the immediate future: "To go to Disneyland."

While Ecaterina, Mary Lou and friends relaxed, another form of women's gymnastics was introduced to the Olympics. Rhythmic gymnastic competition was added to the calendar for the 1984 Games. It eliminates tumbling skills and emphasizes flamboyant acrobatic movements synchronized with the use of hoops, clubs, balls and ribbons. As an art form, it would be analogous to ice dancing versus figure skating.

Held over three evenings, it had just one phase, all-around competition. Marta Bobo of Spain was the leader on the first night with her hoop and ball routines. Doina Staiculescu of Romania took over first place the next night with a sparkling clubs routine that featured behind-the-back catches.

But in the finale, the night before the Closing Ceremonies of the Olympics, Lori Fung of Canada experienced a moment that epitomized the Games' spirit of friendly competition. A 23rd place finisher in the world championships, she had gone to Romania for a month specifically to train with Staiculescu, the classy silver medalist. And now with the gold medal on the line, Lori performed brilliantly in all four routines on the program to edge Doina, who dropped the ribbon in her last event and lost by .025 of a point.

"Winning the gold was the smallest little dream I had," said the Canadian champ, who could now dream big.

Preceding Pages
Lori Fung (CAN) no
1. in rhythmic
gymnastics
Photo: T. Jones

Preceding Pages
Szabo and Pauca
(ROM), dual
champions from
one country.
Photo: T. Jones

The irrepressible
Mary Lou Retton
(USA).
Photo: S. Powell

Handball:
Full House At Fullerton

Joe Gergen

The floor was as green as a desert oasis. And for those teams which would represent the United States of America in the men's and women's handball competition, in was every bit as refreshing. After so many years of wandering, they finally had a court they could call home.

Taraflex was the trade name of the foam rubber composition set atop the basketball court in Titan Gymnasium on the campus of California State University at Fullerton. What the Americans found so irresistible about the setting was its simplicity. The only white lines on the floor, were a center line and the standard 6 meter and 9 meter semicircles around each goal. Nothing but handball lines. Billy Kessler, the USA men's goalkeeper, said it was beautiful.

Such an observation might have confused Europeans, in whose countries the sport is eminently popular and courts are plentiful. But the Americans had to prepare for this, the first major competition ever held in the USA, on a variety of surfaces, including cement, canvas-covered hockey rinks, and wooden gym floors striped for basketball, volleyball and a bewildering variety of schoolchildren's games. For serious training and competition, they traveled to the continent.

Thus, to the home teams, the court at Fullerton was a sight to behold. And, once the competition began, the crowds were a revelation. Each two-game session at Fullerton was sold out, as were all 16,000 tickets for the men's championship doubleheader at the Forum. No longer would the sport— devised as an outdoor game in Europe in the early 1900s— labor in obscurity in the New World. The crowds not only were sizable, they were enthusiastic.

"People from Europe were amazed at the reception the sport received," said Peter Buehning Sr. who, in addition to being Jim Buehning's father, is the president of the USA Team Handball Federation. "We're salesmen for the sport. It confirmed what we knew, that we have a terrifically exciting spectator sport." The sport captivated a new audience with its demand for speed, agility, power and contact which altered noses and inflicted stitches on more than one participant.

Although Yugoslavia was delighted with its gold medals, first for that nation since 1972, there was some disappointment among the champions. "Until now, at big events, we have been just one step behind the Soviets," said Josip Samarzija, coach of the victorious women's team. "We're very sorry they're not here for we had anticipated we would beat them."

The Soviets have never lost a game since women's handball debuted in the 1976 Olympics. But the Yugoslavs had defeated the URS twice in 1984 while preparing for the Olympic Games. "I regret they are not here," said Jasna Kolar-Merdan, the Yugoslav star. "We want to show the world we

are the best."

There wasn't much doubt that the Yugoslavs were the best in the Olympics. They won all five of their games. In Kolar-Merdan, they also produced the outstanding player in the women's field. The slender backcourt player, nicknamed the Gazelle, led all scorers with 48 goals, including an Olympic one-game record of 17 in a 33-20 rout of the USA.

Kolar-Merdan, a 27-year-old mother of one, was anything but a one-woman team. The Yugoslavs, silver medalists at Moscow, were well-balanced offensively and defensively. In fact, it was a teammate, the dynamic Svetlana Dasic-Kitic, who scored the most dazzling goal of the tournament in Yugoslavia's 29-23 victory over KOR, the eventual silver medalists. Dasic-Kitic, a 24-year-old blonde with one of the most powerful shots in the game, intercepted a pass and broke in alone on the Korean goaltender. Soaring into the air over the 6-meter line, faking a shot to her right, she then whipped the ball behind her back and into the other side of the net.

"The shot was the beginning of the celebration," said Dasic-Kitic, whose three goals in a two-minute span enabled Yugoslavia to secure the victory and the championship. "It's not something I normally do, that's for sure." Teammate Ljubinka Jankovic completed the scoring in that game and then turned a somersault at midcourt, which is something she normally doesn't do, either.

But, for all of Yugoslavia's gyrations, the outstanding game in the women's competition featured KOR v. CHN. Smaller but quicker than their occidental opponents, the two teams left spectators breathless with their fast-break attacks. The People's Republic of China, trailing by five goals at one stage of the second half, assumed a 24-22 lead on the strength of a remarkable rally and extraordinary goaltending by Wu Xing-jiang. Twice in the final six minutes, Wu stopped a breakaway, all the while sending shrill alarms to her teammates. But in the last minute of play, her teammates let her down. Leading 24-23, CHN had only to run out the clock. However, an uncertain pass was intercepted by Hyoi-Soon Jeong, who passed to Young-Ja Lee for a breakaway. Lee's shot sailed past Wu with six seconds remaining for a 24-24 tie. Zingjiang slumped to the floor, and her teammates hung their heads. That one goal cost them a chance for the silver medal. They settled eventually for the bronze.

Surprisingly, the USA women, making their first Olympic appearance, played well enough to threaten both CHN and KOR. They upset CHN in the opening round and suffered a narrow loss to KOR. But for an 18-17 loss to FRG, they might have claimed a medal.

Any fanciful medal hopes entertained by American men

**Opposite Page
Vukovic (YUG)
sidearms a shot
against FRG.
Photo: IOPP**

in the wake of the boycott were scotched in their first game loss against the Federal Republic of Germany. For FRG team, it was a springboard to success. Considered too inexperienced by many to be a serious contender, they emerged undefeated from the boycott- weakened "B" group in the 12-team competition, qualifying for the gold-medal game against Yugoslavia, only to suffer an 18-17 defeat.

Yugoslavia, meanwhile, was grateful to escape with a tie from its first game against upstart Iceland. The path to the final was made more difficult by the presence of Romania in the "A" group. Those two teams met on the final day of group competition, and the margin of the 19-18 YUG victory was a penalty shot by Mile Isakovic and the interception of a Romanian pass by Zdravko Radjenovic in the final seconds.

Romania handily defeated Denmark 23-19 to win the bronze medal. "Now," said Nicolae Nedeff, the Romanian coach, "I have to go back home and explain why we didn't win the gold." The explanation was simpler for FRG. It ran up against a more experienced and cohesive team at the Forum in a game which featured the standard male defensive tactics of blocking, grabbing and bearhugging.

Yugoslavia held the ball for the final 30 seconds. In fact, defensive specialist Zdravko Zovko held it considerably longer. At the sound of the final buzzer, he tucked it under his shirt

and danced around the court as if in celebration of an upcoming birth.

Attendance at the Forum was 12,958, still a landmark for the sport in the USA, and those in attendance were treated to a spontaneous victory lap with the YUG flag by the new champions. The next day in their final chance of the Games, the USA men's team defeated Japan, 24-16. The triumph was highlighted by the performance of William Michael Kessler. The 21-year-old goalkeeper not only made 11 saves but supplied the most bizarre moment of the competition by scoring a goal late in the second half. If nothing else, it supplied the competition with a fitting touch of American ingenuity. The American men and women had sacrificed a lot for the moment. They had postponed careers and put off thoughts of family while chasing this dream. The women won twice and the men managed not only one victory and a tie in five games but accounted for the third best defensive average in the tournament.

"What America has accomplished here is a triumph of work and sacrifice," said Juan Roman, manager of the Spanish men's team. "It will be a very short time before America can beat quality teams."

In the meantime, the Americans have the consolation of that beautiful home court, and the memory of capacity crowds

Ognjenovic (YUG)
raises her hand to
block a shot.
Photo: T. Jones

chanting their names and cheering a sport with which they were unfamiliar. "I feel," Peter Buehning said, "we have made the breakthrough."

He had every right to be pleased. The man virtually introduced the sport, which he had first played in his native Germany, to the USA, and coached the first American Olympic team in 1972. His oldest son, Peter Jr., played on the 1976 Olympic team and was a referee in the 1984 competition. And Jim Buehning, a 27-year-old, scored a team-leading five goals in that long-sought triumph.

They have provided the foundation. The future lies with players like Leora (Sam) Jones, a converted basketball player who first glimpsed the sport two years ago and emerged as the fifth-leading scorer in the women's competition with 32 goals. The future lies in the colleges and high schools and a deep pool of athletic talent handball has yet to tap. "If you get a guy like Dr. J (Julius Erving) or Wilt Chamberlain in the game," Jim Buehning said, "no one's going to stop them."

Hockey: The PAK Is Back

by Hal Bock

The year was 1972. The Munich Olympics. In hockey, Pakistan met FRG in a bitterly fought game for the gold medal. The Federal Republic of Germany prevailed, 1-0, but Pakistan did not take the setback lightly. The tumultuous reaction by the losing team resulted in 11 players being banned from the Olympics for life and the team receiving a four-year international suspension which later was rescinded.

So when the men's hockey tournament at the 1984 Games reached its gold medal showdown and Pakistan faced FRG again, there was a grudge factor involved. The Pakistanis play a fluid style, depending on deception for the success. The Federal Republic of Germany prefers the more muscular game that gained favor in Europe following their 1972 Olympic gold medal. Now finesse and passing may make a comeback after Pakistan captured the 1984 gold, 2-1, from their former rivals.

It was not easy. The two teams struggled into overtime before Kaleemullah settled the issue, netting the rebound of a blocked penalty corner kick after 12 minutes in the extra period. Hasan Sardar had forced overtime, tying the score for Pakistan after Michael Peter had given FRG the game's first goal.

The gold medal was the third in Olympic hockey for third-seeded Pakistan, who also won in 1960 and 1968, and thought it should have won in 1972. The FRG men took the silver, matching the medal won by their women's team, and the bronze went to Great Britain. The tournament started poorly for Pakistan, in its opener against New Zealand. NZL used three goals by Peter Daji, two of them coming in the final three minutes of the contest, to gain a 3-3 tie in the opener. Daji's tying goal came with just 30 seconds remaining and left the PAK team shaken. But Coach Zaku Uddin was not upset by the tie. "I'm satisfied," Uddin said. "We played all right. We will settle down in other matches."

He turned out to be right. Pakistan shut out Kenya, 3-0, in its next start and tied the Netherlands 3-3. Unlike the tie with New Zealand, the deadlock against HOL was considered a plus because that team and Australia were the pre-tournament favorites.

Australia was led by a genuine Renaissance man, Rick Charlesworth. He is a doctor, a member of parliament and his country's best field hockey player. He and Terry Walsh gave Australia a powerful one-two scoring punch. But Pakistan shut down Australian scorers when the teams met in the medal semifinals. Sardar had the game's lone goal, his ninth of the tournament.

"It was our turn to win," said Manzoor Atif, the Pakistani team manager. "It's high time after losing four straight times to Australia."

Richard Aggiss, the Australian coach, noted the roughness of the game with close checking and the anguish of his team missing two good scoring opportunities within 10 seconds late in the game. "If you don't score those in international hockey, you lose," he said.

That victory moved Pakistan into the title game against FRG which had shut out Great Britain, 1-0, in the other semifinal. GBR, which had not had an Olympic medal in hockey since 1952, appeared overmatched against Australia but came up with a 3-2 victory to earn the bronze in one of the tournament's biggest upsets. Goalie Ian Taylor was the hero, stopping 18 penalty corners and 26 shots on goal against the tournament's top-seeded team.

"Statistics show we were the better team," said Alan Berry, the Australian team manager. "But there's another statistic having to do with number of goals in the net, and that showed the other team was better."

Great Britain may have benefitted from lack of pressure. Australia had been expected to win a gold medal, and its elimination by Pakistan may have still been haunting the players. Great Britain, though, was playing with nothing to lose, and surprisingly, came up with the win and the bronze medal.

The only hockey medal American men have ever won was a bronze in 1932. They did it without benefit of a victory because just three teams competed in the Olympic tournament that year. The USA team was not so bold as to predict another medal in 1984, but they had hoped to at least win a game. They came close a number of times, but failed again to record their first Olympic hockey victory. Two of the American losses came as a result of penalty stroke shootoffs when games against MAL and KEN ended tied after both regulation and overtime periods had expired. The loss to Malaysia left the USA 12th in the tournament, but Coach Gavin Featherstone sees hope for his program.

"The United States team is in world contention," he said. "We have four years to go for a medal. We think it's realistic to talk about a medal in 1988."

The American women, however, can talk about their medal now. They took a bronze at Los Angeles and, ironically, they won their medal the same way the USA men were beaten twice—in a shootoff. But they needed help to even have a chance for that medal. After completion of the round-robin portion of the tournament, the standings left USA medal hopes squarely in the hands of HOL, which faced Australia for the gold. The HOL team had the edge with Australia needing to win by two or more goals for the gold medal. A victory by

**Opposite Page
Wheatly (CAN)
advances the ball
past Hahn (FRG).
Photo: IOPP**

one goal or a tie would have only been good enough for a silver for the Australians. And a loss by one or two goals would have given the silver to FRG and open the door for the USA women.

Earlier, the American women had scored victories over Canada and New Zealand with Beth Anders leading the way with three goals against Canada—the first hockey victory for any USA Olympic team.

With their fate resting in the hands of the team from HOL, the Americans could do little more than root for the HOL women against Australia. The USA situation would have been better had the Americans beaten Australia in their match, but they lost that contest 3-1. So the Americans needed a 2-0 victory by HOL to get a chance for the medal, and that's exactly what they supplied. The victory clinched the gold for that nation, a silver for FRG. It left the Australians, who had been playing for gold, suddenly struggling for bronze. They didn't get it, either, because the fired-up American women, seizing the opportunity supplied by the HOL victory, won the shootoff, 10-5. It was an improbable turn of events as the USA came down out of the stands to play for the bronze.

"They were playing for themselves," Anders said of HOL. "They weren't playing to put us in. "Nevertheless, that was the effect and the USA profited from the strange system applied in international play to settle such situations.

"I don't think they had enough time emotionally to get into that kind of situation," said USA Coach Vonnie Gros. "I certainly wouldn't vote for the shootoff. Our Federation was pushing to have a medal game. However, if that's the way it is, we will take advantage of it."

The shootoff was settled quickly with USA goalie Gwen Cheeseman stopping four of the first six shots and Anders, the tournament's top scorer, clinching the medal with her second shot and team's seventh straight.

"They didn't miss a stroke," said Cheeseman of her teammates. "They made all 10, so all I had to do was save one of them."

Australian Coach Brian Glencross admitted he never expected his team's medal chances to come down to a penalty stroke playoff. "That was the farthest thing from my mind," he said. "We practice it, but we really haven't emphasized strokes. We don't have a very good track record on it."

Because of the help the Americans received, the fans at East Los Angeles College, where the hockey tournament was played, came up with a new Olympic chant—a variation on the one which rocked most of the venues. In saluting the success of the American team, they chanted "USA-Holland, USA-Holland."

The Olympic tournament champions—Pakistan in the

Photo: D. Cannon

men's tournament and HOL in the women's competition—came into the Games with solid credentials as World Cup champions. Australia had been expected to challenge in both men's and women's play but went home without any medals. Great Britain's bronze from the men's tournament was its first Olympic hockey medal in 32 years. FRG had silvers from both men's and women's teams. And the USA, of course, had never even won an Olympic hockey game, much less a medal, until the Los Angeles Games.

Judo:
The Gentle Giants
Hal Bock

When Jigoro Kano, a Japanese student, decided some years ago that the sport of ju-jitsu was a bit too dangerous for his taste, he developed an alternative called judo. The translation of the word is gentleness, or giving way, but that was hardly the way to describe American Ed Liddie's condition on the opening night of the judo competition at the 1984 Olympic Games.

Liddie, a 25-year-old former New York City school teacher, had been battered by France's Guy Delvingt as the two men struggled for a bronze medal in the 132-pound extra light weight class. He suffered a badly bruised bicep and was disoriented, as Delvingt worked him over.

"I can't look," said his mother, Arlene Liddie, as her son continued to absorb punishment.

An American losing a judo match is hardly uncommon in Olympic competition. After all, the USA came into these Games with just two judo medals in its previous participation so another American loss would raise no eyebrows. What few in the Cal State University Arena could tell, however, was that Liddie, who had worked as a doorman and waiter to support his judo training, was not about to lose. Like a 130-pound bolt of lightning, Liddie dumped Delvingt with a knee-drop, one-arm shoulder throw to seize the advantage. Then Liddie went after his man. There was less than a minute left as the American fell on Delvingt to clinch the medal. Then he collapsed, exhausted and exhilarated.

"I feel like I just died and went to heaven," Liddie said. He had won his medal despite a badly injured arm, which was banged up in a preliminary match with Kim Jae Yup (KOR), who took the silver medal. The division gold went to Japan's Shinji Hosokawa which triggered a four-gold sweep for Japan in the eight-class competition. Before the Games began, Nobuyuki Sato, a former world champion who coaches the Japanese team, had predicted five golds. The man who missed was Seiki Nose, who had to settle for a bronze in the 189-pound middleweight division. It was in that class that the United States of America captured its other judo medal of the Games, a silver by 22-year-old Bob Berland.

Berland and the rest of the USA team had promised America's best judo showing ever, and he delivered. The stunning part of his medal was that just six months before the Olympics, Berland was in a wheelchair, recovering from knee surgery.

For two and a half minutes, Berland and Peter Seisenbacher, a goldsmith from Austria, battled on even terms for the division title. Then the American went down from a sweeping leg throw. "There was a moment of a lack of concentration," he said, "and at this level, you can't afford that. I have

mixed feelings about this medal. I'd like to change the color to gold. But I made history in American judo, and I am proud of that."

Seisenbacher's gold was historic, too. It marked the first time Austria has ever won a world class judo event. Japan usually dominates the competition—a tribute to the sport's roots—and these Olympics followed that pattern.

The star of the Japanese team was 280-pound Yasuhiro Yamashita. He came into the Games with a winning streak of 194 matches, and had not been beaten since 1977 when he was 19. His speed and size have combined to make him unbeatable, and his calm nature belies his judo ability. He is fond of saying, "In my face I am soft, but in my heart I am rigid." In Los Angeles, he was at his rigid best.

Yamashita began by throwing his first opponent, Lahsana Coly (SEN) in just 12 seconds. But against Arthur Schnabel (FRG), the Japanese star suffered a torn calf muscle. That prolonged the bout to three minutes before Yamashita applied a choke hold for the victory. In the gold medal match against Mohamed Rashwan (EGY), Yamashita sidestepped a rush by his opponent, let him fall of his own momentum and fell on him after just 65 seconds. It looked easy, but Yamashita assured the world it was not. "I was lucky to be able to use mat fighting because my leg was hurting and I don't think I would have been able to do a throw," he said. "I try my best in every match, so none are boring. If I tried to compete easily, I would not have won for seven years."

Japan's other gold medals were won by Yoshiyuki Matsuoka in the 143-pound half-lightweight division, and Hitoshi Saito, a 320-pound mountain of a man who won the heavyweight division. Matsuoka had a difficult path to the gold. He seemed uncertain in some preliminary bouts after suffering a serious nose bleed when he banged his head in a throw attempt. He made it to the final by the narrowest of margins, the tie-breaking vote of the referee. One judge had voted for Matsuoka and the other for his opponent Marc Alexandre (FRA), forcing the third ballot. In the final against Jung-Oh Hwang (KOR), Matsuoka took charge with a shoulder throw that proved decisive. Later he said, "I am sorry to worry you with close matches, but I tried my best in each."

Hwang, scheduled to be married at the conclusion of the Games, seemed satisfied with his silver, saying it would make "a good present for my fiancee and mother-in-law."

Saito, whose quickness was astounding for a man of his size, needed just 90 seconds to finish off his first three opponents. But Angelo Parisi, a bronze medalist for Great Britain in 1976 who changed his citizenship after getting married and now was representing France, proved more difficult. He

Opposite Page Adams (GBR) subdues an opponent in the 78kg classification. Photo: T. Duffy

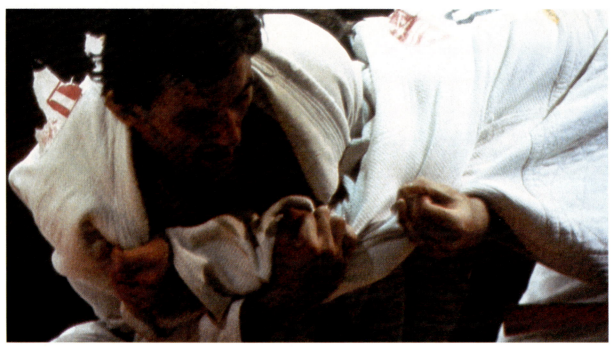

clutched at Saito's judo jacket and forced the match to its full time limit, losing on a penalty for being defensive.

"He weighs quite a lot," Parisi said of the huge Japanese champion. "It takes a lot of strength to move him about."

Saito said he was not pleased by his bulk. "I really want to lose weight," he said. "But I can't because I eat so much."

Saito knows that he operates in the shadow of Yamashita, considered Japan's—and perhaps the world's—premier judo player. "Some day," he said of his countryman, "I will beat Yamashita."

Despite winning half of the possible gold medals, Japan came up empty in three weight divisions—lightweight, half middleweight, and half heavyweight. Two of the golds went to KOR, with Ha Hyoung Zoo taking the half heavyweight crown and Ahn Byeong Keun capturing the lightweight title. Frank Wieneke (FRG) won the half middleweight division.

Despite disappointing losses in three classes, Japan enjoyed its biggest success of the Games in the judo competition with four golds and a bronze.

The tournament was a popular one with Los Angeles audiences, especially its large oriental community. And though competition was hardly what one would describe as gentle, Jigoro Kana, father of the sport, would have been more than pleased.

Modern Pentathlon: The Five Star Battle

Howard L. Levine

Envision a military courier from the Napoleonic era setting off on his horse with an important message to deliver. When his horse is shot out from under him, he duels with his foes until his sword breaks. Resorting to his pistol, he vanquishes his enemies and makes his escape by swimming across a river and running a stretch across land. He reaches his destination and delivers the message.

Rooted in this tradition of the Napoleonic courier, modern pentathlon was introduced into Olympic competition in 1912 and has evolved into a test of five totally different skills: equestrian, fencing, shooting, swimming, and running. Perhaps the most eclectic and demanding of all Olympic events, the modern pentathlon is a struggle involving skill and stamina.

Although nearly all 18 nations had something to cheer about at some point during the four days of competition, the modern pentathlon of the XXIIIrd Olympic Games was really a tale of three countries: Italy, winner of the team gold and individual gold and bronze; the United States of America, winner of the team silver; and Sweden, winner of the individual silver despite a series of disappointing mishaps.

The 52 athletes competed in teams of three men per nation at Coto de Caza, an exclusive 5000 acre residential and resort community carved into the sear hills of Orange County some 100km south of Los Angeles.

They were rated by a complicated scoring system. Each competitor and team began with a base score. Points were added for achievement, deducted for faults. On the first day each pentathlete rode a horse, chosen by lot only 20 minutes before competition started, over a 600-meter course featuring 15 jumps, including one triple and one double.

The following day, the pentathlete competed in a dozen uninterrupted hours of epee fencing. Each competitor dueled in a single-touch bout lasting no longer than three minutes against every other pentathlete. A 300 meter freestyle swim, contested at Heritage Park in nearby Irvine, was staged on the third day. In the shooting phase held on the last morning of competition, each pentathlete fired four rounds of five shots with a 22 caliber pistol at a silhouette target 25 meters away. The competitor had three seconds to raise his arm from a 45 degree angle, aim, and shoot.

In the final event eight hours later, the pentathletes ran a grueling 4000 meter crosscountry race. For the first time in Olympic history, this race featured staggered starting times based on individual standings. The first man across the finish line in Coto de Caza's riding arena (where the competition began three days earlier) won the gold.

Italy will long prize its accomplishments in the modern pentathlon of the 1984 Olympic Games. Its team of Daniele Masala, Carlo Massullo, and Pierpaolo Cristofori won the team championship. Masala won the individual gold medal. Massullo won the bronze. This showing of strength equalled the Soviet Union's 1980 achievement in Moscow.

Masala, a 29-year-old physical education teacher from Rome and 1982 World Champion, started the cross country run with only a 26 point lead over Sweden's Svante Rasmuson. He began 8.5 seconds over Rasmuson. Throughout the winding course, over the hills of Coto de Caza, Rasmuson remained at Masala's heels. As the two tiring runners entered the equestrian arena before more than 8000 cheering spectators and neared the finish line, Rasmuson spurted into the lead. With 60 meters to go, the tall, patrician, blond medical student appeared headed for the gold. Then he stumbled, almost fell to the ground and wound up limping home close behind Masala, who was jubilant in victory. Masala had the gold, Rasmuson the silver. The 13-point margin was the closest since 1968. The finish was undoubtedly the most exciting in Olympic history.

Masala, who had finished fourth in the 1976 Olympics, became the first non Eastern bloc athlete to win a modern pentathlon medal since Sweden's Bjorn Ferm won the gold in 1968 in Mexico City. He is the first Italian gold medalist ever, and the first Italian to win a medal in modern pentathlon since Silvano Abba won a bronze in 1936 in Berlin.

Masala's teammate, Carlo Massullo, who had started the cross country in fifth place, passed two men ahead of him, Paul Four (FRA) and Michael Storm (USA), to win the bronze by 15 points over Great Britain's Richard Phelps. Storm finished fifth and Four sixth. Massullo ran the second fastest cross country. Phelps posted the best cross country time.

Masala's formula for victory was consistency. On the first day he scored a perfect 1100 in riding. Four others (Massullo, Phelps, Japan's Daizou Araki, and Egypt's Ihab Ellebedy) achieved the same record so Masala was tied for first overall after day One. Masala placed fourth in fencing with 34 victories and 17 defeats, good for 956 points. He fell to second in the overall race, trailing Sweden's Rasmuson by 36 points. Masala's time of 3:16.9 placed him eighth in the swim and earned him 1300 more points. At the end of three days he still trailed Rasmuson by 40 points.

Masala vaulted into the lead for the individual gold in the shooting competition. It was not that he shot so well—he only tied for 10th with 193, good for 978 points. But this was 62 points better than Rasmuson's 912 (earned by tying for 24th with 190).

This set the stage for the dramatic cross country final

event. Masala ran the 4000 meters in 12:36.57, the 20th fastest of the day. However, the 1135 points this earned him, won the title. Rasmuson's gallant effort, timed in 13:35.76, was the 16th fastest of the day but fell 13 points short of the gold.

As a team the Italian trio finished no lower than fourth in any discipline. They were fourth in fencing, swimming, and shooting. Their first in the opening (riding) and closing (running) events outclassed everyone else.

For the USA, the team silver medals—won by only three points over France—were that nation's finest achievement since its team silver in 1964 in Tokyo. But there were other triumphs of which the USA team of Michael Storm, Greg Losey and Dean Glenesk could be proud. Storm surged into fourth place overall and contention for an individual medal (which would have been the USA's first since 1960), by winning the shooting with 198 hits, only two below a perfect 200 for 1088 points, and 22 better than his previous best. Another high point for the USA came in the fencing competition, not traditionally a strong American discipline. Toward the end of the long day, Storm, Losey, and Glenesk won seven of nine bouts from a powerful French team and continued on to a third place finish in fencing.

En route to the team silver, the USA finished second in riding, a surprising third in fencing, sixth in swimming, seventh

in shooting and eighth in running. Storm led the team with his individual fifth-place finish. Losey placed 13th and performed particularly well in fencing, winning 32 and losing 19 to tie for fifth in that discipline. Glenesk placed 18th overall and did best in riding, finishing sixth.

For Sweden, a team bronze medal winner in the 1980 Moscow Games, this was a disappointing Olympic modern pentathlon despite Rasmuson's silver medal. First there was the fateful stumble which probably cost Rasmuson the gold. Then there was the elimination of Roderick Martin in shooting for deliberately firing two shots at a single facing of the target. Targets in modern pentathlon face the shooters for only three seconds and then turn away for seven seconds. One shot is required in that three second span. Martin apparently was not ready when the first target of his second round faced him and did not get off a shot. He shot twice at the second facing of the round. The judge, who was standing behind Martin, disqualified him in shooting. Not only did this hurt Martin's individual standing, (he finished 47th overall), but it ruined Sweden's chances for a team medal. Sweden finished 10th in team competition.

To win the team bronze medals, the French team members placed sixth (Paul Four), 10th (Didier Boube), and 17th (Joel Bouzou). France finished first in shooting, second in fencing,

seventh in running, ninth in riding, and 11th in swimming.

The Federal Republic of Germany took pride in two superb individual performances although its highest individual finish overall was 14th (by Achim Bellmann), and the FRG team wound up sixth behind Switzerland and Mexico. Bellmann won the fencing with a 39-12 record. His unorthodox crouching stance not only confused his opponents but earned him the nickname "Spiderman." Christian Sandow swam the fastest 300 meters. His 3:13.85 edged Mexico's Ivar Sisniega, holder of the modern pentathlon world record in this discipline.

For Masala, Rasmuson, and Massullo—Victors Ludorum of the 1984 modern pentathlon, the other competitors, and the enthusiastic sell-out audience, the shadow of the military courier of two centuries ago probably went unnoticed. In 1988, the Seoul Olympics will move the Modern Pentathlon even further from its historical roots. And for the first time in history, competition in this most arduous and varied sport will be open to women.

Rowing: Camelot at Casitas

Christopher Dodd

The road from the Pacific Coast Highway leads uphill towards a hazy hint of the Santa Ynez Mountains. Somewhere behind is the relentless surf of the ocean, and here and there on scrubbled dry earth or etched on a bluff against the dawn is an oil well. Turning to the left off Highway 33, Santa Ana Road climbs more steeply through woodland and orchard to the first-light coffee stall at the Corner Market, then rises sharply to barer, rockier, still blue-rinsed chaparral country. There, a motionless balloon and a turreted tower of glitter rippled by the first rays of sunshine indicate another land. Lo, the level lake, a deep-hued opaque mirror stretching to the pine and live oak slopes of Red Mountain. "Welcome to Camelot," Dick Erickson says.

He is the deep-throated chief coach of the University of Washington's Huskies, looking rather abashed in his official outfit in delicate shades of bubble-gum, caramel, and off-Leander cerise. He is wandering about in the crews area where shining white tents have diamond-shaped roofs, doing his homework on those who will race their sweep-oars or their two-blades-in-the-hand sculling boats fast and furiously on the 2000-meter track. The course stretches away from the launching pontoons towards the start under dark Laguna Ridge. It is now floodlit as the sun creeps over Topa Topa range. The orange and white Albano buoys are pinpointed by sunbeams. The flags of the nations hang limp above the open grandstand. The athletes' rest rooms and massage tent, the fast food, souvenir, and binocular stalls have conical or four-poster roofs, with knobs on. Streamers stir all around. Sprinklers play the flower beds. And everything is pastel, save the stark green strip of the yeomen volunteers and the dark fronds of a majestic line of giant palms.

Once upon a time this was a warm reservoir in Lake Casitas Recreation Area, where anglers chased rich stocks of bass and catfish. But now, inside the high wire after an hour's ride from the University of California at Santa Barbara Olympic Village, it is a tournament arena. Minstrels play flute and harp, barber shop quartets sing fresh as the morning dew, sequined cheerleaders high kick to the Santa Barbara City College band.

The architect Barry Berkus did a fine job in creating the Lake Casitas site which, coupled with early-morning starts to beat the breeze that gets up at ten and the hot midday temperature that follows, served as a place of beauty for preparations and competition.

A few of the eight men's events and all six of the women's were marked by absent friends, a situation felt less by athletes for its effect on their events than because, more than most sports, theirs is a family. Despite this absence, the competition in the fourteen events was fair and fiery, the medals were hard won. In the men's events they were also spread out wide so that happiness was distributed as widely as misery. Golds went to Canada, Finland, the Federal Republic of Germany, Italy, Great Britain, New Zealand, Romania and the United States of America. Australia, Belgium, Denmark, Spain, Norway, and Yugoslavia also reached the medal table, crews from 14 nations sharing the total of 24. Romania's sweep of the women's golds stopped at five when the USA won the eights. Australia, Belgium, Denmark, Federal Republic of Germany and the Netherlands were also among the 18 medals. Much more than in the case of the men, the presence of crews from the Soviet bloc would have changed this pattern considerably.

One race was spiked by mystery, an act of sabotage which appeared in the men's eight like the shadow of death which rowers experience when 500 meters from goal. The night before the preliminary heats a journalist and a British Member of Parliament doodled on the menu at Rocky Galenti's, a cheerful Italian food spot in Santa Barbara. They drank a little wine and drew up a wager on the final outcome of the eight-oared boats in stormy or no-wind conditions, and placed a one pound note per crew on the eventual order. They discussed it for a long time because there were several realistic finishing orders to choose among five of the seven crews. Australia, Canada, Great Britain, New Zealand and the USA were all in the running.

The others in the line-up were France and Chile, so two heats and a "second-chance" repechage, rowing's system of requiring two races before elimination is possible, were needed to remove one crew. New Zealand and the USA won the heats respectively, thus avoiding the repechage. The other five raced again to drop the last, and France faltered suddenly just outside the 100-meter equipment breakage safety net. Crews are responsible for their own equipment, and after 100 meters breakage does not earn a re-start. Their No. 6 man, Jean Jacques Martigne, lost his oar. The gate or keeper, a brass hinged bar which locks the oar into the rowlock at the end of the outrigger, had broken. This is not uncommon, but when the angry and distraught crew reached the finish, officials detached the rowlock and gate immediately. They smelled a rat because something odd had happened to an American crew at the Federation Internationale des Societes d'Aviron junior championships in Jonkoping, Sweden two weeks before. They found that the gate had sheared at its hinge end, not at the more likely screw-thread end, and that its pivot had been filed down, a considerable job of work, according to Keller. The motivation is a mystery. The French would not get near the medals. The menu at Rocky Galenti's had them

Opposite Page Unger (AUT) pulls hard in women's singles sculls. Photo: IOPP

Hamilton, Hughes, Monckton and Ford (CAN) in men's fours-without-cox.
Photo: IOPP

Karppinen (FIN) strokes ahead of Kilbe (FRG) in 2000M single sculls.
Photo:IOPP

Photo: IOPP

down sixth, the only position, it turned out, that the gamblers had both named correctly. And the sheared gate could have been in use for some time. There was no way of telling when it would break. While it was unlikely that the work was done at the Casitas site, the rowlock's gate could have been exchanged there easily enough. This takes a matter of seconds. The French crew was admitted to Lane 7 for the final, an unprecedented move which met with applause from the other team managers. Coaches redoubled their vigilance in boat tents already floodlit at night and 'round the clock.

By this time athletes were used to going to bed at seven p.m. and bussing to the lake to train at first light. In nearby Oakview, locals chewing the dawn around the centre table in Cuddles Coffee Shop were used to reporters and Highway Patrol men staring bleary-eyed into breakfast.

The women's finals came a day before the men's. It was a question of whether spectators would know the tune of "The Three Colors," Romania's national anthem, by heart at the end of the day. Just after 8 o'clock on Saturday August 4, Florica Lavric in the bow of the Romanian four-with coxswain was the first rower to strike gold, and she crossed 2.25 seconds ahead of Marilyn Brain in the bow of the Canadian boat. These crews had been almost level half way along the 1000 meters course, straining their backs against the sun, their coxswains driving

them into it. Australia, the USA, the Netherlands and the Federal Republic of Germany were battling also. Tomorrow had run out on them.

The fours were followed by Marioara Popescu and Elisabeta Oleniuc in the double sculls, who, with almost three seconds in hand, could look back on the struggle for silver and bronze between the Netherlands and Canada. The HOL women won the silver by .62 seconds. Rodica Arba and Elena Horvat had matters slightly easier in the sweep-oared pairs, moving in front early on and leading the CAN and FRG shells across the line.

Then came the coup de grace. The sculling world had been waiting since the 1983 world championships in Duisburg, West Germany, to see the lithe and bronzed Valeria Racila, the girl with the widest smile in Camelot, scull her graceful way in a final. In Duisburg she fell overboard after her rowlock broke. Here she followed her copybook, winning the gold which had had her name etched on it for a year. It finally came out of a GDR shadow, cast in the Lucerne regatta six weeks beforehand.

FRG pulled to an early lead in the quadruple sculls-with-cox, but the Romanians came through chased hard by the Americans. These boats really fly, in close-up resembling a pianist's fingers lightly riffing chord cadences. Five Romanian

golds. They were heading for their sixth in the eights, but they couldn't hold their lead over the USA after half way. The American women had fought hard for this, some of them since before 1980 when they sat dejected on the bank at Henley Royal Regatta in England and watched their men's crews race on the Thames instead of at the Moscow Games. Theirs was a famous, well-deserved, well-rowed-out gold.

Next day was men's day. It dawned bright but when racing began, the lake was shrouded in mist, an English mist, said the British, who came out of it in their four-with-cox to take the gold, overtaking the American crew in a crushing burn in the penultimate 200 meters of the 2000 meters course. Adrian Ellison, wedged on his back in the bows, was thus the first man to cross the final Olympic finish line. Ellison was thrown into the lake, where swimming is not allowed. "It tastes wet," he said.

This was the first of eight gripping finals, presided over, it seems, by courtiers who decreed that as many as possible should eat cake. The USA's Brad Lewis and Paul Enquist caught the Belgians Pierre-Marie Deloof and Dirk Crois in the last five strokes in the double sculls, and they were last chancers among the American fleet. The Romanians Petru Iosub and Valer Toma splayed the field behind them in the pairs-without-cox. Then the "Floating Finn," Pertti Karppinen, interrupted the heartbeats of onlookers as he stalked Peter-Michael Kolbe (FRG) along the course. Two beautiful scullers. Kolbe a sprinter tried to hang on to his virtuoso solo but missed a note perhaps 100 meters from the line. It was at that moment that the power and coordination of the Finn's leg-drive, body-swing, and arm pull and his smooth recovery for the next mighty stroke took him through to his third Olympic gold medal. Such a record is matched only by the Soviet sculler Vyacheslav Ivanov. Bells rang out in Finland for the fire chief who stayed atop the greasy pole. Kolbe graciously acknowledged that the Finn is stronger and better.

Carmine and Giuseppe Abbagnale (ITA), steered by Giuseppe di Capua, took gold in the pairs-with-cox. New Zealanders powered their way to the front in the fours-without-cox in a final where all six runners could have borne heavy backing. The USA and Denmark took the other medals, but the FRG, SUI, and SWE were in contention for most of the race. FRG caught the Australians in the quadruple sculls-without-cox in the nick of time, winning gold by .43 seconds. And in the eights, Canada never did get around to letting the British quippers see them. They charged up the course arriving first, .42 seconds or a canvas ahead of the disbelieving Americans, with Australia, New Zealand, and Great Britain streaming behind. France was sixth, Chile became the firstcrew ever to finish seventh in an Olympic final.

None of this really happened. Folk will point at Olympic records printed out from the vaporized electronic messaging system, and show you photos of crews and videos of a dream at Camelot. Wiseacres in Cuddles and Oakview will tell you that some big shot from Tinsel Town once offered the fishermen of Casitas 7000 pounds of catfish to borrow their lake to make a TV movie. But when trumpets muted, commentators' babble ceased, and cheers evaporated, Camelot floated away with the mist one morning over the Santa Ynez mountains. If you go to Casitas now, all you will see is deer in the chaparral, and an angler in his motor boat beneath the pine and live oak of Red Mountain casting a sinker and a night crawler in the hope of catching a catfish.

Shooting:
Eleventh Hour Shootout

Gary Anderson

When the LAOOC began its preparations for the 1984 Olympics, there were serious doubts as to whether shooting would even be included. When the Olympics were over, not only had shooting taken place, it had set a new athlete participation record played to sell-out crowds. An outstanding new Olympic range had been built, and four new shooting events had become part of the Olympic program to spark the future development of the sport.

Several reasons prompted organizers to doubt whether shooting competition could be held. Until recently, most shooting in the United States of America had been conducted according to rules which differ from those of the world governing body for shooting, the International Shooting Union. Even more fundamentally, prior to 1984, there had not been a single suitable range in the United States for Olympic shooting.

After a five year search for a new range site, only one year before the Games, and truly at the eleventh hour, a cow pasture near Chino, California was selected. It was transformed into an Olympic-quality facility in the space of six months.

Shooting in the Games of the XXIIIrd Olympiad was enhanced by four new events, including three separate women's events. The emergence of special heroes in shooting is rare because success requires specialization in a particular event. The last time a shooter won two individual gold medals was in 1912.

This makes the shooting performance of Wu Xiaoxuan of People's Republic of China very special. The 26-year-old shooting instructor won a bronze medal in women's air rifle, a new Olympic event for men and women, with 389 and then won the women's 50 meter three position rifle event with a score of 581.

Since 1896, only five shooters have repeated as Olympic gold medal winners. Luciano Giovannetti of Italy became the sixth when he won the trap competition. The 38-year-old gun store owner finished the regular competition tied with 19 year old Francisco Boza of Peru and world record holder Dan Carlisle of the USA. Giovannetti earned the victory by breaking 24 of 25 targets in a shoot-off, compared to 23 for Boza and 22 for Carlisle. Just as in Moscow, he was carried off the field on the shoulders of his jubilant teammates.

Ion Corneilieu won the rapid fire pistol event in 1980, was Romania's flagbearer in the 1984 Opening Ceremonies, and came close to successfully defending his Olympic title. This event, which involves shooting a series of five shots at five different targets in as little as four seconds, has two days of competition. Corneliu led after the first day with 299 points, but he fell to 294 on the second day to allow Takeo Kamachi, a 48-year-old veteran of five Olympics, to win the gold medal with a 595 total. Kamachi's win was remarkable because he severed the nerves in two fingers of his shooting hand three years ago and wasn't able to resume training until one year before the Games.

One of the all-time greats in free pistol, Ragnar Skanaker of Sweden, came within a fraction of an inch of winning his second gold medal. He won the gold in 1972 and in a great demonstration of longevity, the world championship in 1982. At the age of 50, he came to Los Angeles shooting better scores than ever. Xu Haifeng (CHN), a 26-year-old shop assistant in a fertilizer outlet who has been in serious training for only two years, denied Skanaker the gold medal by the painfully narrow margin of 566 to 565 points.

Xu's gold medal was indeed special. The free pistol competition finished in the morning of the first day of Olympic competition, and he was the first gold medal winner of the XXIIIrd Olympiad. His medal was also the first Olympic medal ever won by an athlete from People's Republic of China.

One of the major surprises of the Games was the success of the shooters from People's Republic of China. Li Feng, an assistant team manager, said, "We only expected one gold medal." 19-year-old student Li Yuwei brought the total to three by winning the 50 meter running game target event. Li's score of 587 was three points ahead of Columbia's Helmut-Bellingrodt, who won his nation's only medal in Los Angeles.

Shooters like Li and trap silver medalist Boza clearly show that younger shooters are becoming more and more successful. Four of the medalists are still juniors according to International Shooting Union rules. In addition to Li and Boza, 18-year-old Pat Spurgin (USA) won the women's air rifle gold medal, with a score of 393, just two points under the World record, and 16-year-old Ulrike Holmer (FRG) won a silver medal in women's 50 meter three position rifle. Holmer, who works as a sales clerk in her father's butcher shop, is the youngest person ever to win an Olympic shooting medal

Another young shooter, 21-year-old Philippe Heberle of France, won the gold medal in men's air rifle with 589 points.

The bronze medalist in men's air rifle, Barry Dagger of Great Britain, offers a poignant example of how physical size is not important in shooting. Dagger is only 4'9" tall. He started shooting because it was one of the few sports where his size would not be an impediment.

Ed Etzel, a doctoral candidate in psychology from the USA, is arguably the best prone position rifle shooter in the world. No sports event in the world requires greater precision. On a 50 meter target with a ten ring only 12mm in diameter, the world record is a perfect 600 and the Olympic record is 599. Etzel tied the Olympic record.

**Opposite Page
Men's small-bore
rifle competition.
Photo: IOPP**

The sport pistol event for women is a new event which includes 30 slow fire or precision shots and 30 duel shots where the pistol must be raised and fired at a target which is turned to face the shooter for only three seconds. Linda Thom from Canada, a mother of two young children and a professional chef and caterer, tied at 585 with Ruby Fox of the USA. After three additional series of five duel shots, the tie was broken by one point.

The men's 50 meter three position rifle event, a long and difficult test that involves shooting 40 shots each in the prone, kneeling, and standing positions over nearly six hours, was won by Malcolm Cooper, a 36-year-old businessman from Great Britain. He tied the Olympic and world records with his score of 1173, achieving one of the finest shooting performances ever.

The last shooting event, skeet, was won by the USA's Matt Dryke. Using his exaggerated crouching stance, Dryke, the world record holder and world champion, broke 74 of 75 targets the first day, 74 targets on the second day and scored a perfect 50 on the last day. His 198 total tied the Olympic record.

In all, 32 different athletes from 17 nations and five continents won the 33 medals awarded in the shooting competitions of the Games of the XXIIIrd Olympiad. But as in every sport in every Olympics, it is not only the medal winners who gain from the Olympic experience. A record total of 474 participants from 68 nations, several hundred judges and competition officials and the sport itself were all victorious in many special ways.

Carlisle (USA) reloads in trap shooting. Photo: IOPP

Swimming: Wet and Wild

Bill Cutting with Robert Ingram

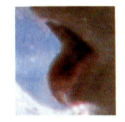

**Opposite Page
Davis (CAN) winner
of the 200M
breaststroke.
Photo: IOPP**

Los Angeles, California. If ever a more appropriate site was chosen for an Olympic swimming competition, it would be hard to imagine. Just a racing dive from the Pacific Ocean; a medley relay from the San Fernando Valley where backyard pools dot the landscape like freckles on a swimmer's back; and a mere 1500 meter freestyle from Mission Viejo, the very cradle of swimming. What Indianapolis is to motor racing; what Innsbruck is to snow skiing; what Monte Carlo is to joie de vivre; so Southern California is to international competitive swimming.

That significance was lost on no one who was present for the seven days of Olympic swimming competition. Many of the competitors—from the USA as well as from foreign countries— matriculated at MVSC, Mission Viejo Swimmers College. And while the thousands of spectators who jammed the gleaming new University of Southern California Olympic Swim Stadium constituted arguably the most knowledgeable swimming crowd in the history of Olympic competition, they were undoubtedly the most enthusiastic.

It began early with hype. Going into the Games, Michael Gross (FRG), a.k.a. "The Albatross", was pretty much expected to take every event he could wrap his talons around. So named for his gangly stature (2.02m) and his wingspan (2.2m), it was clear from the start that the pressure was on Gross to sweep his events. He lived up to his reputation in the men's 100 meter butterfly, taking the gold medal and wresting the Olympic and world record time of 53.08 away from Pablo Morales (USA), the runner-up. But it was in the 200 meter fly, that Gross ran afowl of expectations, finishing a shocking second to 17-year- old upstart John Sieben of Brisbane, Australia. Sieben who, at 1.7m tall is a relative sparrow next to Gross, trailed him by two body lengths at the 50 meter mark. But he catapulted into first place and touched the wall in a time of 1:57.04., .01 better than Gross' world mark. The Australian, who had never even broken two minutes until the morning preliminaries, said after the race, "Normally, I've had pretty bad luck finishing. This time, everything went right."

Everything went superbly for Gross in the 200 meter freestyle, as he toppled his own best by .11 and set another world mark at 1:47.44. Meanwhile, the USA's Steve Lundquist, a muscular, rangy blond from Georgia, with a smile as big as his talent, stunned the crowd by becoming the first swimmer ever to break 1:02 in the 100 meter breaststroke, in a time of 1:01.65. "Lunk" had to accept preeminence at the expense of his rival and teammate, John Moffet. Moffet's is a classic story of Olympic fortitude. World record holder going into the event, he pulled an upper thigh muscle during the morning 100 meter preliminaries. The pain was so intense by the afternoon final, that his piston-like frog kick was useless. Dead last at the turn, he finished a heroic fifth at 1:03.29. Canada's Victor Davis, second to Lundquist in the 100 meter breaststroke, roared back to take the 200 meter in 2:13.34, more than a second faster than his own previous world record in that event. Glenn Beringen (AUS) trailed 2.5 seconds later to take the silver. Etienne Dagon's (SUI) bronze was the first medal his country had ever won in swimming competition.

In the oddest women's 100 meter freestyle finish ever, Olympic Village roommates Nancy Hogshead and Carrie Steinseifer (USA), were declared co-gold medalists with an identical time of 55.92. The Swiss timing system clocked them to the nearest hundredth of a second, which is as close as the International Swimming Federation (FINA) will calculate. Theirs was the first instance in which a gold medal was awarded to two swimmers in the same event. Annemarie Verstappen (HOL) took the bronze. In the women's 200 meters, Mary Wayte and Cynthia Woodhead (USA) swept the field in a slow winning time of 1:59.23. Verstappen took the bronze in that event also.

Canada's Alex Baumann, proved he belongs in a class by himself. The 20-year-old from Sudbury, Ontario, became the first swimmer from his country to win a gold medal in swimming in 72 years. He succeeded in gritty fashion in perhaps the two most grueling events in the sport: the 200 and 400 meter individual medleys (IM). In the 400 meter IM, Baumann bettered his own world record by .12 with a time of 4:17.41. Baumann, who comes from an immigrant family from Czechoslovakia, has missed major international meets during the past few years due to the deaths of his father and brother, and because of nagging shoulder ailments. "He's had the courage and fortitude to face life," says Dr. Jeno Dihanney, Baumann's coach and family friend." He was ready to quit swimming because of personal setbacks. But I told him that, 'life is waiting.'" Baumann was waiting for no one in the 200 meter IM five days later. He set another world mark with a time of 2:01.42. "It's been a long time coming", he said of Canada's medal drought. "Now we have four gold medals on the Canadian swim team. I really feel good. I can't get down, I'm still flying above the clouds." World records continued to fall like ten-pins.

In one of the most agonizing finishes in any of the swimming events, the USA 4x200 meter freestyle relay team of Mike Heath, David Larson, Jeff Float and Bruce Hayes bettered the team from FRG, anchored by the omnipresent Gross. The relay started out with Heath blazing a 1:48.67 leg against Thomas Fahrner. Larson was off the blocks and into his first

Andrews (USA) on her way to the gold medal in the 100M backstroke.
Photo: T. Duffy

Left to Right
Gross (FRG) new
world and Olympic
record in the 100M
butterfly.
Photo: IOPP

Gaines' (USA) medal
ceremonies for the
100M freestyle.
Photo: T. Duffy

O'Brien (USA) gold
medal winner in the
1500M freestyle.
Photo: T. Duffy

Carey (USA) 1984
with Kiykawa (JPN)
1932, 100M back-
stroke champions.
Photo: IOPP

CHN collides with YUG in a hard contested match.
Photo: T. Duffy

Diving & Synchronized Swimming: Aqua-batics

Russ Ewald

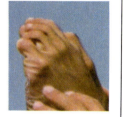

**Opposite Page
Louganis (USA) in
men's springboard
finals.
Photo: T. Duffy**

Divers seem to defy those laws of nature that govern everyone else—things such as space, time and the force by which terrestrial bodies tend to fall to the center of the earth. Which is why the spectators at University of Southern Califonia (USC) Swim Stadium held their collective breaths as Greg Louganis stepped to the edge of the 10 meter platform poised to execute the most difficult, most important dive of his career; the one that had come to be called "the death dive".

The 24-year-old Louganis, blessed with a powerful, nearly flawless body, had dominated diving for half a decade, so much so, he was regarded as the greatest diver in history. Louganis hadn't lost on the platform in international competition, nor on the springboard in any kind of meet during the three years prior to the 1984 Olympic Games.

In spite of his success, going into the '84 Games, Louganis still sought his first gold medal in Olympic competition, where the audience would probably be bigger than in all other meets put together. In the first of the two men's diving events, the three-meter springboard, he was so far ahead he needed less than one point on his last dive to win the gold medal. He got 92.40.

But Louganis, who has a theater arts degree from the University of California at Irvine, saved his best performance for the most dramatic moment. On the final day of the Olympics, he turned in such a near-flawless exhibition that his score on the platform may never be duplicated.

Mere mortals may content themselves with ordinary things. But Louganis is no mere mortal. He is perfection incarnate. And so, on the 10 meter platform, with a score of 618.09 going into his tenth and final dive, he wasn't satisfied with winning his second Olympic gold medal, Louganis was after something far greater: a score of 700 or better for ten dives. "There's no doubt about it," said Ron O'Brien, co-coach of the USA diving team and Louganis' personal coach, "it's tantamount to someone leaping nine meters in the long jump or running 9.5 for the 100 meters." Since it was an extraordinary score, it would require an extraordinary dive to pull off. And so Louganis chose a reverse three and a half tuck somersault, the "death dive", named for the Soviet diver Sergei Shalibashvili, who died attempting it in international competition. The Soviet slammed his head into the tower on the second somersault, fracturing his skull. He died one week later of a massive cerebral hemorrhage.

Louganis poised himself at the top of the platform for a surprisingly short amount of time. Slowly his leg muscles tensed and he rose on his toes, then pushed himself up and away from the tower. He soared through the California sky and began to spin in slow motion: once, twice, three times, plus one more half for good measure. Then, with little more than a small splash, he ripped the surface of the pool. He averaged a score of 8.9 from each judge on each dive. His final score of 710.91 was far above his previous bests of 687.90 at the previous year's world cup and 688.05 in the preliminaries. No one else had even come close to those scores.

O'Brien was ecstatic: "It was the most dominant display in diving history." There are several reasons why Louganis is so superior to other divers. "His overall strength is his greatest attribute," analyzed O'Brien. "It gives him the ability to make adjustments in the air that others can't. He gets so high on his takeoff that he has more time in flight than anyone else."

Although Louganis makes its look so easy off the board, he still finds it difficult to cope with the mental pressure inherent in a sport where most of the time is spent waiting to perform and the dive takes but a few seconds. "Part way through the competition I was thinking that I was diving well, and it was kind of scary," Louganis reflected afterward. "You have to have just enough of a distraction so you can concentrate on what you want to be doing. "You can say to yourself, 'don't mess up.' Many times you get stuck in that and that's when you start holding back. I didn't want to do that today. I wanted to go all out."

Louganis found a way to calm himself before his final dive, when he would be seeking to break the 700-point milestone. He grabbed "Gar"—the stuffed bear given him for good luck by Mary Jane O'Brien, his coach's wife—and took the stuffed animal into the restroom for a long talk. "I like to talk to Gar," Louganis explained, "because he doesn't talk back."

Bruce Kimball, the other USA entrant, was far back of Louganis, but he felt good anyway. He had come through with his highest score ever, enough to edge Li Kongzheng (CHN) for the silver medal. Three years ago, Kimball wasn't thinking of medals, only surviving. He suffered near-fatal injuries in an auto accident when a van crossed a double yellow line and hit his car head-on. But nine months later he made the USA team for the world championships.

That competitive spirit was evident in the platform finals when Kimball vaulted from fourth place entering the eighth round, to second by the finish, three dives later. This was a source of satisfaction for Bruce's father, Dick Kimball, a member of the USA staff and Bruce's coach since he began diving at the age of four.

In the springboard event, while Louganis was competing against his own records, Tan Liangde and Li Hongping of the People's Republic of China and Ron Merriott, another USA

competitor, were in a tight battle for the silver and bronze medals after the five compulsory dives, they were within one point after the five compulsory dives.

Tan, a 19-year-old from Canton, hit his eighth-round inward two and a half pike for a big score to open up a lead. Merriott, a former world trampoline champion used his exceptional spring off the board to good effect in his final dives, closing the gap. But he was nosed out by less than a point, settling for the bronze medal.

Unlike the men's competition, the women's events provided some surprise winners. They were Canada's Sylvie Bernier in springboard and the Peoples Republic of China's Zhou Jihong in platform, who proved you don't have to be big to be successful in diving. Bernier stands 1.57 meters and weighs 50 kilograms, Zhou 1.52 meters and 41.8 kilograms.

The 20-year-old Bernier had always been a high finisher in major international meets but never a champion. She had the double distinction of being her country's first-ever gold medalist in diving and the only diving medalist at the Los Angeles Games from outside of the USA and CHN.

Sylvie never knew where she stood throughout the competition. "That's good for me," she revealed. "I've been diving for 12 years and I know for me it's not good to know where I am. The pressure is good to a certain point, but at this time, I didn't want to know. I tried many times to look at the board and see where I was, but it never worked. I knew before I came here that I just wanted to be myself and listen to music."

When Bernier completed her final dive, she went up to her coach, who told her, "You're ahead, but it's not over. If Kelly McCormick does a dive for 70 points, she's going to beat you."

McCormick, the USA trials winner and Pan American champion in 1983, was a close second from the third round on. She couldn't quite catch Bernier on her final attempt, getting all 8s on a back two and a half tuck to wind up three points back. Her low score on a reverse two and a half tuck two rounds earlier had been her downfall.

McCormick, 24, is the daughter of Pat McCormick, the only diver ever to win two Olympic gold medals in each of two successive Games (1952 and 1956). Asked if she thought about her mother during the competition, Kelly replied, "If I would have done that, I think I would have been a lot more nervous. I couldn't imagine watching my daughter in the Olympics. It would drive me up the wall."

Chris Seufert, the oldest USA Olympic diver at 27, was only fifth after the five compulsories. But she hit her optionals better than anyone to earn the bronze medal. After the com-

petition, she immediately hugged winner Bernier.

Platform champion Zhou, just 19, was the youngest diving gold medalist at the Games. She was almost apologetic following her victory. "I think I performed up to my potential," she said, "but unfortunately my teammate did not. She normally would have done better than I."

Zhou was talking about veteran diver, Chen Xiaoxia, 21 (CHN), who dominates meets in her country but suffers from nerves outside it. She was the event's favorite but finished only fourth.

Wendy Wyland and Michele Mitchell were seeking the USA's first gold medal in the women's platform since 1964. Lapses in the compulsories ruled that out, but they came back in the optionals to earn medals. "The best performance of mine was at the U.S. trials," said 22-year-old silver medalist Mitchell, who rebounded from shoulder surgery in February to set a national scoring record at the trials. "It's a performance I don't know if I can repeat." Mitchell scored 45 points less in the Olympics than at the trials.

Although Wyland was world champion as a 17-year-old in 1982, she wasn't disappointed with the bronze medal. "This one means a lot to me," she said. "I don't think there are too many people in the world who can say they got a third place in the Olympics." An all-women event made its Olympic debut

in the 1984 Games. Synchronized swimming, it reminded some of the Esther William movies of 30 years ago which featured beautiful water ballets in extravagant tropical settings. The setting at the Olympic Swim Stadium was not tropical, but the event was, all seemed to agree, just as lush. Synchronized swimmers disdain the ballet metaphor. They claim they are water gymnasts—not dancers. But to anyone watching the paired swimmers performing their graceful, routines, mirroring each other, the argument over what to call them seemed quite beside the point.

Tracie Ruiz and Candy Costie had been working on their mirroring routines for so long, they started to mirror one another on dry land as well as in the water. Both women are about the same height and weight and share a similar bone structure. They were born only a month apart. Their long hours of practice together made the similarity even greater. Their coach, Charlotte Davis said, "They'll say the same thing or react the same way in a certain situation. Or they'll show up at the same place in the same clothes."

There was a time when the two women were fierce rivals. That was in Seattle, Washington, eleven years ago, when they were ten-years-old and members of rival swim clubs. But when their clubs merged a year later, the two girls began a 10-year partnership which found its culmination in the 1984 Olympics.

Costie and Ruiz (USA) won the synchronized swimming gold medal.
Photo: T. Duffy

Following Page Classic piked position reverse dive by Wyland (USA).
Photo: T. Duffy

Ruiz and Costie made a rapid rise from the USA novice age group to international competition. During their early years, they never dreamed of winning gold medals, simply because synchronized swimming wasn't in the Olympics until this year.

At the 1982 world championships in Guayaquil, Ecuador, they were beaten by the Canadian pair of Sharon Hambrook and Kelly Kryczka when Costie finished only 23rd in the figures portion, although Ruiz was first. The two Americans returned to workouts with renewed vigor. They dropped out of the University of Arizona—where they had athletic scholarships—to practice under the guidance of their club coach, Charlotte Davis. Beginning their workouts in the pool as early as 4:30 in the morning, they would practice for up to seven hours with workouts in speed swimming, weights, aerobics and dance as well as synchronization.

Further north, synchronized swimmers in Canada were not resting on their laurels. Hambrook, 20, and Kryczka, 22, used metronomes and psychic exercises to get their hearts to beat as one. At the 1984 Canadian trials, they performed without an audience so the Americans were not able to view their routine.

The long-awaited United States-Canada duel and curiosity over the new Olympic sport attracted sellout crowds to all the sessions, the first of which was the routine portion of the prelims on the ninth day of the Games.

It was a shaky beginning for the sport. At first, the teams from the United States of America and France were penalized one point each for performing too short a routine. But then it was discovered the timers had started their watches on the swimmers' entry into the water rather than when their musical accompaniment began. With the correction, Ruiz and Costie qualified first followed closely by Hambrook and Kryczka.

During their preliminary routine, Ruiz and Costie unveiled a unique movement dubbed "threading the needle." This new maneuver had the two women spinning underwater with their toes touching on top of the water and then performing a move that makes it appear as if their legs are going under and up through the opening created by their other legs.

The next day's figures, were very important to the competitors. They counted not only as the final 50 percent of the preliminaries but also as 50 percent of the final score. In addition, they would be used as the figures portion for the solo competition. Out of 36 possible figures that the competitors were required to know, six were randomly selected for the Olympic event. Ironically, it turned out to be the same group of six figures chosen at the world championships two years ago. But Costie, who had lost more than 6.81 kilograms since her poor performance at Guayaquil, was prepared. And Ruiz showed she was still the best.

Ruiz finished far ahead in first and Costie was fifth (fourth among duet competitors). The Americans thus took a .5 lead over the Canadians into the last half of the finals—the routine which would take place the following day. Hambrook and Kryczka had finished third and fourth, respectively in the figures (second and third among duet entries—their teammate, solo performer Carolyn Waldo was second to Ruiz).

An important bonus for the USA team was that their combined preliminary routine and figures score gave them top seeding for the finals, allowing them to perform their routine last.

"This has always been a difficult group of figures for me, but this is the best I've done," said a relieved Costie, who improved eight points over her 1982 score.

"Boy, am I glad that's over," said Davis. "The Canadians have always been the favorites going into the figures, but we've done our homework."

Debbie Muir, the Canadian coach, was philosophical about her team's runner-up position. "We're going to swim well tomorrow. It won't matter whether we're the last team performing or next-to-last," she commented about the important order of the finalists.

Hambrook summed up the competitors' outlook toward the significant figures portion. "For the routine, you use the adrenaline and excitement of the crowd, while in the figures you have to maintain control and be calm throughout. It's intense concentration for four hours, rather than four minutes, so you have to control yourself."

Prior to the last two routines by the favorites, Japan assured itself of at least the bronze medal by scoring higher than the preceding teams from France, Mexico, the Netherlands, Switzerland and Great Britain. The Japanese duet of Saeko Simura and Miwako Motoyoshi demonstrated exquisite choreography and synchronization.

It was the Canadians' turn next. They astonished the 12,000 spectators with a combination of flashy movements, power moves and athleticism. Finishing with a flourish, they drew a rousing ovation as they moved to the lively beat of "Rock Around the Clock" and closed with the last of their unprecedented three dramatic lifts. Their score put them in first place at the time, clinching at least the silver medal.

However, the USA team, because of its high figures score, needed a score of only 97.7 to take the gold medal. It had received 98.4 in the preliminary routine.

Ruiz and Costie didn't play it safe, though. They began with a daring display of endurance, performing the first 53 seconds with their heads under water. Then, they wooed the audience further into their routine when Costie slipped underwater and lifted Ruiz into the air by the shoulders so that it looked as if she were doing a handstand on the surface of the water. The pair's showmanship appeared with their break dancing moves, and they concluded in a saluting position to the tune "Yankee Doodle Dandy," bringing the clapping crowd to its feet. The entertaining routine, which drew one score of 10 (from the USA judge) and the rest 9.9s, earned Ruiz and Costie the gold medal by more than a point.

In her hour of victory, Ruiz couldn't hold back the tears. They were tears of joy, but also of a sadness for the end of her long relationship with partner Costie.

"We're like sisters," she said. "I know we'll stay in contact, but everything will be different from this moment on. I guess that's how life goes on."

Ruiz was just as proud that synchronized swimming was a part of the Olympics as she was of her medal.

"I think just making it to the Olympic Games is something in itself," she emphasized. "Then, to have it be a history-making event at the same time is like icing on the cake. It can't get any better than that."

Costie seconded Ruiz, explaining, "It's great to be here because we want the public to know that synchronized swimming is a sport, and that it takes a lot of training."

While the Americans celebrated, the Canadians questioned the judging. "When we came out of the water, our coach said she couldn't see one mistake," said Hambrook. "You can't expect any more from us."

The solo competition, which was added to the Olympic schedule just over two months before the Games, was less controversial. With each country allowed just one entry, there were 17 competitors. But one stood out—you could say knees and thighs above the rest—defending champion Ruiz, who had not lost a solo event in the last four years.

There was little suspense to the routine portion, the last half of the event, because the gaps were so great between first and second and second and third after the figures competition. Ruiz held a big lead. Canada's Waldo was comfortably in second and Japan's Motoyoshi in third by more than a point.

To get up for her solo routine after the excitement of the duet gold medal, Ruiz put on a new suit and hat. She began her performance with a spectacular body flip into the water. "I knew the entry wasn't even judged," she said afterward. "But I just wanted to show we're athletes like gymnasts."

Ruiz averaged scores of 9.9 and got one 10 (from the Italian

judge) to hold on to her lead and win her second gold medal. Waldo remained in second, coming close to Ruiz' routine score with a total of an average mark of 9.86. Motoyoshi was third to collect her second bronze medal.

What can Ruiz do for an encore? She doesn't know.

"Nobody's done this before," she answered. "So I don't know what I'll be doing. I'll sit back and see what's offered."

**Left to Right
Besson and Hermine
(FRA) perform a
duet routine in
synchronized
swimming.
Photo: IOPP**

**Great Britain in
synchronized swim
Photo: T. Duffy**

Photo: IOPP

**Kimura and
Motoyoshi (JPN)
take home the
bronze.
Photo: IOPP**

Costie and Ruiz
(USA) were just as
stunning under
water as on top.
Photo: S. Powell

Volleyball: The Rugged Road

Bill Cutting with Steven Newman

In 1983, a year and a half before the 1984 Olympic Games, 15 members and 3 coaches of the USA men's volleyball team went on a retreat of sorts. The entire squad spent three frigid January weeks traversing 80 rugged miles of Canyonlands National Park in southern Utah—much of it in snowshoes and all of it laboring under the weight of 27kg packs. It was all part of an outdoor survival course designed to test the mettle of individuals tough enough to take on the challenge. Since it's difficult to fit a volleyball inside a backpack and still leave room for trivial items such as food, water and a change of underwear, it is presumed that the team concentrated on a more elevated curriculum. In fact, that is precisely what they did.

"In order to complete our total training program," said Assistant Coach Bill Neville, "to ensure that the team was ready, individually and collectively for any situation, and to provide the most positive and influential experience, we wanted to involve the team in a wilderness situation that would uniquely tap the human resources required in every stress situation. We wanted our players to be totally prepared when they marched into the Olympic Stadium in 1984, to represent the United States."

What followed 18 months later confirmed the coaching staff's "wilderness" method of preparing for international volleyball competition. For by the time Olympic competition was over, the USA men's volleyball team had:

—survived a tough opening field of 10 teams,

—climbed all over every challenger it met, and in the process,

—reached the summit of a sport that had denied it so much as an Olympic qualifying berth in 16 years of trying.

What's more, in testing their mettle, the USA men took home a medal—gold to be precise—the first of any that an American squad has won in the history of Olympic volleyball.

The women's environment was considerably more hostile. After powering their way through an opening field of seven other teams, a tip-top squad from the People's Republic of China savaged the USA women in a straight-set final.

Though invented in the United States, the sport of volleyball has, for the past forty years, remained the virtual private property of countries outside of the western hemisphere. Japan, for one, is credited with formulating and refining international volleyball to such a degree that they are now considered among the world's finest players. And the men's team from the Soviet Union was regarded as almost unbeatable going into the 1984 Olympics. Despite its heritage and the fact that Southern California beaches are a checkerboard of courts, volleyball never gained the preeminence in the USA that basketball has, even though it was patterned after it. In fact, competitive volleyball bears little resemblance to the schoolyard version that is played in most circles. Complex offenses and defenses, combined with sets, fakes, blocks and spikes (in which the ball can travel at over 160km/hr) all make world-class volleyball one of the most exciting sports in Olympic competition.

So it was no surprise that capacity crowds jammed the Long Beach Arena for nearly every match in the 1984 Olympic volleyball tournament. Women's competition began with two qualifying pools: BRA, FRG, CHN, USA in Pool A; and KOR, JPN, PER, CAN in Pool B. Round-robin matches whittled the field down to a medal round of four: CHN, JPN, PER and USA. Round-robin competition was highlighted by spirited play from the underdogs, especially the Federal Republic of Germany, which posted its first win in Olympic volleyball with a courageous 15-9, 16-14, 15-11 match against a solid team from Brazil, and went on to take sixth place.

In medal round play the pool winners were matched to pool runners-up, the winners going on to meet for the gold and silver, and the losers playing for the bronze. From the very beginning, women's competition had been considered too close to call, with CHN, JPN and the USA all shooting for the top spot. As one observer noted, the only real upset would come if a team emerged that was not from that trio. That question was put to rest by the medal round. It matched the unbeaten USA v. PER and JPN v. CHN. That round also brought no surprises. The USA, thanks to solid play from sharpshooters Flo Hyman and Rita Crockett, and setter Debbie Green, got by a stubborn team from PER in straight sets. The team from CHN, meanwhile, overwhelmed JPN 15-10, 15-7, 15-4. That set up the final round match for first and second place between the USA and CHN. In the months prior to the 1984 Olympics, the USA and CHN met eight times. The powerhouse women's team from the People's Republic of China came away victorious in seven of those matchups. However, in their only 1984 Olympic meeting prior to the final, it was the USA that held sway, in a no-holds-barred matchup that went on to a 15-12 fourth game. What's more, the USA had the momentum. By virtue of a win against Peru, they advanced their unbeaten record to 5-0.

In the final, CHN, behind breathtaking spikes by Lang Ping, and Zhang Rongfang, seemed to have the ability to pull strength and shotmaking from the rafters. Overall, their play was characterized by a crisp ability to block, pass and dig for shots at will. They trounced the Americans in straight sets, 16-14, 15-3, 15-9. The only contest was the first set. The USA appeared to rally for a moment, but a pair of serving recep-

**Opposite Page
Saunders, Powers,
and Salmons (USA)
in a match with
TUN.
Photo: T. Jones**

tion errors handed the set to CHN. The USA strategy appeared to be to rely on high outside sets. But effective blocking by the Great Wall of China quickly upended that plan. The second set lasted just 20 minutes, the third only 27. After a convincing loss at the hands of the USA team days before, the final win was a triumphal reaffirmation for the CHN team and coach Yuan Weimin. USA coach Arie Selinger, who brought the same team to Los Angeles that he would have taken to Moscow in 1980, claimed that his squad had accomplished its goal by even finishing in the medals. Still, from so close a vantage point as second place, seeing the gold medal around the neck of another had to be a heartbreak.

The men's competition was never knotted so tightly as the women's. But the reason had less to do with who was present, than with who was not. By virtue of its home team status, the strongest team in USA volleyball history was assured an automatic berth in the Olympic tournament. Also present in the original line-up: ARG, CAN, CHN, EGY, ITA, JPN, KOR, TUN and BRA. But the absence of the Soviet Union, the world's most prolific volleyball champion, along with upstart Poland, cast a shadow over the men's tournament. As a measure of their importance to the men's tournament, it must be noted that three of the teams in the original 10-team pool qualified for Olympic competition by placing second to the

URS in international matches. Another strong contender: Brazil, runner-up to the Soviet Union in the 1982 world championships featured setter William Da Silva. He was thought to be the equal of Viatcheslauf Zajtsez (URS), long considered the world's best. For its part, the USA could count on several advantages along the way: setter Dusty Dvorak, all-around starter Karch Kiraly, exquisite depth and an enthusiastic home-town crowd. All in all a vigorous, though flawed, tournament was promised.

Throughout the opening rounds, Italy, Canada and Japan jockeyed for supremacy in Pool B. CHN, whose youthful men's team was not nearly so strong as its women's, was still in the running. Pool A's most surprising starter was KOR, whose complex offense behind Lee Jong Kyung and Chang Yoon Change, contributed to an early defeat for BRA. ARG, much improved over any international team they have ever fielded, was actually considered a medal contender at the outset. Two others, ITA and CAN were tough enough to be considered spoilers for favorites USA and BRA. And TUN was expected to slug it out for a single victory with EGY, from Pool B.

As the early rounds developed, CAN and ITA shaped up as dark horses in Pool B. ITA drew first blood in their initial encounter and would go on to an identical match record. CAN, on the strength of brawny left-side shooters John Barrett and

Photo: T. Jones

Paul Gratton, actually won the preliminary pool standings. JPN managed to finish in a virtual dead heat with the two, but because of the scoring system, ended up outside of the medal round. In Pool A, convincing victories over ARG, TUN and KOR assured the Americans a medal round spot. BRA, on the other hand, was not so blessed. It was desperate for a victory over the USA, since its loss at the hands of KOR put its medal round status in jeopardy. Only a victory over the USA in the final preliminary round would keep them in from sinking into ignominy. Before the match, Bebeto de Freitas, Brazil's head coach told the team it was "now or never". The emotional Brazilians came out blazing. Bernard Rajzman, a 10-year veteran pounded spikes around and through the USA. Jose Montanaro consistently beat the block with quick sets and raw power. Between them, Rajzman and Montanaro accounted for 54 of the 93 kills delivered by BRA during the match. BRA fought its way to a straight set rout of the USA, 15-10, 15-11, 15-2. In the other preliminary final, an inspired Canadian team trounced JPN in straight sets.

That set up in the semi-final pairings: USA against CAN, and BRA v. ITA, which finished the preliminary round with a methodical but effective match against EGY. In the opener, Brazil initially appeared confused and inconsistent, dropping the first set to Italy. But they stormed back and, in an offen-

sive flurry, managed to convert 86 of 131 kill opportunities. The final three games were literally no contest. Brazil finished the match 12-15, 15-2, 15-3, 15-5. Canada never really got on track during its semi-final with the United States of America. Pat Powers lived up to his name, unleashing shot after shot, converting kill opportunities into points. The straight-set score was 15-6, 15-10, 15-7. The USA banished Canada from the gold medal round.

In a way, it really mattered little who would triumph in the championship round. Both BRA and the USA were already guaranteed the best finishes their men's teams had ever recorded in an Olympic volleyball tournament, since neither had ever taken home a medal of any kind. However, nobody was ready to concede the gold, least of all the inspired Americans who wanted to avenge their loss of the previous week. Was that one a rollover? Karch Kiraly, to no one's particular surprise, noted offhandedly that the second game had significance while the first didn't.

The USA hit the packed arena like a fire out of control. Before the first ball was even served, the sellout crowd of 12,000 was on its feet, screaming for the home team. The USA played overwhelming defense, blocking 17 shots to Brazil's 7. This was in marked contrast to its three-set loss to Brazil earlier in the week. One of Brazil's most powerful

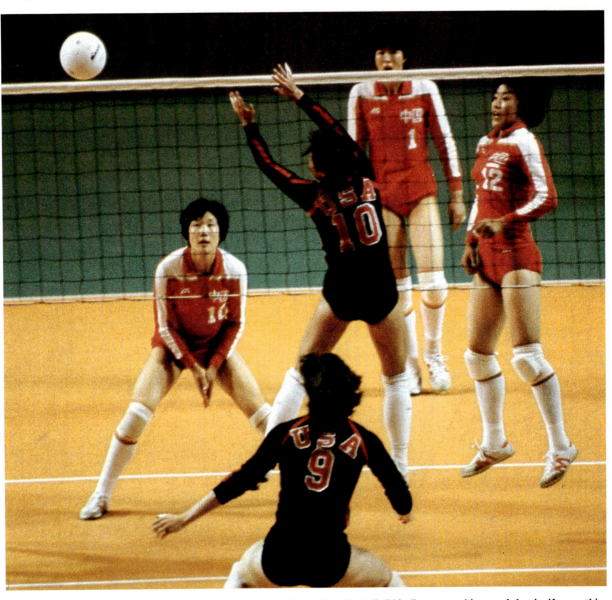

weapons throughout the tournament, a devastating run-and-jump power serve that incapacitated even the USA, was impotent this time around. Pat Powers and Steve Timmons were the sparkplugs of the squad, providing the power that kept the USA rolling along. Dvorak worked to put the ball in front of the spikers with deadly-accurate setups that converted into points 66 of 115 times. At every point, the USA partisans were on their feet, screaming their approval, waving American flags and chanting the by-now ubiquitous U-S-A! Brazil was not only overwhelmed by the style of play, they were overcome by its exuberance. The win came on a solo block by Dvorak and Long Beach Arena exploded. The final score in three sets was 15-6, 15-6, 15-7.

Italy won the bronze in a 3-set match 15-11, 15-12, 15-8, that was actually closer than it appeared. The final standings ended with Canada in fourth place, followed by KOR, ARG, JPN, CHN, TUN with its first victory in volleyball ever, and EGY.

Anticipating mitigating commentary that would follow the USA as surely as champagne followed victory, Karaly later defended the URS-less gold medal, "We proved it," he emphasized. "We beat the Soviets four straight. We've beaten Bulgaria eight straight. We've beaten Poland 11 out of 13. And we beat Cuba six times. This was all in the last year. And those are the four teams who were supposed to have been our biggest competition."

The results of the 1984 Olympic volleyball tournament should and will stand for every team involved. The USA, BRA and ITA, CAN, JPN, CHN and ARG all showed the world that they can play on any court with any team in any competition.

Still, the absence of Eastern bloc teams from 1984 Olym-

pic volleyball did indicate one thing, and that is, if everything goes as expected, we're in for one whale of a tournament in Seoul in 1988.

CHN goes low
in volleyball.
Photo: T. Jones

The USA men in
a game with the
team from TUN.
Photo: T. Jones

CHN duels JPN in
women's volleyball.
Photo: T. Jones

Some volleyball fans
had mixed emotions
about the outcome.
Photo: T. Jones

Weightlifting: Pumping Iron Into Gold

Berl Rosenthal

Shortly after the weightlifting program at the 1984 Olympic Games had ended, Herb Glossbrenner, a long-time statistician for the U.S. Weightlifting Federation, was asked to assess the competition.

"This whole meet was one big B session," he replied.

Glossbrenner's evaluation, while appearing to be harsh, was indeed true.

Weightlifting was perhaps the Olympic sport hardest hit by the Soviet-led boycott. All 10 of the sport's 1983 world champions were from Eastern bloc nations, six from the Soviet Union, three from Bulgaria, and one from GDR, and all were missing from the Los Angeles Games. Prior to World War II, the Italians, French and Germans were the most successful lifters. It wasn't until the post-war years, with nearly 500,000 registered athletes in the sport that the Soviet Union became a world leader in weightlifting. Its 33 Olympic gold medals is almost double that of the USA, the closest runnerup. So instead of having the creme de la creme of the world's weightlifters— the A lifters—the Olympics had to settle for the second team.

Therefore, the overall level of competition in the Olympics was far below that of the 1983 world championships, and thus, no world records were broken.

The fans who attended the weightlifting competition at Loyola Marymount's Albert Gersten Pavilion were denied the opportunity of seeing many outstanding athletes, such as Naim Suleimanov of Bulgaria, whom many observers say has the wherewithal to become the greatest lifter in history; super-heavyweight Anatoly Pisarenko of the Soviet Union, a two-time world champion; Stefan Topurov of Bulgaria, the first lifter to hoist triple his body weight overhead, and Blagoi Blagoev of Bulgaria, the weightlifter of the year in 1982 and 1983.

Of the world's 100 top-ranked lifters (10 in each weight category), only six competed in the Games. And only one of the 30 medal winners in the 1983 world championships, featherweight Gelu Radu of Romania, the bronze medalist in the 60 kilogram division, was at the Olympics.

Even the pro-USA flag-waving fans did not get the chance to see the top two USA weightlifters in action. Heavyweight Jeff Michels of Chicago, America's best lifter, was bothered by an ankle injury and finished only third in the USA Olympic trials in the 110 kilogram. He wound up on the team as an alternate.

The other top USA lifter missing from the Games was Curt White (82.57 kilograms), who eliminated himself from the team with mistakes during the trials. Needing to jerk 177.72 kilograms to assure himself a spot on the team, White decided to try 185 kilograms instead. He missed all three attempts at 185.

Despite the failures of Michels and White, USA hopes were high going into the Games. USA weightlifting officials predicted the Americans would produce their best showing since 1960, the last time they won a gold medal. Chuck Vinci won the 56 kilogram title that year in Rome.

But, as it turned out, the Americans, who had dominated the Games from 1948-1956, winning a total of 12 gold medals, were being overly optimistic. They ended up winning only two medals, a silver and a bronze.

Instead, the surprising athletes from the People's Republic of China, who had not participated in the Games since 1952, and Romania, were the two countries that dominated the weightlifting competition at the Los Angeles Olympics.

The People's Republic of China led the way with a quartet of gold medals, all during the first four days of competition, while Romania wound up with the most medals—eight in all—including two golds, five silvers and one bronze.

Two hundred thirteen athletes from 52 countries participated in the Olympic weightlifting competition. It took place in 10 weight classifications and was divided into two sessions, A and B.

The two elements of weightlifting include the two-handed clean-and-jerk sequence, and the two hands snatch sequence. Modern-day weightlifting not only requires tremendous power, but suppleness, agility and concentration, because of the tempo of the Olympic sport.

The resurrected sports program of the People's Republic of China began to show its strength on the opening night of the weightlifting competition, when Zeng Guoqiang, a baby-faced 19- year-old student at the Canton Institute of Athletics, earned the gold medal in the 52 kilogram class and countryman Zhou Peishun finished second. Those were the first two medals the People's Republic of China ever had received in Olympic weightlifting. The two each lifted a total of 235.45 kilograms, but Zeng, who was born 13 years after his nation had last competed in the Olympics, was awarded the gold medal because his body weight was 98 grams less than his teammate.

"I feel I made a good contribution for my country," the proud Zeng said after receiving the gold medal. Zeng had been lifting weights since he was 12 years old. "I always liked it since I was a child," he said.

Zhou, 22, was unruffled by the fact that his weight cost him a gold medal. "It's according to the rules, so I don't have any special feeling." he said.

The bronze medal went to Kazushito Manabe of Japan.

**Opposite Page
Chen (CHN), gold medalist at 60kg.
Photo: D. Cannon**

Manabe, who had been favored for the gold, said he was hampered by wrist and elbow injuries. "I kept it secret until now," he said.

The weightlifting competition continued with an Oriental flavor on the second day, as CHN again finished one-two and JPN was third in the 56 kilogram class. The winner was favored Wu Shude, a 25-year-old coach from the province of Nan Ning. He came from behind on the final attempt, lifting 147.72 kilograms for a combined total of 267.95 kilograms, beating countryman Lai Runming by 2.5 kilograms for the gold medal. The victory marked the end of a long development period for Wu, the fifth-place finisher in the 1983 world championships. "I started lifting in 1973," he said. "At that time, it was just for fun mostly. After doing it for two or three years, I got to like it more and more. Although I got the gold medal, I don't feel I have reached my personal best level," he added. "I hope to get an even higher result in the 1985 world championships." Wu maintained that he wasn't overly concerned about the possibility of failing on his last attempt. "I was relaxed because it would have been the same," he noted. "My country would have gotten the gold medal either way."

Lai, 21, lifted 265.45 kilograms for the silver medal. The bronze went to Japan's Masahiro Kotaka, whose total was 252.95 kilograms. Takashi Ichiba, also of Japan, who entertained the fans with a backflip on the platform before each lift, finished fourth with 250.45 kilograms.

Albert Hood, the 19-year-old breakdancing weightlifter from Los Angeles, placed eighth with a USA record total of 242.95 kilograms, including 112.72 kilograms in the snatch lift, another USA record. Hood, wearing his "lucky breakdancing headband," tried for another record in the clean and jerk, but after shouldering 137.72 kilograms, dropped the weight. "I blacked out," said Hood, the youngest member of the USA team. "You know how it is when you pass out? That was the effect. It's like somebody is putting a choke hold on you. The problem was I was kind of scared to jerk it. The bar fell on me once before, early in 1984."

The third night of weightlifting produced one of the Games' most emotional awards ceremonies. There, two countries, separated by decades of political tension, joined each other for the first time on an Olympic victory stand. Receiving the gold medal in the 60 kilogram division was Chen Weiqiang of Peoples Republic of China (CHN) and collecting the bronze was Tsai Wen- Yee of Chinese Taipei (TPE). Together with silver medalist Gelu Radu of Romania, the athletes clasped hands on the victory podium following the medal presentations.

Chen, a 26-year-old postgraduate physical education student from Guandung Province, won a gold medal by lifting 282.95 kilograms in the combined snatch and clean and jerk competition.

He and Tsai, a 27-year-old teacher, who lifted 272.95 kilograms, congratulated each other on their performances. Then, Tsai said he hoped that the sporting spirit of the competition would remain paramount and that it would "not get into the political realm. This is very important to me."

Huang Quinghui, the CHN weightlifting coach, was asked what the success of his team would mean to weightlifting in his country, following Chen's upset victory over Radu. "It is a very long story," he said. "It can't be told here."

Radu, the third-place finisher in the 1983 World Championships at Moscow, earned the Olympic silver medal by lifting a total of 280.45 kilograms.

The People's Republic of China's remarkable victory streak continued in the 67.5 kilogram class, as Yao Jingyuan, a 26-year-old physical education teacher from Liau Ning, captured the gold medal by hoisting a total of 320.68 kilograms.

"We didn't expect so many gold medals," said Yao, the fifth-place finisher in the 1983 world championships. "We expected one of the first three places in these four categories."

Andrei Socaci of Romania and Jouni Gronman of Finland each lifted 313.06 kilograms, but Socaci was given the silver

medal because he weighed slightly less than Gronman—the deciding factor in case of a tie in weightlifting.

"I'm 18 years old," was Socaci's reaction. "This was my first international competition where there is such a degree of movement, so many people, and so much international attention. I did come here with expectations for a medal, but certainly not a silver or a gold." Gronman, who said a silent prayer on the platform before each lift, said, "I had enough self-confidence, but I didn't have the strength" to win.

Domination by CHN ended after Yao's triumph. As most experts predicted before the Olympics, weightlifting excellence for CHN in the lighter categories might be possible—in the heavier categories it would be doubtful.

CHN Team Coach Huang Qianghui explained, "We have to stop today. We don't have any more promising lifters. Four gold medals is it. It is difficult to find heavyweights in our country." CHN's weightlifting program has been on the rise since 1974, when it was readmitted to the International Weightlifting Federation, but no one expected that nation to do so well in the Olympics.

"It will be a great impact for all sports," Huang finally admitted. "It means our country can win gold medals in an international sports meeting, and young children will follow them. It will give them courage."

Still, Huang was frank when asked if his team would have won any medals—gold or otherwise—in weightlifting if the boycott had not occurred.

"No, I don't think so," he said. "The Soviet Union, Bulgaria, Hungary, Poland and GDR all have great weightlifters."

CHN's medal feast ended on the fifth day of competition, as Karl-Heinz Radschinsky of FRG won the 75 kilograms division with a total lift of 340.68 kilograms, Jacques Demers of Canada took the silver medal with 335.68 kilograms and Dragomir Cioroslan of Romania got the bronze with 333.18 kilograms.

Instead of the CHN national anthem, which had become familiar to the weightlifting fans, "Deutschland Uber Alles" was played when Radschinsky became the first non-People's Republic of China lifter to win a gold medal.

Radschinsky, 30, owner of a gym in Bavaria, said he was not in good physical shape for the Olympics. "I started training for the Olympics in January of 1984, but I had a lot of misfortune," he said. "I tore a muscle in my lower back in a test competition in Munich, and I trained very little after that."

Demers, 24, was one of four CAN lifters awaiting trial on charges of illegally bringing steroids into Canada after the 1983 World Championships. The trial has been postponed until 1985.

The veteran Cioroslan of Romania, the fifth-place finisher in the Moscow Olympics, third in the world championships and the favorite at Los Angeles, announced that he would retire after the competition. "I have been in the sport 15 years and I am 30 now," he said. "I think that is enough."

On the next day of competition, Romania got its first Olympic gold medal in weightlifting, as Petre Becheru hoisted a total of 355.68 kilograms to win the 82.5 kilogram division.

Australia's Robert Kabbas, a three-time Olympian, won the silver medal with a total of 343.18 kilograms, a British Commonwealth record. Kabbas was a favorite with the crowd because of his emotional reactions to his successful lifts.

Obviously I'm happy to break both the National and Commonwealth records," said Kabbas. "As far as my own preparation style goes, that's always been mine and nobody else's. It gets the crowd happy and behind me, and that's fine, but that's not the purpose of it. I don't try to copy anyone else."

The crowd also appreciated third-place finisher Ryoji Isaoki of Japan. He was given a standing ovation after collapsing in agony on his final attempt, a lift of 207.95 kilograms, which would have given him the gold medal if he had been successful. Isaoka hoisted the bar to his shoulders in the clean and jerk movement, but couldn't jerk it above his head.

Nica Vlad, a 20-year-old Army captain from Bucharest who

Left to Right
Wu (CHN),
victorious in
56kg.
Photo: D. Cannon

Becheru (ROM),
no. 1 In 82.5kg
on the victory
stand.
Photo: D. Cannon

Vlad (ROM) in a
snatch in the
90kg class.
Photo: D. Cannon

likens weightlifting competition to an individual battle of man against iron, gave Romania its second consecutive gold medal. He won the 198-pound class with a total of 393.40 kilograms, an Olympic record. Vlad also set Olympic records of 172.84 kilograms for the snatch competition, and 220.45 kilograms for the clean and jerk. The blond-haired, blue-eyed Vlad was asked afterward how he approached the bar before a lift. "It's like a personal combat against the weight," he said.

Petre Dumitru, a 26 year old, two time Olympian from Romania, finished second in the 90 kilogram class with 360.68 kilograms and Britain's David Mercer won the bronze medal with 353.18 kilograms. It was the first Olympic weightlifting medal for Great Britain in two decades.

There were two dramatic moments during the 90 kilogram competition. First, the USA's Derrick Crass, a 24-year-old bartender from Colorado Springs, Colorado, hit his head with the bar and collapsed while attempting to snatch 130.22 kilograms. Crass was stretched out on the platform for several minutes, before being taken to a hospital for X-rays. Examination later revealed that, although he suffered a dislocated right elbow and a strained right knee, there were no serious skull injuries.

Denis Garon of Canada also collapsed on the platform while attempting to lift 192.84 kilograms in the clean and jerk. His powers of recuperation were remarkable. Just a short time after his collapse, Garon returned and successfully lifted the weight. The courage and accomplishment of Garon emotionally affected the audience, and the gritty weightlifter was accorded a standing ovation.

There were a number of interesting developments in the 100 kilogram division that followed next in the competition. The first involved Rolf Milser, (FRG). A three-time Olympian, he almost abandoned weightlifting after the 1980 USA Olympic boycott to devote his time to coaching. But Milser, who helps design weight training programs for other athletes, including FRG Jurgen Hingsen, the world record holder in the decathlon, decided to give the Olympics one more shot. It paid off in a gold medal. Milser won it with a total of 385 kilograms, including an Olympic clean and jerk record of 217.95 kilograms on his final attempt. That gave him the edge over Vasile Gropa of Romania, who had matched Milser's clean and jerk standard, moments earlier.

"It was not a matter of absolute strength tonight, but rather one of nerves," said Milser. "I could have done more in the clean and jerk, but I took 217 in order to get the gold medal. I want to thank the American public for their enthusiasm. I need that kind of an atmosphere in order to do well. I once again thank you for your enthusiasm and your cheer." Gropa, the favorite, won the silver medal with a total of 382.5 kilograms, and Pekka Niemi of Finland, winner of the B session, took the bronze medal with a total of 367.5 kilograms. Niemi, who compiled a better total than five lifters in the A session, was the first athlete from the B session ever to win an Olympic medal. The 32-year-old technical teacher from Tampere, deemed his chances at a medal so slim that he had left the weightlifting arena before the medals ceremony and was not present for the awards presentations. Instead he was at the Los Angeles Coliseum watching the athletic competition. It was there that he learned that he had won a medal when he checked a computer message terminal. "It was a great surprise," said the startled Niemi. "After I found out that I won, I thought, 'What is the possibility to go back to Loyola?' But there was no transport. My family knew that I had won the medal before I did," continued Niemi. "They heard it on TV." Niami finally got his medal on the closing day of the Games—six days after he had earned it.

Winning the bronze medal was a surprise for Niemi. Winning the gold climaxed a great career for Milser. After blowing kisses to the fans and pumping his fists into the air following his victory, the 33-year-old Milser, a businessman from Duisburg, announced his retirement.

"I've been weightlifting for 19 years, and I think that's enough," said Milser, who had competed in six world championships, five European championships and 115 German championships.

Norberto Oberburger, 24, who has been lifting for nine years, gave Italy its first Olympic weightlifting gold medal in 60 years, capturing the 110 kilogram class with a lift of 390.79 kilograms.

"At one point, this was very far away, but slowly and surely I have fought for it," said Oberburger, who had become a father only three days earlier.

Stefan Tasnado of Romania totaled 380.68 kilograms for the silver medal, and the USA's Guy Charlton, a 30-year-old construction worker from Colorado Springs, gave the USA its first medal in eight years, winning the bronze with 378.18 kilograms.

Carlton, the only member of the 1980 U.S. Olympic weightlifting team to compete in Los Angeles, almost gave up the sport after the boycott of the Moscow Games. He changed his mind, though, and continued training for 1984. Carlton endured some difficult financial problems, but his wife, Jan, said, "It's worth it because this is what he wanted to do and he wouldn't have been happy if he didn't lift weights."

The weightlifting competition concluded with Dinko Lukim, a 24-year-old millionaire tuna fisherman from Australia, winning the superheavyweight title and earning acclaim as "the world's strongest man."

Lukim, the first-ever Olympic weightlifting gold medalist from Australia, lifted a total of 413.29 kilograms, to defeat Mario Martinez of the USA. Bidding to become the first American gold medalist in 24 years, Martinez had to settle for the silver medal with a total of 410.79 kilograms. Manfred Nerlinger of FRG was awarded the bronze medal with 398.29 kilograms.

Lukim's family owns a fleet of tuna boats in Port Lincoln, Australia. "I train for six months and then go out on a boat for six months," said the powerful Lukin. "I'm going to go fishing for six months now."

Martinez isn't nearly as wealthy. Formerly a prison guard, he drives a courtesy bus for a rental car company at San Francisco International Airport.

While the Games ended on positive notes for Lukim, Martinez and Nerlinger, they did not for Mahmound Tarha of Lebanon and Ahmed Tarbi of Algeria. Tarha, the fourth-place finisher in the 52 kilogram class, and Tarbi, ninth in the 56 kilogram division, were banned for life by the International Weightlifting Federation and disqualified from the Games by the International Olympic Committee's Executive Board for using steroids during the Olympics. Both tested positively for anabolic steroids.

Petre (ROM) silver medalist in 90kg. classification. Photo: D. Cannon

Wen (TPE) strains against the bar in the 60kg class. Photo: D. Cannon

Kabbass (AUS), silver medalist in the B2.5 class. Photo: D. Cannon

Mercer (GBR), bronze in 90kg. Photo: D. Cannon

Wrestling: Meeting At The Mat

Mike Chapman

Randy Lewis, a member of the highly-regarded 1984 United States of America Olympic free-style wrestling team said, "It would be nice if all the top wrestlers were here. But they're not, so I just did the best I can."

That statement exemplified the spirit of the USA team at the Games of the XXIIIrd Olympiad. Because they knew they were part of one of the best USA squads ever assembled, the freestylers were disappointed they were not allowed the opportunity to test themselves against the wrestlers of the Soviet Union, long considered the world's premier matmen.

So, the Americans had to be content to perform at the very highest level possible.

Blocking the Soviet bloc from their minds, they wrestled with an intensity and an aggressiveness that matched the fiery spirit of their legendary coach, Dan Gable. When the smoke had cleared and the last match had been wrestled at the Anaheim Convention Center, USA had won 40 of its 45 freestyle matches . . . and seven gold medals and two silvers. Only one American—Joe Gonzales, a medal contender at 52 kilograms who suffered a neck injury and subsequently performed below par—failed to place.

Lewis, a former two-time National Collegiate Athletic Association (NCAA) champion at the University of Iowa and the 1983 Pan-American Games champ, romped to the 62 kilograms title with five wins, all by technical superiority (the match ends when one wrestler takes a 12-point lead).

In fact, Lewis's most difficult struggle came in trying to earn a spot on the USA team. It was a long and fierce battle that began on the mats and finished up in the courtroom, and left the entire sport gasping for breath, and searching for peace.

Lewis decisioned former Oklahoma State star Lee Roy Smith in two wrestleoffs in June of 1984, but Smith was given fresh life when a protest committee ruled there were questionable calls in the second match. Smith won the next two bouts, earning a place on the team, but Lewis's family took the matter to federal arbitration. For over a month, the Lewis and Smith groups battled back and forth, until Lewis emerged as the team's representative.

While Lewis and Gable were contending with various off-mat problems, the wrestlers were going about their business with machine-like precision. Bobby Weaver, a tireless dynamo at 48 kilograms, breezed to his title with three lopsided victories, then delighted the crowd with his enthusiasm. He raced the length of the arena twice, the second time carrying his eight- month old son, Bobby Jr., in his arms. "He's not used to the crowd yet," said Weaver of the infant. "He was pro-

bably in shock like I was."

The final victory, which came with a pin in two minutes and fifty-eight seconds over Japan's Takashi Irie, was the climax of a great career. The former Lehigh University star, like Lewis a member of the 1980 Olympic team, had won four national titles and was a runnerup in the 1979 world championships.

"I think we would have given the Soviet Union all they wanted," said Lewis after winning his gold medal. "Last year, I pinned the member of the Soviet Union team who is the current world champion at my weight, and Bobby has beaten them a number of times."

Gable, who once won 180 straight matches and waltzed to the gold medal at 68 kilograms in 1972 in Munich without surrendering a single point in six matches, agreed that the Soviets could have had their hands full.

Other 1984 Olympic champions, however, were not quite so certain. "Right now, I'm an Olympic champion, but I might not be the best in the world," said Ed Banach, one half of the bruising twin brother combination from Port Jervis, New York. Banach, a three-time NCAA champion at Iowa under Gable, was totally dominant in the 90 kilogram weight class, allowing just seven points in his five bouts.

"I beat everyone in the tournament and it was a shame for me that the Soviet Union opponents weren't here," said Banach. "If they were here, I'd be able to push them all the way because I've been wrestling so well."

Big brother Lou, five minutes younger and about fifteen pounds heavier than Ed, was even more philosophical in explaining his feelings after winning the gold medal. "Sure," he said, "there's a better man somewhere. There's always a better man somewhere. But on this particular day, things clicked for me."

The Banachs weren't the only brother act doing a bang-up job in the wrestling competition. In fact, the brothers Schultz, of Palo Alto, California, did too much banging up in the view of some officials. In back-to-back matches, Dave, the defending world champion at 74 kilograms, and Mark, at 82 kilograms, sent their opponents to the sidelines with injuries.

Dave, wrestling Saban Sejdi of Yugoslavia, strained his opponent's knee with a leg twisting device used to turn the foe toward his back for valuable points. Shortly after Sejdi was carried from the mat, Mark caught top-ranked Resit Karabachak of Turkey in a vicious bar arm, slamming him to the mat for what appeared to be a pin in just thirty seconds.

A meeting of mat officials convened immediately, and the result was that Schultz was disqualified for using a legal hold with illegal force. Karabachak, on the other hand, was knocked

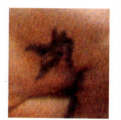

Opposite Page Ljungbeck (SWE) subdues Ronnie Sigde (NOR) in a 57kg Greco-Roman. Photo: IOPP

from the entire meet with a fractured left elbow.

The results of the matches were twofold: the rules committee, concerned with possible "brutality" on the part of the USA brothers, decided to monitor each and every match the Schultzes participated in from that point on; and Gable suggested the former University of Oklahoma stars actually became better wrestlers.

"I think it's worked positively on them," Gable said of the extra officials appointed to their matches. "It's made them realize they have to be versatile, that they have to rely more on control wrestling (than power wrestling). The Schultzes sometimes get a little lazy, and this has made them have to wrestle more."

But bad for the competition. Dave never really was extended, and defeated former world champion, Martin Knosp of FRG, in a classic match for the gold medal, 4-1. Mark, overcoming the setback of his opening loss disqualification, had little trouble with the remainder of his field. He scored four easy wins, including a technical superiority win over Japan's Hideyuki Nagashima in the finale, 13-0.

"I was really bothered by the fact that I was considered brutal," said Dave," because I've always made the greatest attempt to stay in the rules and to wrestle a fair match. The only thing I'm interested with is scoring points, pinning and-

winning on the mat. Most of these guys are my friends. It's rather ridiculous to think that I would intentionally injure them."

Soviet boycott or not, the USA's top hope for a gold medal probably was in the unlimited category, where 120.45 kilogram Bruce Baumgartner rules the mat. The former Indiana State collegiate star went 9-0 in a tour of the Soviet Union in 1983, and breezed to the Olympic crown in Anaheim with three easy wins. In the final match, he decisioned Canada's Bob Molle, fifth in the world meet last year, 10-2

The three titles the USA didn't win went to Yugoslavia, Japan and Korea. At 52 kilograms, Saban Trstena decisioned Korea's Kim Jong-Kyu for his second world title, giving Yugoslavia a gold medal. At 57 kilograms Hideaki Tomiyama became a three-time world champion with an 8-3 win over Barry Davis of Cedar Rapids, Iowa.

Davis, at 22 the youngest member of the USA team, gave Tomiyama a courgeous battle, but couldn't match the cagey veteran in the crucial flurries. Tomiyama, who said he plans to train in Iowa City under Gable in order to learn the "Yankee spirit" (a quality of winning the close matches), was inspired by the presence of his father and grandfather. He had never lost a bout at which his grandfather was present, and immediately after the vitory he ran over to where he was sitting,

Eto (JPN)
struggles to
avoid a takedown
in Greco-Roman
57kg class.
Photo: D. Cannon

and bowed.

At 68 kilograms, You In-Tak of Korea outlasted the USA's Andy Rein, to win his gold medal. Rein was the aggressor for most of the match, and the highly-partisan crowd was keenly disappointed that Rein was not given the victory due to what it perceived as stalling on the part of the Korean wrestler.

Two world champions of the past wound up third in Anaheim. At 48 kilograms, Son Gab-Do of Korea, super world champ in 1983, lost a close match to the runnerup, Takashi Irie. And at 52 kilograms, Yuji Takada, a four-time world champion, was edged by Saban Trstena.

When the final match had expired, the crowd of 6000-plus came to its feet and chanted "Gable, Gable, Gable" in an effort to coax the coach, winner of a record seven straight NCAA team titles at Iowa, to take a bow. Finally, Gable appeared riding on the shoulders of Ed Banach, who carried his college and Olympic coach to the center of the arena. The team gathered about in a show of support for thirty-five year old coach considered by most wrestling authorities the most influential force in the history of the sport. "The guy's super," said Weaver of Gable. "He's the best thing that ever happened to me. He's helped me out a lot the last couple of years."

"Dan Gable is the most consistent person I've ever met in my life in honesty and justice," said Lou Banach.

The American wrestling success actually began with the competition in Greco-Roman, a sport little known and little practiced in the USA. Ever since Civil War days when Union soldiers participated in pick-up matches during the lulls between battles, the wide open freestyle form of wrestling has been the favorite in the United States of America. Even Abe Lincoln considered himself a pretty fair country wrestler, freestyle rules.

Greco-Roman, popular in Europe and Asia since the days of Homer, limits hold to above the waist, eliminating the use of legs for any purpose other than standing. Prior to these Games, USA had never won a medal of any sort in Greco-Roman competition.

The boycott by the Soviet bloc countries helped open up the Greco-Roman field tremendously, and Jeff Blatnick, Steve Fraser, Greg Gibson and Jim Martinez responded magnificently. Gibson, a Marine who starred collegiately at Oregon, muscled his way to a silver medal at 100 kilograms, while Martinez, a former University of Minnesota collegian, took the bronze medal in the 68 kilogram class.

Fraser, an extremely physical wrestler from the University of Michigan, was superb in his pounding style. Wading into foe after foe, he stunned the world wrestling community by winning the gold medal in the 90 kilogram class. The deputy

sheriff from Ann Arbor, Michigan turned in a surprising triumph over Sweden's handsome Frank Andersson, thereby derailing Andersson's hopes of a glorious return to his homeland. With the King of Sweden watching from the stands, Fraser scored a 4-1 victory over the former three-time world champion to gain the finals. There, Fraser defeated Ilie Matei of Romania, 1-1 criteria (Fraser scored the last takedown) to turn the near impossible into reality.

Then Jeff Blatnick captured the hearts of American viewers. Labelled "an unlikely hero", Blatnick battled cancer in 1982 and won. The emotional surge of his scoring three straight wins over Thomas Johansson (SWE), to capture the super heavyweight title made him sob uncontrollably. Later that night, a full house at the site of the Olympic baseball game, watching the poignant scene of Blatnick's crying on a huge television screen, responded with a standing ovation.

Only Romania, with two golds, one silver and two bronzes, was able to surpass the USA effort in Greco-Roman wrestling.

Greco coach Ron Finley, a fourth place finisher in Greco-Roman in the 1964 Olympics and head coach at the University of Oregon, gave much of the credit for the team's success to a former Soviet Union wrestler, Paval Kastsen.

"Paval was one of the big reasons we did so well," said Finley. "He emigrated to the USA five years ago and is a full-fledged American citizen. He is a great technician."

Finley believes the accomplishments of the 1984 team will help boost the cause of Greco-Roman wrestling in the USA." Many of our athletes who traditionally have been only interested in freestyle are talking about Greco. I think Greco-Roman wrestling is here to stay."

Though many of the 1984 United States wrestlers were disappointed in the Soviet boycott and the freestyle team was racked by controversy, the XXIIIrd Games were a golden moment for this rugged sport. In twenty combined weight classes, America captured nine gold medals, three silvers and one bronze. It was the most magnificent wrestling performance in the history of the USA.

Hu (CHN) and
Halonen (FIN) in
52kg match in
Greco-Roman.
Photo: IOPP

Petkovic (YUG)
and Overmark
(FIN) in the
Greco-Roman 82kg.
Photo: IOPP

Yachting: Fickle Zephyrs

Chris Caswell

To the landlubber, wind is just wind. But to a sailor, it is an infinitely variable quantity, and each racing skipper has certain types of winds in which he performs well. Anything else is like forcing a runner to race on a strange surface, or asking a pole vaulter to use an unfamiliar pole. Skill, speed, tactics, and even luck are the essential ingredients in sailing success. But still, the yachting events, unlike any other sport, depend upon wind. And for the 300 sailors from 62 countries who arrived at Long Beach Harbor prepared for steady sea breezes, the fickle zephyrs that greeted them posed a problem that resulted ultimately in several classes.

Many had committed years of practice to sailing in the winds that blow through the Catalina Channel every August. You could see the frustration on their faces as they walked to the water's edge each morning and stared out to sea, hoping for the dark shadows that would mean an afternoon breeze. But wind, so crucial to sailing was the only item not provided by Long Beach.

Unlike the Olympic yachting events in Munich in 1972 or Montreal in 1976, the Long Beach racing site was not permanently constructed. Located approximately 48 km south of Los Angeles, the site was just a sandy beach area days before the Olympics, and it returned to its natural state within hours after the Closing Ceremonies. But in between, it took on the overnight vigor of a gold rush town. House trailers were used for staff and committees, more than 65 tents (up to a circus-like 2424 square meters) housed teams, repair facilities, and measurement areas. The sandy beach was covered with 57,575 square meters of used Astroturf purchased from a football stadium to protect the small sailboats which were pulled ashore each night. One European competitor surveyed the carpeted beach, smiled, and said, "Only in America . . . ".

When the racing had ended, the yachting events had become an unprecedented near-sweep for the USA with three gold and four silver medals. Tiny New Zealand emerged as a major power in the sailing world with two golds and a bronze, while Canada was a surprise with two bronzes and one silver. Many traditionally strong sailing nations, such as Great Britain, Australia, the Federal Republic of Germany, and Italy were left with only a single medal each.

The Soling class, a 7.8 meter three-man sailboat, provided the most resounding victory for America, with Robbie Haines placing so high in the first six races that he didn't have to sail in the last. A two-time world champion, Haines was also the USA representative before the 1980 boycott. Afterwards, Haines noted that the USA elimination series had caused more tension than the Olympics and, when asked how he felt

throughout the racing, his one word response was "mellow".

The biggest upset in the Olympics was in the Tornado class, a 6 meter catamaran that zips along at speeds of up to 35 miles per hour. Going into the competition, the class had literally been dominated by two-time world champion, American Randy Smyth. But Chris Cairns of Australia suddenly appeared with an innovative sail shape and promptly won the last two worlds. Smyth initiated an intensive test program to develop what he hoped would be an equally fast sail, but there was no time to test it before the Olympics. So the stage was set for a showdown between Smyth and Cairns. No one, however, had reckoned on a lanky lobster fisherman from New Zealand named Rex Sellers who showed that consistency, as well as speed, can win a gold medal.

Smyth proved the effectiveness of his new sail in the first race with a winning margin of nearly a minute, while Cairns sailed in a distant fourth. Sellers, almost unnoticed in the shadow of the two giants, led part of the race before dropping to third with gear damage. Smyth fouled a competitor in the second race and dropped out, Cairns managed to slump to 16th, and Sellers, the model of consistency, finished second. Sellers was soon far enough ahead of the fleet that his gold medal was assured after only six races. When asked if he would sail the last race, the exuberant Sellers said, "I will if I am still walking after tonight's celebration."

He didn't make it to the last race, which was a battle between Smyth, Cairns, and Denmark's Paul Elvstroem for the remaining two medals. Elvstroem, known in the sailing world as "The Great Dane," had won four gold medals in a row ('48, '52, '56, '60) as well as 13 world championships. At 56, Elvstroem was nearly twice the age of his competitors, most of whom were not even born when he was already an Olympic legend. Sailing with his daughter Inge Trine as crew, Elvstroem knew his chances of winning a fifth gold medal or any medal at all were slim at the 1984 Olympics. "That means nothing," he said, "nothing at all. I'm here for enjoying, that's all. We will not be surprised if it goes badly here. In the old days, it was first or nothing. Racing is seamanship, and I like to be perfect on the water. I still like it but we are relaxed. I'm only thankful that I can compete with my daughter. We take it 100 percent for fun." That attitude took them to within .7 of a point of a bronze medal. "If only we'd passed just one more boat in any race," he sighed afterwards.

The Star is a 6.6 meter two-man keel sailboat which is the oldest Olympic class, dating back to 1932. An array of world and Olympic champions filled the fleet, so it was anybody's guess who would win the gold medal. But the stage was set when Bill Buchan of the USA won the first race in short order.

**Opposite Page
Spinnakers fill with wind in 470 class yachting competition.
Photo: S. Powell**

Left to Right
Peponnet and Pillot
(FRA) guide their
470 around a buoy.
Photo: S. Powell

Van den Berg (HOL)
pilots his Wingglider
to the gold medal.
Photo: IOPP

Coutts (NZL) checks
his sail in the Finn
class.
Photo: S. Powell

Foster (GBR), first
woman to pilot a
racing craft in
Olympic competition.
Photo: S. Powell

Soling class competition. Photo: S. Powell

He dropped back with gear failure in the second race, and the last race became a match among Italy, the Federal Republic of Germany, Sweden, and the USA for the gold medal. That race started badly for the American crew. A wind shift dropped them to the back of the fleet, and they were starting to worry about even getting the bronze. But the winds shifted back, putting the Americans just behind Italy. When Italy accidentally touched one of the buoys and had to circle back, losing time, it became Buchan's race. He picked off Italy and two others to win by seconds. Italy ultimately got the bronze, and the Federal Republic of Germany the silver.

One of the "old men of the sea," Buchan has sailed a star boat for 33 of his 49 years. "I frankly don't find age to be a factor," he said. In point of fact, age has been a factor—a positive factor in the Olympic yachting gold list. The historical roster of veteran gold medal winners includes: Hilary Smart (USA) 56, Herbert Williams (USA) 48, Durward Knowles of the Bahamas 46, Valentin Mankin of the Soviet Union, 41.

It was a particularly proud moment for Buchan because on that same day, his son Carl, a crew in the Flying Dutchman class, also won a gold medal. The Flying Dutchman, a 6 meter high-tech dinghy where the crew hangs suspended by a trapeze wire, has been dominated by the Europeans in recent years. But a concerted American effort to develop better boats and sailors added the USA to the four other contenders for the gold: Canada, Great Britian, Denmark, and the Federal Republic of Germany. Had the winds blown harder, it would have favored the European crews, but Americans Jonathan McKee and Carl Buchan sailed consistently to win the gold. Terry McLaughlin of Canada took the silver, and Great Britain's Jonathan Richards received the bronze.

The International 470 class, a 4.5 meter version of the Flying Dutchman, was expected to be swept by New Zealand, winner of the last three worlds, although USA's Steve Benjamin was also a candidate. But it was Luis Doreste of Spain who surprised everyone with his victory. Benjamin, with one bad start, was also disqualified from another race for crossing the starting line early. Those two errors cost him the gold. Third went to Thierry Peponnet of France, while Great Britain, in sixth place, made history with Cathy Foster, the first woman to skipper an Olympic racing yacht. Her performance was hampered by the light winds, but she won the breezy final race by more than one minute.

The Finn, a 4.7 meter singlehander, was the most controversial class, with disputes before and during the racing. The USA representative, chosen during a trials series months earlier, had been the subject of a protest that went through several higher courts with each reversing the previous decision. Just days before the Olympics, John Bertrand was finally named as USA skipper. He proved his ability by winning the first race. That victory was overturned on a protest by New Zealand's Russell Coutts, who went on to win the gold medal. Bertrand won the silver, and Canada's Terry Nielson the bronze.

The Windglider, a sailing surfboard, is the newest Olympic class. It was nearly eliminated from Olympic competition after rounds of international lawsuits regarding patent rights. While the board sailers have been viewed as toys in the USA, they are a highly competitive class in Europe. Thus, it was no surprise that world champion Stephan Van Den Berg of the Netherlands swept the class. The surprise was that the USA's Scott Steele, who had won a light wind elimination series, was the silver medalist. But it was those same light winds for the first races that allowed him to build up a points lead that cushioned his lower finishes later in the series. New Zealand's Bruce Kendall took the bronze, and the International Yacht Racing Union decided that since 38 countries had competed, a boardsailing class would be recommended for the 1988 Games.

As the makeshift town that had been constructed before the site was dismantled, and the competitors congratulated one another with a celebratory beer; even as the Closing Ceremonies were taking place and the world was saying goodbye to the Olympic Games for another four years, the fickle zephyrs returned. Absent for most of the racing, at the end they built to an intensity that made the 62 national flags on the breakwater snap and dance in the fading light.

Doreste (ESP) pilots his 470 to gold, with help from Molina.
Photo: S. Powell

Richards and Allam (GBR) sail their Flying Duchman through heavy swells.
Photo: S. Powell

Baseball: Bidding for Medal Status

Harvey Frommer

In the stands, fans stamped their feet, waved banners, played with beach balls, paraded with flags, chanted and roared and leaped to their feet in human waves. On the field, teams from eight nations competed for the championship. Their play was characterized by the ping of aluminum bats, the accents of their native tongues, the between-innings huddles of Asian teams fine-tuning themselves, exchanging insights, respectfully receiving suggestions from their coaches.

This was the atmosphere in the baseball demonstration tournament of the Games of the XXIIIrd Olympiad, an atmosphere that merged the tension of the World Series with the international fervor of the World Cup.

A record 385,290 attended the baseball tournament that overall was underscored by tight, suspenseful, crisply played games. There were, however, some one-sided contests: a 12-0 USA victory over the Dominican Republic sparked by a pair of two-run homers by outfielder Will Clark; a 16-1 USA victory over Italy that included a nine run first inning; a 10-0 victory by Chinese Taipei over Italy that featured Yeh Chih-Shien's home run and triple, and Japan's 19-1 clobbering of Nicaragua.

Japan and the USA, survivors of the eight team round robin competition, met in the championship game before 55,325, surpassing the record for the largest regular season crowd in Dodger Stadium history. The powerhouse American team, its roster stocked with eleven of the seventeen players chosen in the first round of the USA's major league baseball draft, entered the championship contest unbeaten in four games. The highly regarded Americans had a team batting average of .322, nine home runs, and 35 runs batted in. The Japanese club had not even qualified for the Olympics but was added after the baseball field was expanded to eight teams. Defeated in six of the seven pre-Olympic exhibition games it had played against the USA, Japan was the decided underdog.

A third inning home run by University of California at Los Angeles junior Shane Mack off Japanese starter Akimitsu Ito into the left field seats gave the USA an early lead. The highly pro-American crowd created human waves in the stands sensing an American triumph and shouted "USA, USA, USA!" Their jubilation was premature and short-lived.

Japan countered with two runs in the fourth inning making the most of two walks, two singles, and a throwing error by USA catcher John Marzano. The disciplined Japanese notched another run in the fifth inning. In the bottom of the seventh, the Americans loaded the bases, and Yukio Yoshida was called on to relieve. The gutsy right-hander, who had started throwing side-armed at age 17 when he broke a bone

in his shoulder, had hurled nine demanding innings the day before allowing just four hits and one run. "Even if my arm is broken," he had said, "I will pitch in the championship game if I am needed."

Submarining the ball to the plate, Yoshida struck out Shane Mack to end the USA rally. A 115 meter, three run homer blasted to left field by Japanese first baseman Katsumi Hirosawa gave Japan a 6-1 lead, silenced the partisan crowd, and sent USA starter John Hoover to the showers. He was replaced by the University of Southern California's Sid Akins, but the damage had been done.

The drama, however, still played on. Exhausted, struggling Yoshida side-armed his way through the eighth inning holding the USA scoreless. Throughout the baseball tournament, the Japanese constantly had pitchers warming up in their bullpen. Now there was an absence of action in the bullpen. It was Yoshida's game to save or lose. Cory Snyder tagged a two run homer off the spent Yoshida in the ninth inning to make the score 6-3. For the USA, it turned out Snyder's home run was a pyrrhic feat. While Yoshida had bent, he did not break. He retired Flavio Alfaro on a flyball to center field for the final out. Japan had won the game!

Exultant in triumph, Japanese players surged together on the playing field. Wild abandon replaced traditional reserve as they tossed their gloves and their coaches into the air.

"It was the greatest victory in the history of Japanese baseball," said their elated manager Reiich Matsunaga. Dejected USA manager Rod Dedeaux explained, "We pecked away, but we could never really get the big hit."

Moments after the championship game concluded, the All-American Olympic Marching Band assembled on the rim of the outfield grass at Dodger Stadium and performed a medley of American songs while attendants rushed to set up temporary structures for the final ceremonies.

"Winners of the gold medal, the team from Japan," was the announcement. Members of the Japanese team wearing their black and white road uniforms took the high step on the victory stand in the middle of the infield, just in front of home plate.

"Winners of the silver medal, the team from the United States of America," the announcement continued. "Winners of the bronze medal, the team from Chinese Taipei." The third place team, elegant in blue blazers and white pants, assembled. International Olympic Committee President Juan Antonio Samaranch presided over the special medal presentation.

At midnight's stroke, the sky above Dodger Stadium, high above Chinatown, was emblazoned with the rainbow colors of exploding fireworks. The stars in motion logo flared into

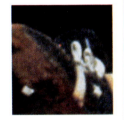

Opposite Page
Hoover (USA) leaps to avoid the spikes of an oncoming runner.
Photo: A. Chung

a gigantic sparkler deep in the recesses of center field.

The night before, victories by the USA and Japan in the semi-final contests enabled them to meet in the championship game. Left-handed Yukio Arai's dramatic bouncing ball single into centerfield edged Japan past Chinese Taipei, 2-1, in the bottom of the tenth inning. The USA defeated Korea 5-2 behind five shutout relief innings by pitcher Don August.

Perhaps the best played game of the tournament was the battle for third place between Korea and Chinese Taipei, which had four players on its roster who had once been participants in the Little League World Series at Williamsport, Pennsylvania. The game lasted three hours and forty-one minutes, the longest in Olympic baseball history. Inning after inning, the two teams prodded and probed like a pair of welterweight boxers searching for an opening. TPE starter Chuang Sheng-Hsiung had a no-hitter for six and one third innings but lost it when Kang Ki Wong, who was batting just .156 for the tourney, managed a single to centerfield. The game remained scoreless through regulation time. In the eleventh inning, an arm-weary, Chuang was relieved by Tu Fu-Ming. Chuang had struck out thirteen batters and had allowed no runs in ten and one third innings to bring his tournament total to 21 and one third scoreless innings and 20 strikeouts. The game moved through the eleventh, the twelfth, the thirteenth inn-

ing. In the top of the fourteenth inning, Chinese Taipei scored three times, capped by Lin Hua-Wei's triple and Yang Ching-Long's home run. Tu handled the Koreans easily in their last at bats in the bottom of the fourteenth inning to preserve Chinese Taipei's victory and threw his glove up in the air after recording the final out.

One of the most disappointing teams in the tournament was the Dominican Republic which had the youngest player in the competition on its roster, 16-year-old pitcher Ramon Martinez. A replacement for Cuba which was ranked the number one amateur club in 1983 after winning the Pan Am Games, the Dominicans were hampered by not having much time to prepare as a team for Olympic baseball competition. Winless in three games, DOM produced only eight runs to 35 scored by their opponents.

One of the more intriguing aspects of the baseball tournament was the strange intermingling of international journalists in the press box at Dodger Stadium. A gracious host, the Los Angeles Dodger organization provided ample food and piles of printed material to keep the media men and women informed. The food apparently satisfied everyone's appetite, but the printed data wasn't quite enough to provide a cram course for journalists who knew little about the fine distinctions between a sacrifice squeeze and an intentional pass.

L.A. Dodger
Stadium, site for the
baseball
competition.
Photo: A. Chung

Thus, tutoring took place while the games were in progress. It was refreshing to see wizened, cynical American writers explain to a French journalist why a game was not declared a tie and had to proceed to extra innings until a decision was reached. A British reporter was tutored in the nuances of the hit and run play, catcher's interference and the outfielder hitting the relay man.

Played in more than 50 countries on five continents, baseball had been staged as a demonstration sport in the Olympics six previous times. However, those competitions were primitive. Just two teams played one exhibition game on makeshift diamonds.

This time around things were vastly different. For the first time baseball players marched in the Opening and Closing Ceremonies, lived in official Olympic villages, and were awarded special exhibition contest medals of gold, silver, and bronze.

The championship game between Japan and the USA drew just a thousand fans less than the all-time Dodger Stadium single game mark set in the World Series. An average of 48,161 fans came out to each game and it wasn't as if there were no other attractions available.

With its record attendance marks and its high caliber of play, baseball dramatically staked its claim to full-fledged medal status in the 1988 Olympics in Seoul, Korea.

Tennis: A Smashing Success

Donna K. Doherty

These words are uttered everyday around the world on tennis courts: "Linesmen ready? Players ready? Play." But never did they carry such historical weight as they did at the new Los Angeles Tennis Center during the second week of the 1984 Olympics.

After an absence of 60 years, tennis was back in the Games, this time as a demonstration sport, but with the promise of official medal status for the 1988 Games in Seoul, Korea. The historical significance of the presence of the sport in Los Angeles was nearly overshadowed by the fact that many of its competitors were professionals. Competitors were strewn together. There were amateurs from tennis non-powers such as Haiti and Indonesia, up against pros who earned six-figure salaries, and all combined in a 32-player draw. What they did have in common was that they were all 20-years-old or younger, and that winners would go home with only a medal, a facsimile one at that, not a check.

There were those expected to win, whose paths turned out to be rockier than expected. And there were those who made the unexpected a thing of joy to watch. The boyish blond Swede, Stefan Edberg, a shy, lithe serve-and-volley stylist, an oddball in a country of baseline-hitters. And little Steffi Graf, a sprite from FRG who demonstrated a game and court savvy far beyond her 15 years. She won the women's title. Many of the young players recorded personal bests—wins over players ranked far above them, who they might never have had the opportunity to meet under ordinary tournament conditions.

Edberg upstaged Jimmy Arias, the young American pro with the howitzer forehand. When Swede Mats Wilander withdrew with a wrist injury, some people were practically putting the gold around Arias' neck. He felt the pressure of a crowd that loudly demonstrated its nationalistic biases, a departure from the traditional tennis crowd's habit of rooting for the underdog.

The top-seeded woman, American Kathleen Horvath, felt just the opposite pressure—a crowd openly rooting for her Yugoslavian opponent in their quarterfinal match. Crushed and near tears, she exclaimed to the press, "I'm ashamed to be an American. Here I am in the USA and the people are rooting against me." They were, rather, rooting for Sabrina Goles and not against Horvath, who requested that the umpire ask the crowd to be quiet so she could regain some concentration.

The seeds fell in the withering 90-degree heat like dry leaves on an August afternoon. Second-seeded Australian Pat Cash, 19, a 1984 Wimbledon semifinalist was put out in the opening round practically before anyone in the stadium had arrived, by unseeded and unheralded Paolo Cane of Italy. Cane made the draw only when an opening was created by the Soviet boycott.

The second round claimed another top player, American Andrea Jaeger, who had not played a regular tour match since the French Open in May 1984. Jaeger defaulted in the first round with a chronically sore shoulder. Speculation had been high as to whether Jaeger, who was named to the team as a wild-card pro entry, would even show up in Los Angeles. "Now is not the time I should be playing tennis," she explained after struggling to beat Danish player Tine Scheuer-Larsen, "but this is the Olympics. It's a once-in-a-lifetime opportunity." The following day, after trying to counterattack the Dane's high-bouncing balls, she could not lift her arm, and withdrew from the tournament.

The allure of the Olympic atmosphere was not lost on the tennis players who, every step of the way in this demonstration, were made to feel just like the other athletes in the Games. They paraded in during the spectacular Opening Ceremonies and stayed in the Olympic Village at the University of California at Los Angeles (UCLA). And when Edberg and Graf won their respective divisions, each was honored with the same flag-and-anthem ceremonies as their counterparts in sports with full medal status. Only upon close inspection did their facsimile medals reveal themselves to be different from the "real" things, but the thrill was there nevertheless.

The road to the final was an uneven one for both medalists. Edberg's semifinal meeting with Arias was anxiously awaited as the classic pairing of the big serve-and-volley style against a wily patient baseline game. The drama, however, disappeared as quickly as Arias did. He was unable to run around the kick serve, unable to get his ground strokes in gear, unable to stop a man who was playing the best match of his life. It was Arias' worst loss as a pro, 6-2, 6-1. And it came at the hands of a quiet Swede who had made the Olympics his goal seven months earlier.

To play so well in a semifinal against a man he'd never played before was almost eerie for Edberg, because he knew he had to sustain the magnificent momentum for his final against the hard-serving Mexican, Francisco Maciel. Maciel eliminated two seeds back to back, then defeated the Italian spoiler Cane, who was plagued by abdominal cramps.

In the final, Edberg served and volleyed his way to a 6-1 win in the first set, while Maciel, hobbled by painful blisters on both feet, could not move effectively to take the net himself. His wounds were wrapped before the second set, which rejuvenated his game enough to force the Swede into a

**Opposite Page
Edberg (SWE) gold-
medalist in men's
tennis.
Photo: A. Chung**

tiebreaker. "I was fighting in the tiebreaker because I love to play them," Edberg said later. "I had a little bit of luck when he fell down at 6-5, and then double-faulted."

Edberg won the match 6-1, 7-6 on a service ace and jumped the net to shake hands with Maciel, who had never expected to end up the silver medalist.

The women, meanwhile, sensed that it could be anyone's tournament, especially when Goles continued to play the giant-killer and upset France's Catherine Tanvier in the semifinal. Goles concentrated on playing her own baseline game, ignoring the wrap protecting Tanvier's pulled thigh muscle.

Graf, meanwhile, was busy eliminating Pascale Paradis (FRA), which set up a meeting with Raffaella Reggi, the feisty Italian whose ascent from the bottom of the draw seemed to please the crowd as much as it did her. Reggi battled gamely against Graf, saving two match points before going down 7-6, 6-4, and sending Graf into the final against Goles.

Graf and Goles provided one of the best matches of the tournament: a pair of stoic baseliners, each armed with impressive forehands and an excess of courage. Neither was afraid to discontinue the baseline strategy when they sensed a drop shot here or an angled short ball there could end a point. Goles started fast, winning the first set 6-1 while Graf did her sleeping cat routine. It took her awhile to test her opponent's range. She knew Goles was a dangerous opponent, a fine clay-court player who had advanced her professional ranking earlier in the year. But what she didn't know was that Goles was hurt. She had pulled her shoulder in the first set, perhaps trying to hit the ball too hard to take that early lead. Graf found her length on her ground strokes, keeping the ball deep, but noticed that Goles was missing what seemed to be easy balls.

With the third set tied at 3-3, the medical team applied ice and massage to what had now become spasms in Goles' back. She came back on the court and broke Graf's serve, but Graf knew it would be a strain for her to bend low, and fed her an array of low balls to both sides. It took its toll, and Graf won the third set and the match 1-6, 6-3, 6-4. Goles was distraught. She cried heartily walking off the court and again at the medal presentation. "If someone told me before I would win the silver, I would have felt great," Goles said, "but now I don't feel so good because I think I had a chance for the gold."

The losing semifinalists, Arias, Cane, Reggi, and Tanvier were all awarded bronze medals. Later that evening at the championship dinner given by the International Tennis Federation (ITF), Edberg and Graf each received a specially designed sculpture from ITF President Philippe Chatrier, whose dream for the return of tennis to the Olympics had materialized in a far more gratifying fashion than even he could have hoped for.

It was Jack Kramer, the tournament director, who had the final word: "Tennis is in, and it will now take its rightful place among the other sports in the world at the Olympics."

Graff (FRG) gold medal-winner in women's tennis.
Photo: A. Chung

Goles (YUG) women's silver-medalist.
Photo: A. Chung

Results/Statistics

The Countries and Their Abbreviations

AFG Afganistan
AHO Netherlands/Antilles
ALB Albania
ALG Algeria
AND Andorra
ANG Angola
ANT Antigua
ARG Argentina
AUS Australia
AUT Austria
BAH Bahamas
BAN Bangladesh
BAR Barbados
BEL Belgium
BEN Benin
BER Bermuda
BHU Bhutan
BIR Burma
BIZ Belize
BOL Bolivia
BOT Botswana
BRA Brazil
BRN Bahrain
BRU Brunei
BUL Bulgaria
CAF Central African
CAN Canada
CAY Cayman Islands
CGO Congo
CHA Chad
CHI Chile
CHN People's Republic of China
CIV Ivory Coast
CMR Cameroon
COL Colombia
CRC Costa Rica
CYP Cyprus
DEN Denmark
DJI Djibouti
DOM Dominican Republic
ECU Ecuador
EGY Egypt
ESA El Salvador
ESP Spain
ETH Ethiopia

FIJ Fiji
FIN Finland
FRA France
FRG Federal Republic of Germany
GAB Gabon
GAM Gambia
GBR Great Britain
GDR German Dem. Republic
GEQ Equatorial Guinea
GHA Ghana
GRE Greece
GRN Grenada
GUA Guatemala
GUI Guinea
GUY Guyana
HAI Haiti
HKG Hong Kong
HOL Netherlands
HON Honduras
HUN Hungary
INA Indonesia
IND India
IRL Ireland
IRN Iran
IRQ Iraq
ISL Iceland
ISR Israel
ISV Virgin Islands
ITA Italy
IVB British Virgin Islands
JAM Jamaica
JOR Jordan
JPN Japan
KEN Kenya
KOR Korea
KUW Kuwait
LAO Laos
LBA Libya
LBR Liberia
LES Lesotho
LIB Lebanon
LIE Liechtenstein
LUX Luxembourg
MAD Madagascar
MAL Malaysia
MAR Morocco
MAW Malawi

MEX Mexico
MGL Mongolia
MLI Mali
MLT Malta
MON Monaco
MOZ Mozambique
MRI Mauritius
MTN Mauritania
NCA Nicaragua
NEP Nepal
NGR Nigeria
NGU Papua New Guinea
NIG Niger
NOR Norway
NZL New Zealand
OMA Oman
PAK Pakistan
PAN Panama
PAR Paraguay
PER Peru
PHI Philippines
POL Poland
POR Portugal
PRK DPR Korea
PUR Puerto Rico
QAT Qatar
ROM Romania
RWA Rwanda
SAM Western Samoa
SAU Saudi Arabia
SEN Senegal
SEY Seychelles
SIN Singapore
SLE Sierra Leone
SMR San Marino
SOL Solomon Islands
SOM Somalia
SRI Sri Lanka
SUD Sudan
SUI Switzerland
SUR Surinam
SWE Sweden
SWZ Swaziland
SYR Syria
TAN Tanzania
TCH Czechoslovakia
THA Thailand

TOG Togo
TON Tonga
TPE Chinese Taipei
TRI Trindad and Tobago
TUN Tunisia
TUR Turkey
UAE United Arab Emirates
UGA Uganda
URS USSR
URU Uruguay
USA United States of America
VEN Venezuela
VIE Vietnam
VOL Upper Volta
YAR Yeman Arab Republic
YMD Yeman Democratic
     Republic
YUG Yugoslavia
ZAI Zaire
ZAM Zambia
ZIM Zimbabwe

Abbreviations

mm	= millimeter
cm	= centimeter
m	= meter
km	= kilometer
mg	= milligram
g	= gram
gr	= grain
kg	= kilogram
m/sec	= minute/seconds
pt	= point

Times

01:25:06.42
hours:minutes:seconds.tenths and
hundredths of seconds

Metric/English Conversion

1mm	= .039"
1cm	= .394"
1m	= 1.094 yd
1km	= .6214 mi
1mg	= .015 gr
1g	= .0353 oz
1kg	= 2.205 lbs
1"	= 2.54 cm
1'	= .3048 m
1 yd	= .9144 m
1 mi	= 1609.3 m
1 oz	= 28.35 g
1 lb	= 453.6 g

* Metric conversions are approximate
  Statistics and Results by the LAOOC

Archery
El Dorado Park

Women August 11

1	Seo, Hyang-Soon	KOR	2568
2	Li, Lingjuan	CHN	2559
3	Kim, Jin-Ho	KOR	2555
4	Ishizu, Hiroko	JPN	2524
5	Meriluoto, Paivi	FIN	2509
6	Dachner, Manuela	FRG	2508
7	King, Katrina	USA	2508
8	Wu, Yanan	CHN	2493
9	Breton, Aurora	MEX	2481
10	Hokari, Minako	JPN	2481

Men August 11

1	Pace, Darrell	USA	2616
2	McKinney, Richard	USA	2564
3	Yamamoto, Hiroshi	JPN	2563
4	Matsushita, Takayoshi	JPN	2552
5	Poikolainen, Tomi	FIN	2538
6	Bjerendal, Goran	SWE	2522
7	Vervinck, Marnix	BEL	2519
8	Koo, Ja-Chung	KOR	2500
9	Wittig, Harry	FRG	2497
10	Ganreiter, Armin	FRG	2494

Athletics
The Los Angeles Memorial Coliseum

Women 100 M — August 05 World Record: 10.79 Olympic Record: 11.01 Wind: 1.2M/Sec Temp: 27C

1	Ashford, Evelyn	USA	10.97*
2	Brown, Alice	USA	11.13
3	Ottey-Page, Merlene	JAM	11.16
4	Bolden, Jeanette	USA	11.25
5	Jackson, Grace	JAM	11.39
6	Bailey, Angela	CAN	11.40
7	Oakes, Heather	GBR	11.43
8	Taylor, Angella	CAN	11.62

Women 200 M — August 09 World Record: 21.71 Olympic Record: 22.03 Wind: -0.1M/Sec Temp: 25C

1	Brisco-Hooks, Valerie	USA	21.81*
2	Griffith, Florence	USA	22.04
3	Ottey-Page, Merlene	JAM	22.09
4	Cook, Kathryn	GBR	22.10
5	Jackson, Grace	JAM	22.20
6	Givens, Randy	USA	22.36
7	Bacoul, Rose Aimee	FRA	22.78
8	Gaschet, Liliane	FRA	22.86

Women 400 M — August 06 World Record: 47.99 Olympic Record: 48.88 Temp: 28C

1	Brisco-Hooks, Valerie	USA	48.83*
2	Cheeseborough, Chandra	USA	49.05
3	Cook, Kathryn	GBR	49.42
4	Payne, Marita	CAN	49.91
5	Leatherwood, Lillie	USA	50.25
6	Thimm, Ute	FRG	50.37
7	Crooks, Charmaine	CAN	50.45
8	Waithera, Ruth	KEN	51.56

Women 800 M — August 06 World Record: 1:53.28 Olympic Record: 1:53.43 Temp: 28C

1	Melinte, Doina	ROM	1:57.60
2	Gallagher, Kim	USA	1:58.63
3	Lovin, Fita	ROM	1:58.83
4	Dorio, Gabriella	ITA	1:59.05
5	Baker, Lorraine	GBR	2:00.03
6	Wysocki, Ruth	USA	2:00.34
7	Klinger, Margrit	FRG	2:00.65
8	O'Shea, Caroline	IRL	2:00.77

Women 1500 M — August 11 World Record: 3:52.47 Olympic Record: 3:56.56 Temp: 28C

1	Dorio, Gabriella	ITA	4:03.25
2	Melinte, Doina	ROM	4:03.76
3	Puica, Maricica	ROM	4:04.15
4	Gerdes, Roswitha	FRG	4:04.41
5	Benning, Christine	GBR	4:04.70
6	Boxer, Christina	GBR	4:05.53
7	McRoberts, Brit	CAN	4:05.98

Women 1500 M (cont.)

8	Wysocki, Ruth	USA	4:08.92
9	Lovin, Fita	ROM	4:09.11
10	Scott, Debbie	CAN	4:10.41
11	MacDougall, Lynne	GBR	4:10.58
12	Van Hulst, Elly	HOL	4:11.58

Women 3000 M — August 10 World Record: 8:26.78 Olympic Record: 8:43.32 Temp: 24C

1	Puica, Maricica	ROM	8:35.96*
2	Sly, Wendy	GBR	8:39.47
3	Williams, Lynn	CAN	8:42.14
4	Bremser, Cindy	USA	8:42.78
5	Buerki, Cornelia	SUI	8:45.20
6	Cunha, Aurora	POR	8:46.37
7	Budd, Zola	GBR	8:48.80
8	Hansen, Joan	USA	8:51.53
9	Rodger, Dianne	NZL	8:56.43
10	Possamai, Agnese	ITA	9:10.82
	Kraus, Brigitte	FRG	DNF
	Decker, Mary	USA	DNF

Women Marathon — August 05 Temp: 27C

1	Benoit, Joan	USA	2:24.52*
2	Waitz, Grete	NOR	2:26.18
3	Mota, Rosa	POR	2:26.57
4	Kristiansen, Ingrid	NOR	2:27.34
5	Moller, Lorraine	NZL	2:28.34
6	Welch, Priscilla	GBR	2:28.54
7	Martin, Lisa	AUS	2:29.03
8	Ruegger, Sylvie	CAN	2:29.09
9	Fogli, Laura	ITA	2:29.28
10	Toivonen, Tuija	FIN	2:32.07
11	Smith, Joyce	GBR	2:32.48
12	Milana, Alba	ITA	2:33.01
13	Rasmussen, Dorthe S	DEN	2:33.40
14	Rowell, Sarah	GBR	2:34.08
15	Keskitalo, Sinikka	FIN	2:35.15
16	Teske, Charlotte	FRG	2:35.56
17	Malone, Annemarie	CAN	2:36.33
18	Hamrin, Marie-Louise	SWE	2:36.41
19	Sasaki, Nanae	JPN	2:37.04
20	Moro, Paola	ITA	2:37.06

*Best Olympic Performance

Women 100 M Hurdles — August 10 World Record: 12.36 Olympic Record: 12.56 Wind: -0.7M/Sec Temp: 24C

1	Fitzgerald-Brown, Benita	USA	12.84
2	Strong, Shirley	GBR	12.88
3	Turner, Kim	USA	13.06
4	Chardonnet, Michele	FRA	13.06
5	Nunn, Glynis	AUS	13.20
6	Savigny, Marie Noelle	FRA	13.28
7	Denk, Ulrike	FRG	13.32
8	Page, Pamela	USA	13.40

Women 400 M Hurdles — August 08 World Record: 54.02 Olympic Record: 55.17 Temp: 28C

1	El Moutawakel, Nawal	MAR	54.61*
2	Brown, Judi	USA	55.20
3	Cojocaru, Cristina	ROM	55.41
4	Usha, P.T.	IND	55.42
5	Skoglund, Ann Louise	SWE	55.43
6	Flintoff, Debbie	AUS	56.21
7	Helander, Tuija	FIN	56.55
8	Farmer, Sandra	JAM	57.15

Women 4 X 100 M — August 11 World Record: 41.53 Olympic Record: 41.60 Temp: 28C

1	Brown, Alice	USA	41.65
	Bolden, Jeanette	USA	
	Cheeseborough, Chandra	USA	
	Ashford, Evelyn	USA	
2	Bailey, Angela	CAN	42.77
	Payne, Marita	CAN	
	Taylor, Angella	CAN	
	Gareau, France	CAN	
3	Jacobs, Simone	GBR	43.11
	Cook, Kathryn	GBR	
	Callender, Beverley	GBR	
	Oakes, Heather	GBR	
4	Bacoul, Rose Aimee	FRA	43.15
	Gaschet, Liliane	FRA	
	Loval, Marie France	FRA	
	Naigre, Raymonde	FRA	

† = New World Record
* = New Olympic Record

Women 4 X 100 M (cont.)	5	Oker, Edith	FRG	43.57
		Schabinger, Michaela	FRG	
		Gaugel, Heide	FRG	
		Thimm, Ute	FRG	
	6	Clarke, Eldece	BAH	44.18
		Davis, Pauline	BAH	
		Greene, Debbie	BAH	
		Fowler, Oralee	BAH	
	7	Bernard, Janice	TRI	44.23
		Forde, Gillian	TRI	
		Hope Washington, Ester	TRI	
		Williams, Angela	TRI	
	8	Cuthbert, Juliette	JAM	53.54
		Jackson, Grace	JAM	
		Findlay, Veronica	JAM	
		Ottey-Page, Merlene	JAM	

Women 4 X 400 M
August 11 World Record: 3:15.92
Olympic Record: 3:19.23
Temp: 28C

	1	Leatherwood, Lillie	USA	3:18.29*
		Howard, Sherri	USA	
		Brisco-Hooks, Valerie	USA	
		Cheeseborough, Chandra	USA	
	2	Crooks, Charmaine	CAN	3:21.21
		Richardson, Jillian	CAN	
		Killingbeck, Molly	CAN	
		Payne, Marita	CAN	
	3	Schulte-Mattler, Heike	FRG	3:22.98
		Thimm, Ute	FRG	
		Gaugel, Heide	FRG	
		Bussmann, Gaby	FRG	
	4	Scutt, Michelle	GBR	3:25.51
		Barnett, Helen	GBR	
		Taylor, Gladys	GBR	
		Hoyte-Smith, Joslyn	GBR	
	5	Oliver, Ilrey	JAM	3:27.51
		Green, Cynthia	JAM	
		Rattray, Cathy	JAM	
		Jackson, Grace	JAM	
	6	Lombardo, Patrizia	ITA	3:30.82
		Campana, Cosetta	ITA	
		Masullo, Marisa	ITA	
		Rossi, Erica	ITA	
	7	Valsamma, M.D.	IND	3:32.49
		Rao, Vandana	IND	
		Abraham, Shinx K.	IND	
		Usha, P. T.	IND	
		Mathieu, Evelyn	PUR	DNS
		De Jesus, Madeline	PUR	
		Lind, Angelita	PUR	
		Mathieu, Marie Lande	PUR	

Women High Jump
August 10 World Record: 2.07
Olympic Record: 1.97
Temp: 28C

				175	180	185	188	191	194	197	200	202	207	
1	Meyfarth, Ulrike	FRG	-	o	o	o	o	o	xo	o	o	xxx	*
2	Simeoni, Sara	ITA	-	o	o	-	o	o	xo	o	xxx		
3	Huntley, Joni	USA	-	o	xo	o	o	xo	xo	xxx			
4	Ewanje-Epee, Maryse	FRA	-	o	o	o	o	o	xxx				
5	Brill, Debbie	CAN	-	o	o	o	xxo	o	xxx				
6	Browne, Vanessa	AUS	o	o	xxo	xo	o	xo	xxx				
7	Zheng, Dazhen	CHN	-	o	o	o	o	xxx					
8	Ritter, Louise	USA	-	o	xo	xo	o	xxx					
9	Elliot, Diana	GBR	-	o	o	o	xxx						
10	Yang, Wenqin	CHN	-	o	o	o	xxx						

Women Long Jump
August 09 World Record: 7.43
Olympic Record: 7.06
Temp: 22C

1	Stanciu, Anisoara	ROM	6.96
2	Ionescu, Vali	ROM	6.81
3	Hearnshaw, Susan	GBR	6.80
4	Thacker, Angela	USA	6.78
5	Joyner, Jackie	USA	6.77
6	Lorraway, Robyn	AUS	6.67
7	Nunn, Glynis	AUS	6.53
8	Ferguson, Shonel	BAH	6.44
9	Lewis, Carol	USA	6.43
10	Scott, Dorothy	JAM	6.40

† = New World Record
* = New Olympic Record

Women Shot Put
August 03 World Record: 22.53
Olympic Record: 22.41

1	Losch, Claudia	FRG	20.48
2	Loghin, Mihaela	ROM	20.47
3	Martin, Gael	AUS	19.19
4	Oakes, Judith	GBR	18.14
5	Li, Meisu	CHN	17.96
6	Head, Venissa	GBR	17.90
7	Cady, Carol	USA	17.23
8	Craciunescu, Florenta	ROM	17.23
9	Griffin, Lorna	USA	17.00
10	Yang, Yanqin	CHN	16.97

Women Discus
August 11 World Record: 73.26
Olympic Record: 69.96

1	Stalman, Ria	HOL	65.36
2	Deniz, Leslie	USA	64.86
3	Craciunescu, Florenta	ROM	63.64
4	Lundholm, Ulla	FIN	63.84
5	Ritchie, Meg	GBR	62.58
6	Manecke, Ingra	FRG	58.56
7	Head, Venissa	GBR	58.18
8	Martin, Gael	AUS	55.88
9	Walsh, Patricia	IRL	55.38
10	DeSnoo, Laura	USA	54.84

Women Javelin
August 06 World Record: 74.76
Olympic Record: 68.40

1	Sanderson, Tessa	GBR	69.56*
2	Lillak, Tiina	FIN	69.00
3	Whitbread, Fatima	GBR	67.14
4	Laaksalo, Tuula	FIN	66.40
5	Solberg, Trine	NOR	64.52
6	Thyssen, Ingrid	FRG	63.26
7	Peters, Beate	FRG	62.34
8	Smith, Karin	USA	62.06
9	Gibson, Sharon	GBR	59.66
10	Sulinski, Cathy	USA	58.38

Women Heptathlon
August 03

1	Nunn, Glynis	AUS	6390
2	Joyner, Jackie	USA	6385
3	Everts, Sabine	FRG	6363
4	Greiner, Cindy	USA	6281
5	Simpson, Judy	GBR	6280
6	Braun, Sabine	FRG	6236
7	Hidding, Tineke	HOL	6147
8	Hagger, Kim	GBR	6127
9	Dressel, Birgit	FRG	6082
10	Schneider, Corinne	SUI	6042

Women 800 M Wheelchair
August 11 World Record: 2:18.2
Temp: 27C

1	Hedrick, Sharon	USA	2:15.73†
2	Saker, Monica	SWE	2:20.86
3	Cable, Candace	USA	2:28.37
4	Hunter, Sacajuwea	USA	2:32.22
5	Orvefors, Anna-Maria	SWE	2:32.49
6	Ieriti, Angela	CAN	2:41.43
7	Hanson, Connie	DEN	2:41.53
8	Lauridsen, Ingrid	DEN	2:43.06

Men 100 M
August 04 World Record: 9.93
Olympic Record: 9.95
Wind: .2M/Sec Temp: 23C

1	Lewis, Carl	USA	9.99
2	Graddy, Sam	USA	10.19
3	Johnson, Ben	CAN	10.22
4	Brown, Ron	USA	10.26
5	McFarlane, Michael	GBR	10.27
6	Stewart, Ray	JAM	10.29
7	Reid, Donovan	GBR	10.33
8	Sharpe, Tony	CAN	10.35

Men 200 M
August 08 World Record: 19.72
Olympic Record: 19.83
Wind: −0.9M/Sec Temp: 28C

1	Lewis, Carl	USA	19.80*
2	Baptiste, Kirk	USA	19.96
3	Jefferson, Thomas	USA	20.26
4	Silva, Joao Batista	BRA	20.30
5	Luebke, Ralf	FRG	20.51
6	Boussemart, Jean-Jacques	FRA	20.55
7	Mennea, Pietro	ITA	20.55
8	Mafe, Adeoye	GBR	20.85

Men 400 M	August 08 World Record: 43.86 Olympic Record: 43.86 Temp: 28C			
	1	Babers, Alonzo	USA	44.27
	2	Tiacoh, Gabriel	CIV	44.54
	3	McKay, Antonio	USA	44.71
	4	Clark, Darren	AUS	44.75
	5	Nix, Sunder	USA	44.75
	6	Uti, Sunday	NGR	44.93
	7	Egbunike, Innocent	NGR	45.35
		Cameron, Bertland	JAM	DNS
	DNS = Did Not Start			

Men 800 M	August 06 World Record 1:41.73 Olympic Record: 1:43.50 Temp: 28C			
	1	Cruz, Joaquim	BRA	1:43.00*
	2	Coe, Sebastian	GBR	1:43.64
	3	Jones, Earl	USA	1:43.83
	4	Konchellah, Billy	KEN	1:44.03
	5	Sabi, Donato	ITA	1:44.53
	6	Koech, Edwin	KEN	1:44.86
	7	Gray, Johnny	USA	1:47.89
	8	Ovett, Steve	GBR	1:52.28

Men 1500 M	August 11 World Record: 3:30.77 Olympic Record: 3:34.91 Temp: 24C			
	1	Coe, Sebastian	GBR	3:32.53*
	2	Cram, Steve	GBR	3:33.40
	3	Abascal, Jose	ESP	3:34.30
	4	Chesire, Joseph	KEN	3:34.52
	5	Spivey, Jim	USA	3:36.07
	6	Wirz, Peter	SUI	3:36.97
	7	Vera, Andres	ESP	3:37.02
	8	Omar, Khalifa	SUD	3:37.11
	9	Rogers, Anthony	NZL	3:38.98
	10	Scott, Steve	USA	3:39.86

Men 3000 M Steeplechase	August 10 World Record: 8:05.04 Olympic Record: 8:08.02 Temp: 22C			
	1	Korir, Julius	KEN	8:11.80
	2	Mahmoud, Joseph	FRA	8:13.31
	3	Diemer, Brian	USA	8:14.06
	4	Marsh, Henry	USA	8:14.25
	5	Reitz, Colin	GBR	8:15.48
	6	Ramon, Domingo	ESP	8:17.27
	7	Kariuki, Julius	KEN	8:17.47
	8	Debacker, Pascal	FRA	8:21.51
	9	Ekblom, Tommy	FIN	8:23.95
	10	Hackney, Roger	GBR	8:27.10

Men 5000 M	August 11 World Record: 13:00.41 Olympic Record: 13:20.34 Temp: 24C			
	1	Aouita, Said	MAR	13:05.59*
	2	Ryffel, Markus	SUI	13:07.54
	3	Leitao, Antonio	POR	13:09.20
	4	Hutchings, Tim	GBR	13:11.50
	5	Kipkoech, Paul	KEN	13:14.40
	6	Cheruiyot, Charles	KEN	13:18.41
	7	Padilla, Doug	USA	13:23.56
	8	Walker, John	NZL	13:24.46
	9	Canario, Ezequiel	POR	13:26.50
	10	Waigwa, Wilson	KEN	13:27.34

Men 10000 M	August 06 World Record: 27:22.04 Olympic Record: 27:38.35 Temp: 26C			
	1	Cova, Alberto	ITA	27:47.54
	2	Vainio, Martti	FIN	27:51.10
	3	McLeod, Michael	GBR	28:06.22
	4	Musyoki, Mike	KEN	28:06.46
	5	Antibo, Salvatore	ITA	28:06.50
	6	Herle, Christoph	FRG	28:08.21
	7	Bitok, Sosthenes	KEN	28:09.01
	8	Kanai, Yutaka	JPN	28:27.06
	9	Jones, Steve	GBR	28:28.08
	10	Treacy, John	IRL	28:28.68

Men Marathon	August 12			
	1	Lopes, Carlos	POR	2:09:21
	2	Treacy, John	IRL	2:09:56
	3	Spedding, Charles	GBR	2:09:58
	4	So, Takeshi	JPN	2:10:55
	5	DeCastella, Robert	AUS	2:11:09

Men Marathon (cont.)				
	6	Ikangaa, Juma	TAN	2:11:10
	7	Nzau, Joseph	KEN	2:11:28
	8	Robleh, Djama	DJI	2:11:39
	9	Kiernan, Jerry	IRL	2:12:20
	10	Dixon, Rodney	NZL	2:12:57
	11	Pfitzinger, Peter	USA	2:13:53
	12	Jones, Hugh	GBR	2:13:57
	13	Gonzalez, Jorge	PUR	2:14:00
	14	Seko, Toshihiko	JPN	2:14:13
	15	Salazar, Alberto	USA	2:14:19
	16	Terzi, Mehmet	TUR	2:14:20
	17	So, Shigeru	JPN	2:14:38
	18	Salzmann, Ralf	FRG	2:15:29
	19	Joergensen, Henrik	DEN	2:15:55
	20	Ahmed, Salah	DJI	2:15:59

Men 110 M Hurdles	August 06 World Record: 12.93 Olympic Record: 13.24 Wind: −0.4M/Sec Temp: 28C			
	1	Kingdom, Roger	USA	13.20*
	2	Foster, Gregory	USA	13.23
	3	Bryggare, Arto	FIN	13.40
	4	Mckoy, Mark	CAN	13.45
	5	Campbell, Anthony	USA	13.55
	6	Caristan, Stephane	FRA	13.71
	7	Sala, Carlos	ESP	13.80
	8	Glass, Jeff	CAN	14.15

Men 400 M Hurdles	August 05 World Record: 47.02 Olympic Record: 47.63 Temp: 27C			
	1	Moses, Edwin	USA	47.75
	2	Harris, Danny	USA	48.13
	3	Schmid, Harald	FRG	48.19
	4	Nylander, Sven	SWE	48.97
	5	DiaBa, Amadou	SEN	49.28
	6	Hawkins, Tranel	USA	49.42
	7	Zimmerman, Michel	BEL	50.69
	8	Amike, Henry	NGR	53.78

Men 20 Km Walk	August 03			
	1	Canto, Ernesto	MEX	1:23:13★
	2	Gonzalez, Raul	MEX	1:23:20
	3	Damilano, Maurizio	ITA	1:23:26
	4	Leblanc, Guillaaume	CAN	1:24:29
	5	Mattioli, Carlo	ITA	1:25:07
	6	Marin, Jose	ESP	1:25:32
	7	Evoniuk, Marco	USA	1:25:42
	8	Andersen, Erling	NOR	1:25:54
	9	Moreno-Moreno, Josequerub	COL	1:26:04
	10	Smith, David	AUS	1:26:48
	★ = Best Olympic Performance			

Men 50 Km Walk	August 11			
	1	Gonzalez, Raul	MEX	3:47:26★
	2	Gustafsson, Bo	SWE	3:53:19
	3	Bellucci, Sandro	ITA	3:53:45
	4	Salonen, Reima	FIN	3:58:30
	5	Ducceschi, Raffaello	ITA	3:59:26
	6	Schueler, Carl	USA	3:59:46
	7	Llopart, Jorge	ESP	4:03:09
	8	Pinto, Jose	POR	4:04:42
	9	Alcalde, Manuel	ESP	4:05:47
	10	Canto, Ernesto	MEX	4:07:59
	★ = Best Olympic Performance			

Men 4 X 100 M	August 11 World Record: 37.86 Olympic Record: 38.19 Temp: 28C			
	1	Graddy, Sam	USA	37.83*†
		Brown, Ron	USA	
		Smith, Calvin	USA	
		Lewis, Carl	USA	
	2	Lawrence, Albert	JAM	38.62
		Meghoo, Gregory	JAM	
		Quarrie, Donald	JAM	
		Stewart, Ray	JAM	
	3	Johnson, Ben	CAN	38.70
		Sharpe, Tony	CAN	
		Williams, Desai	CAN	
		Hinds, Sterling	CAN	
	4	Ullo, Antonio	ITA	38.87
		Bongiorni, Giovanni	ITA	
		Tilli, Stefano	ITA	
		Mennea, Pietro	ITA	
	† = New World Record * = New Olympic Record			

Men 4 X 100 M (cont.)

5	Koffler, Jurgen	FRG	38.99	
	Klein, Peter	FRG		
	Evers, Juergen	FRG		
	Luebke, Ralf	FRG		
6	Richard, Antoine	FRA	39.10	
	Boussemart, Jean-Jacques	FRA		
	Gasparoni, Marc	FRA		
	Marie Rose, Bruno	FRA		
7	Thompson, Daley	GBR	39.13	
	Reid, Donovan	GBR		
	McFarlane, Michael	GBR		
	Wells, Allan	GBR		
8	Silva, Arnaldo	BRA	39.40	
	Santos, Nelson Rocha	BRA		
	Nakala, Katsuko	BRA		
	Correia, Paulo	BRA		

Men 4 X 400 M

August 11 World Record: 2:56.16
Olympic Record: 2:56.16 Temp: 28C

1	Nix, Sunder	USA	2:57.91
	Armstead, Ray	USA	
	Babers, Alonzo	USA	
	McKay, Antonio	USA	
2	Akabusi, Kriss	GBR	2:59.13
	Cook, Garry	GBR	
	Bennett, Todd	GBR	
	Brown, Philip	GBR	
3	Uti, Sunday	NGR	2:59.32
	Ugbusien, Moses	NGR	
	Peters, Rotimi	NGR	
	Egbunike, Innocent	NGR	
4	Frayne, Bruce	AUS	2:59.70
	Clark, Darren	AUS	
	Minihan, Gary	AUS	
	Mitchell, Rick	AUS	
5	Tozzi, Roberto	ITA	3:01.44
	Nocco, Ernesto	ITA	
	Ribaud, Roberto	ITA	
	Mennea, Pietro	ITA	
6	Louis, Richard	BAR	3:01.60
	Peltier, David	BAR	
	Edwards, Clyde	BAR	
	Forde, Elvis	BAR	
7	Govile, John	UGA	3:02.09
	Kyeswa, Moses	UGA	
	Rwamuhanda, Peter	UGA	
	Okot, Mike	UGA	
8	Sokolowski, Michael	CAN	3:02.82
	Hinds, Doug	CAN	
	Saunders, Bryan	CAN	
	Bethune, Tim	CAN	

Men High Jump

August 11 World Record: 2.38
Olympic Record: 2.36 Temp: 26C

			215	218	221	224	227	229	231	233	235	240
1	Moegenburg, Dietmar	FRG	o	-	o	-	o	-	o	o	o	xxx
2	Sjoeberg, Patrik	SWE	-	-	o	-	xo	o	xo	xo	xxx	
3	Zhu, Jianhua	CHN	o	-	o	-	o	-	o	x-	xxx	
4	Stones, Dwight	USA	-	o	-	o	-	x-	o	xxx		
5	Nordquist, Doug	USA	-	o	-	o	o	o	xxx			
6	Ottey, Milt	CAN	o	-	o	xo	xo	o	xxx			
7	Liu, Yunpeng	CHN	o	-	o	o	xxo	xo	xxx			
8	Cai, Shu	CHN	o	-	xo	o	xo	o-	xx			
9	Niemi, Erkki	FIN	o	-	xo	xxo	xxx					
10	Thraenhardt, Carlo	FRG	xo	-	xx-	x						
	Dalhaeuser, Roland	SUI	-	-	xxx							
	Goode, Milton	USA	-	-	xxx							

- = Passes   o = Cleared   x = Missed

Men Pole Vault

August 08 World Record: 5.83
Olympic Record: 5.78

			510	520	530	540	545	550	555	560	565	570	575	580
1	Quinon, Pierre	FRA	-	-	-	-	xo	-	-	-	x-	o	o	xxx
2	Tully, Mike	USA	-	-	-	o	-	o	-	xxo	-	-	xxx	
3	Bell, Earl	USA	-	-	o	-	o	-	o	-	xxx			
3	Vigneron, Thierry	FRA	-	-	o	-	-	-	o	-	xxx			
5	Pallonen, Kimmo	FIN	-	-	xo	-	xo	-	xxx					
6	Lytle, Doug	USA	-	-	-	o	-	o	-	xxx				
7	Boehni, Felix	SUI	-	-	o	-	-	-	xxx					
8	Barella, Mauro	ITA	xxo	-	xxo	xxx								
9	Ruiz, Alberto	ESP	o	-	xxx									
10	Yang, Weimin	CHN	xo	xxx										

- = Passes   o = Cleared   x = Missed

Men Long Jump

August 06 World Record: 8.90
Olympic Record: 8.90 Temp: 28C

1	Lewis, Carl	USA	8.54
2	Honey, Gary	AUS	8.24
3	Evangelisti, Giovanni	ITA	8.24
4	Myricks, Larry	USA	8.16
5	Liu, Yuhuang	CHN	7.99
6	Wells, Joey	BAH	7.97
7	Usui, Junichi	JPN	7.81
8	Kim, Jong-Il	KOR	7.81
9	Alli, Yusuf	NGR	7.78
10	Corgos, Antonio	ESP	7.69

Men Triple Jump

August 04 World Record: 17.89
Olympic Record: 17.30 Temp: 26C

1	Joyner Al	USA	17.26
2	Conley, Mike	USA	17.18
3	Connor, Keith	GBR	16.87
4	Zou, Zhenxian	CHN	16.83
5	Bouschen, Peter	FRG	16.77
6	Banks, Willie	USA	16.75
7	Agbebaku, Ajayi	NGR	16.67
8	Mccalla, Eric	GBR	16.66
9	Taiwo, Joseph	NGR	16.64
10	Herbert, John	GBR	16.40

Men Shot Put

August 11 World Record: 22.22
Olympic Record: 21.35 Temp: 28C

1	Andrei, Alessandro	ITA	21.26
2	Carter, Michael	USA	21.09
3	Laut, Dave	USA	20.97
4	Wolf, Augie	USA	20.93
5	Guenthoer, Werner	SUI	20.28
6	Montelatici, Marco	ITA	19.98
7	Tallhem, Soeren	SWE	19.81
8	DeBruin, Erik	HOL	19.65
9	Akonniemi, Aulis	FIN	18.98
10	Weil, Gert	CHI	18.69

Men Discus

August 10 World Record: 71.86
Olympic Record: 68.28 Temp: 24C

1	Danneberg, Rolf	FRG	66.60
2	Wilkins, Mac	USA	66.30
3	Powell, John	USA	65.46
4	Hjeltnes, Knut	NOR	65.28
5	Burns, Art	USA	64.98
6	Wagner, Alwin	FRG	64.72
7	Zerbini, Luciano	ITA	63.50
8	Fernholm, Stefan	SWE	63.22
9	DeBruin, Erik	HOL	62.32
10	Weir, Bob	GBR	61.36

Men Hammer Throw

August 06 World Record: 84.14
Olympic Record: 81.80

1	Tiainen, Juha	FIN	78.08
2	Riehm, Karl-Hans	FRG	77.98
3	Ploghaus, Klaus	FRG	76.68
4	Urlando, Giampaolo	ITA	75.96
5	Bianchini, Orlando	ITA	75.94
6	Green, Bill	USA	75.60
7	Huhtala, Harri	FIN	75.28
8	Ciofani, Walter	FRA	73.46
9	Weir, Bob	GBR	72.62
10	Girvan, Martin	GBR	72.32

Men Javelin

August 05 World Record: 104.80
Olympic Record: 94.58 Temp: 27C

1	Haerkoenen, Arto	FIN	86.76
2	Ottley, David	GBR	85.74
3	Eldebrink, Kenth	SWE	83.72
4	Gambke, Wolfram	FRG	82.46
5	Yoshida, Masami	JPN	81.98
6	Vilhjalmsson, Einar	ISL	81.58
7	Bradstock, Roald	GBR	81.22
8	Babits, Laslo	CAN	80.68
9	Olsen, Per Erling	NOR	78.98
10	Petranoff, Tom	USA	78.40

† = New World Record
* = New Olympic Record

Decathlon	August 09 World Record: 8798		
	Olympic Record: 8618		
	1 Thompson, Daley	GBR	8797 *
	2 Hingsen, Juergen	FRG	8673
	3 Wentz, Siegfried	FRG	8412
	4 Kratschmer, Guido	FRG	8326
	5 Motti, William	FRA	8266
	6 Crist, John	USA	8130
	7 Wooding, Jim	USA	8091
	8 Steen, Dave	CAN	8047
	9 Werthner, Dr. Georg	AUT	8012
	10 Ruefenacht, Michele	SUI	7924

Men 1500 M Wheelchair	August 11 World Record: 3:48.1		
	Temp: 27C		
	1 VanWinkel, Paul	BEL	3:58.50
	2 Snow, Randy	USA	4:00.02
	3 Viger, Andre	CAN	4:00.47
	4 Fitzgerald, Mel	CAN	4:00.65
	5 Geider, Juergen	FRG	4:00.71
	6 Trotter, Peter	AUS	4:00.83
	7 Hansen, Rick	CAN	4:02.75
	8 Martinson, Jim	USA	4:21.37

Basketball

The Forum

Women — Gold/Silver Game

August 07

	USA	
Edwards, Teresa	USA	2
Henry, Lea	USA	4
Woodard, Lynette	USA	7
Donovan, Anne	USA	6
Boswell, Cathy	USA	4
Miller, Cheryl	USA	16
Lawrence, Janice	USA	14
Noble, Cindy	USA	10
Mulkey, Kim	USA	6
Curry, Denise	USA	6
McGee, Pamela	USA	6
Menken-Schaudt, Carol	USA	4
Summitt, Pat, Coach	USA	
Total		**85**

Choi, Aei-Young	KOR	20
Park, Yang-Gae	KOR	0
Kim, Eun-Sook	KOR	0
Lee, Hyung-Sook	KOR	6
Choi, Kyung-Hee	KOR	0
Lee, Mi-Ja	KOR	0
Moon, Kyung-Ja	KOR	0
Kim, Hwa-Soon	KOR	15
Jeong, Myung-Hee	KOR	0
Kim, Young-Hee	KOR	0
Sung, Jung-A	KOR	11
Park, Chan-Sook	KOR	3
Cho, Seung-Youn, Coach	KOR	
Total		**55**

Women — Bronze Game

August 07

CHN		CAN	
Chen, Yuefang	0	Polson, Lynn	6
Li, Xiaoqin	11	McAra, Tracie	0
Ba, Yan	0	Pendergast, Anna	0
Song, Xiaobo	16	Huband, Debbie	12
Qiu, Chen	5	Sealey, Carol Jane	0
Wang, Jun	0	Lang, Alison	7
Xiu, Lijuan	13	Smith, Bev	13
Zheng, Haixia	0	Sweeney, Sylvia	4
Cong, Xuedi	10	Clarkson-Lohr, Candi	4
Zhang, Hui	0	Kordic, Toni	0
Liu, Qing	8	Blackwell, Andrea	6
Zhang, Yueqin	0	Thomas, Misty	5
Yang, Boyong, Coach		McCrae, Don, Coach	
Total	**63**	**Total**	**57**

Men — Gold/Silver Game

August 10

	USA	
Alford, Steve	USA	10
Wood, Leon	USA	6
Ewing, Patrick	USA	9
Fleming, Vern	USA	9
Robertson, Alvin	USA	6
Jordan, Michael	USA	20
Kleine, Joseph	USA	4
Koncak, Jon	USA	2
Tisdale, Wayman	USA	14
Mullin, Chris	USA	4
Perkins, Samuel	USA	12
Turner, Jeffrey	USA	0
Knight, Robert, Coach	USA	
Total		**96**

Beiran, Jose Manuel	ESP	0
Llorente, Jose Luis	ESP	2
Arcega, Fernando	ESP	2
Margall, Jose Maria	ESP	10
Jimenez, Andres	ESP	16
Romay, Fernando	ESP	5
Martin, Fernando	ESP	14
Corbalan, Juan Antonio	ESP	6
Solozabal, Ignacio	ESP	0
De La Cruz, Juan Domingo	ESP	0
Lopez, Juan Maria	ESP	6
San Epifanio, Juan Antoni	ESP	4
Diaz-Miguel, Antonio, Coach	ESP	
Total		**65**

Men — Bronze Game

August 09

YUG		CAN	
Petrovic, Drazen	12	Kelsey, Howard	2
Petrovic, Aleksandar	15	Simms, Tony	10
Zorkic, Nebojsa	4	Pasquale, Eli	16
Zizic, Rajko	0	Tilleman, Karl	13
Sunara, Ivan	4	Kazanowski, Gerald	8
Mutapcic, Emir	2	Triano, Jay	10
Hadzic, Saabit	0	Hatch, John	0
Knego, Andro	4	Herbert, Gord	0
Radovanovic, Ratko	8	Wennington, Bill	11
Nakic-Vojnovic, Mihovil	2	Raffin, Romel	0
Dalipagic, Drazen	37	Wiltjer, Greg	12
Vukicevic, Branko	0	Meagher, Dan	0
Novosel, Mirko, Coach		Donohue, Jack, Coach	
Total	**88**	**Total**	**82**

Boxing

The Los Angeles Memorial Sports Arena

Light Flyweight

August 11

1	Gonzales, Paul	USA
2	Todisco, Salvatore	ITA
3	Mwila, Keith	ZAM
3	Bolivar, Jose Marcelino	VEN

Flyweight

August 11

1	McCrory, Steven	USA
2	Redzepovski, Redzep	YUG
3	Can, Eyup	TUR
3	Bilali, Ibrahim	KEN

Bantamweight

August 11

1	Stecca, Maurizio	ITA
2	Lopez, Hector	MEX
3	Walters, Dale	CAN
3	Nolasco, Pedro J.	DOM

Featherweight

1	Taylor, Meldrick	USA
2	Konyegwachie, Peter	NGR
3	Aykac, Turgut	TUR
3	Catari Peraza, Omar	VEN

Lightweight

1	Whitaker, Pernell	USA
2	Ortiz, Luis F.	PUR
3	Ndongo Ebanga, Martin	CMR
3	Chun, Chil-Sung	KOR

† = New World Record
* = New Olympic Record

Light Welterweight	August 11		
	1	Page, Jerry	USA
	2	Umponmaha, Dhawee	THA
	3	Fulger, Mircea	ROM
	3	Puzovic, Mirk O	YUG

Welterweight	August 11		
	1	Breland, Mark	USA
	2	An, Young-Su	KOR
	3	Nyman, Joni	FIN
	3	Bruno, Luciano	ITA

Light Middleweight	August 11		
	1	Tate, Frank	USA
	2	O'Sullivan, Shawn	CAN
	3	Zielonka, Manfred	FRG
	3	Tiozzo, Christophe	FRA

Middleweight	August 11		
	1	Shin, Joon-Sup	KOR
	2	Hill, Virgil	USA
	3	Zaoui, Mohamed	ALG
	3	Gonzalez, Aristides	PUR

Light Heavyweight	August 11		
	1	Josipovic, Anton	YUG
	2	Barry, Kevin	NZL
	3	Moussa, Mustapha	ALG
	3	Holyfield, Evander	USA

Heavyweight	August 11		
	1	Tillman, Henry	USA
	2	Dewit, Willie	CAN
	3	Musone, Angelo	ITA
	3	Vanderlijde, Arnold	HOL

Super-Heavyweight	August 11		
	1	Biggs, Tyrell	USA
	2	Damiani, Francesco	ITA
	3	Wells, Robert	GBR
	3	Azis, Salihu	YUG

Canoeing
Lake Casitas

Women Kayak-1 500 M	August 10 Wind: 0 M/Sec Temp: 18C			
	1	Andersson, Agneta	SWE	1:58.72
	2	Schuttpelz, Barbara	FRG	1:59.93
				+ 1.21
	3	Derckx, Annemiek	HOL	2:00.11
				+ 1.39
	4	Marinescu, Tecla	ROM	2:00.12
				+ 1.40
	5	Basson, Beatrice	FRA	2:01.21
				+ 2.49
	6	Conover, Sheila	USA	2:02.38
				+ 3.66
	7	Guay, Lucie	CAN	2:02.49
				+ 3.77
	8	Blencowe, Elizabeth	AUS	2:02.63
				+ 3.91
	9	Smither, Lesley	GBR	2:04.09
				+ 5.37

Women Kayak-2 500 M	August 10 Wind: 0 M/Sec Temp: 28 C			
	1	Andersson, Agneta	SWE	1:45.25
		Olsson, Anna	SWE	
	2	Barre, Alexandra	CAN	1:47.13
		Holloway, Sue	CAN	+ 1.88
	3	Idem, Josefa	FRG	1:47.32
		Schuttpelz, Barbara	FRG	+ 2.07
	4	Constantin, Agafia	ROM	1:47.56
		Ionescu, Nastasia	ROM	+ 2.31
	5	Dery, Shirley	USA	1:49.51
		Klein, Leslie	USA	+4.26
	6	Hettich, Bernadette	FRA	1:51.40
		Mathevon, Catherine	FRA	+ 6.15
	7	Ofstad, Kari	NOR	1:51.61
		Wahl, Anne	NOR	+ 6.36
	8	Perrett, Lucy	GBR	1:51.73
		Smither, Lesley	GBR	+ 6.48
	9	Kuppens, Marleen	BEL	1:51.92
		Thijs, Lugarde	BEL	+ 6.67

Women Kayak-4 500 M	August 11 Wind: 0 M/Sec Temp: 20 C			
	1	Constantin, Agafia	ROM	1:38.34
		Ionescu, Nastasia	ROM	
		Marinescu, Tecla	ROM	
		Stefan, Maria	ROM	
	2	Andersson, Agneta	SWE	1:38.87
		Olsson, Anna	SWE	+ 0.53
		Karlsson, Eva	SWE	
		Wiberg, Susanne	SWE	
	3	Barre, Alexandra	CAN	1:39.40
		Guay, Lucie	CAN	+ 1.06
		Holloway, Sue	CAN	
		Olmsted, Barb	CAN	
	4	Conover, Sheila	USA	1:40.10
		Dery, Shirley	USA	+ 2.15
		Klein, Leslie	USA	
		Turner, Ann	USA	
	5	Idem, Josefa	FRG	1:42.68
		Schmidt, Regina	FRG	+ 4.34
		Schuttpelz, Barbara	FRG	
		Skolnik, Judith	FRG	
	6	Legraid, Wenche	NOR	1:42.97
		Ofstad, Kari	NOR	+ 4.63
		Rasmussen, Ingeborg	NOR	
		Wahl, Anne	NOR	
	7	Lawler, Janine	GBR	1:46.30
		Perrett, Lucy	GBR	+ 7.96
		Smither, Lesley	GBR	
		Watson, Deborah	GBR	

Men Kayak-1 500 M	August 10 Wind: 0 M/Sec Temp: 14 C			
	1	Ferguson, Ian	NZL	1:47.84
	2	Moberg, Lars-Erik	SWE	1:48.18
				+ 0.34
	3	Bregeon, Bernard	FRA	1:48.41
				+ 0.57
	4	Diba, Vasile	ROM	1:48.77
				+ 0.93
	5	Upson, David	GBR	1:49.32
				+ 1.48
	6	Scarpa, Daniele	ITA	1:49.60
				+ 1.76
	7	Del Riego, Guillermo	ESP	1:49.71
				+ 1.87
	8	Scholl, Reiner	FRG	1:49.89
				+ 2.05
	9	Janic, Milan	YUG	1:49.90
				+ 2.06

Men Kayak-2 500 M	August 10 Wind: 0 M/Sec Temp: 28 C			
	1	Ferguson, Ian	NZL	1:34.21
		MacDonald, Paul	NZL	
	2	Bengtsson, Per-Inge	SWE	1:35.26
		Moberg, Lars-Erik	SWE	+ 1.05
	3	Fisher, Hugh	CAN	1:35.41
		Morris, Alwyn	CAN	+ 1.20
	4	Scarpa, Daniele	ITA	1:35.50
		Uberti, Francesco	ITA	+ 1.29
	5	Fedosei, Nicolae	ROM	1:35.60
		Velea, Angelin	ROM	+1.39
	6	Hervieu, Francis	FRA	1:36.40
		Legras, Daniel	FRA	+ 2.19
	7	Seack, Matthias	FRG	1:36.51
		Seack, Oliver	FRG	+ 2.30
	8	Sheriff, Andrew	GBR	1:36.73
		West, Jeremy	GBR	+ 2.52
	9	Bachmayer, Werner	AUT	1:37.05
		Hartl, Wolfgang	AUT	+ 2.84

Men Canadian-1 500 M	August 10 Wind: 0 M/Sec Temp: 16 C			
	1	Cain, Larry	CAN	1:57.01
	2	Jakobsen, Henning L.	DEN	1:58.45
				+ 1.44
	3	Olaru, Costica	ROM	1:59.86
				+ 2.85
	4	Renaud, Philippe	FRA	1:59.95
				+ 2.94
	5	Gronlund, Timo	FIN	2:01.00
				+ 3.99
	6	Inoue, Kiyoto	JPN	2:01.79
				+ 4.78
	7	Faust, Hartmut	FRG	2:01.86
				+ 4.85
	8	Rozanski, Robert	NOR	2:02.12
				+ 5.11
	9	Lopez, Francisco	ESP	2:03.95
				+ 6.94

Men Canadian-2 500 M	August 10 Wind: 0 M/Sec Temp: 28 C			
	1	Ljubek, Matija	YUG	1:43.67
		Nisovic, Mirko	YUG	
	2	Potzaichin, Ivan	ROM	1:45.68
		Simionov, Toma	ROM	+ 2.01
	3	Miguez, Enrique	ESP	1:47.71
		Suarez, Narciso	ESP	+ 4.04
	4	Hoyer, Didier	FRA	1:47.72
		Renaud, Eric	FRA	+ 4.05
	5	Botting, Steve	CAN	1:48.81
		Smith, Eric	CAN	+ 5.14
	6	Faust, Wolfram	FRG	1:48.97
		Wienand, Ralf	FRG	+ 5.30
	7	Jamieson, Eric	GBR	1:49.59
		Train, Andrew	GBR	+ 5.92
	8	Fukuzato, Shusei	JPN	1:50.22
		Izumi, Hiroyuki	JPN	+ 6.55
	9	Young, J. Bret	USA	1:50.55
		Merritt, Bruce	USA	+ 6.88

Men Canadian-1 1000 M	August 11 Wind: 0 M/Sec Temp: 18 C			
	1	Eicke, Ulrich	FRG	4:06.32
	2	Cain, Larry	CAN	4:08.67 + 2.35
	3	Jakobsen, Henning L.	DEN	4:09.51 + 3.19
	4	Gronlund, Timo	FIN	4:15.58 + 9.26
	5	Olaru, Costica	ROM	4:16.39 + 10.07
	6	Train, Stephen	GBR	4:16.64 + 10.32
	7	Merritt, Bruce	USA	4:18.17 + 11.85
	8	Inoue, Kiyoto	JPN	4:18.72 + 12.40
	9	Lopez, Francisco	ESP	4:23.92 + 17.60

Men Kayak-1 1000 M	August 11 Wind: 0 M/Sec Temp: 18 C			
	1	Thompson, Alan	NZL	3:45.73
	2	Janic, Milan	YUG	3:46.88 + 1.15
	3	Barton, Greg	USA	3:47.38 + 1.65
	4	Sundqvist, Kalle	SWE	3:48.69 + 2.96
	5	Genders, Peter	AUS	3:49.11 + 3.38
	6	Boccara, Philippe	FRA	3:49.38 + 3.65
	7	Diba, Vasile	ROM	3:51.61 + 5.88
	8	Jackson, Stephen	GBR	3.52.25 + 6.52
	9	Alegre, Pedro	ESP	3:53.20 + 7.47

Men Kayak-2 1000 M	August 11 Wind: 0 M/Sec Temp: 23 C			
	1	Fisher, Hugh	CAN	3:24.22
		Morris, Alwyn	CAN	
	2	Bregeon, Bernard	FRA	3:25.97
		Lefoulon, Patrick	FRA	+ 1.75
	3	Kelly, Barry	AUS	3:26.80
		Kenny, Grant	AUS	+ 2.58
	4	Kent, Terry (Olney)	USA	3:27.01
		White, Terry	USA	+ 2.79
	5	Seack, Matthias	FRG	3:27.28
		Seack, Oliver	FRG	+ 3.06
	6	Scarpa, Daniele	ITA	3:27.46
		Uberti, Francesco	ITA	+ 3.24
	7	Menendez, Herminio	ESP	3:27.53
		Del Riego, Guillermo	ESP	+ 3.31
	8	Andersson, Bengt	SWE	3:29.39
		Sundqvist, Kalle	SWE	+ 5.17
	9	Debucke, Patrick	BEL	3:32.92
		Hanssens, Patrick	BEL	+ 8.70

Men Kayak-4 1000 M	August 11 Wind: 0 M/Sec Temp: 28 C			
	1	Bramwell, Grant	NZL	3:02.28
		Ferguson, Ian	NZL	
		MacDonald, Paul	NZL	
		Thompson, Alan	NZL	
	2	Bengtsson, Per-Inge	SWE	3:02.81
		Karls, Tommy	SWE	+ 0.53
		Moberg, Lars-Erik	SWE	
		Ohlsson, Thomas	SWE	

Men Kayak-4 1000 M (cont.)				
	3	Barouh, Francois	FRA	3:03.94
		Boccara, Philippe	FRA	+ 1.66
		Boucherit, Pascal	FRA	
		Vavasseur, Didier	FRA	
	4	Constantin, Ionel	ROM	3:04.39
		Fedosei, Nicolae	ROM	+ 2.11
		Letcaie, Ionel	ROM	
		Velea, Angelin	ROM	
	5	Bourne, Grayson	GBR	3:04.59
		Sheriff, Andrew	GBR	+ 2.31
		Smith, Kevin	GBR	
		West, Jeremy	GBR	
	6	Gonzalez, Ivan	ESP	3:04.71
		Ramos, Luis Gregorio	ESP	+ 2.43
		Roman, Juan Jose	ESP	
		Sanchez, Juan Manuel	ESP	
	7	Doak, John	AUS	3:06.02
		Doak, Robert	AUS	+ 3.74
		Martin, Raymond	AUS	
		Wooden, Scott	AUS	
	8	Hessel, Bernd	FRG	3:06.47
		Kegel, Oliver	FRG	+ 4.19
		Schmidt, Detler	FRG	
		Scholl, Reiner	FRG	
	9	Brien, Don	CAN	3:06.66
		Holmes, Mark	CAN	+ 4.38
		Irvine, Don	CAN	
		Shaw, Colin	CAN	

Cycling

Olympic Velodrome, California State University
Dominguez Hills
Artesia Freeway
Mission Viejo

Women Individual Road Race 79.2 Km	July 29			
	1	Carpenter-Phinney, Connie	USA	2:11:14
	2	Twigg, Rebecca	USA	G
	3	Schumacher, Sandra	FRG	G
	4	Larsen, Unni	NOR	G
	5	Canins, Maria	ITA	G
	6	Longo, Jeannie	FRA	+1:21
	7	Soerensen, Helle	DEN	+2:14
	8	Enzenauer, Ute	FRG	G
	9	Seghezzi, Luisa	ITA	G
	10	Parks, Janelle	USA	G

G = GROUP

Men 1000 M	July 30			
	1	Schmidtke, Fredy	FRG	54.459
	2	Harnett, Curtis	CAN	54.187
	3	Colas, Fabrice	FRA	54.014
	4	Samuel, Gene	TRI	53.980
	5	Adair, Craig	NZL	53.760
	6	Weller, David	JAM	53.537
	7	Alexandre, Marcelo O.	ARG	53.499
	8	O'Reilly, Rory	USA	53.420
	9	Baudino, Stefano	ITA	53.173
	10	Isler, Heinz	SUI	53.036

Men Sprint	August 03			1 R.D.	2 R.D.	3 R.D.
	1	Gorski, Mark	USA	10.49	10.95	-
	2	Vails, Nelson	USA	-	-	-
	3	Sakamoto, Tsutomu	JPN	11.06	11.03	-
	4	Vernet, Philippe	FRA	-	-	-
	5	Scheller, Gerhard	FRG	11.36		
	6	Alexandre, Marcelo O.	ARG	-		
	7	Tucker, Kenrick	AUS	-		
	8	Schmidtke, Fredy	FRG	-		

Men 4000 M Individual Pursuit	August 01			
	1	Hegg, Steve	USA	51.548
	2	Golz, Rolf	FRG	50.736
	3	Nitz, Leonard Harvey	USA	50.698
	4	Woods, Dean	AUS	50.689

Men Points Race	August 03			
	1	Ilegems, Roger	BEL	37
	2	Messerschmidt, Uwe	FRG	15
	3	Youshimatz, Jose Manuel	MEX	29
	4	Mueller, Joerg	SUI	23
	5	Curuchet, Juan Esteban	ARG	20
	6	Clarke, Glenn	AUS	13

<table>
<tr><td colspan="6">

Men
Points Race
(cont.)

</td></tr>
</table>

Men **Points Race** **(cont.)**	August 03	7	Fowler, Brian	NZL	12
		8	Van Egmond, Derk Jan	HOL	56
		9	Marcussen, Michael	DEN	21
		10	Stieda, Alex	CAN	17

Men **4000 M** **Team Pursuit**	August 03				
		1	Grenda, Michael	AUS	54.137
			Nichols, Kevin	AUS	
			Turtur, Michael	AUS	
			Woods, Dean	AUS	
		2	Grylls, David	USA	53.362
			Hegg, Steve	USA	
			McDonough, R. Patrick	USA	
			Nitz, Leonard Harvey	USA	
		3	Alber, Reinhard	FRG	54.216
			Gola, Rolf	FRG	
			Günther, Roland	FRG	
			Marx, Michael	FRG	
		4	Amadio, Roberto	ITA	53.952
			Brunelli, Massimo	ITA	
			Colombo, Maurizio C.	ITA	
			Martinello, Silvio	ITA	

Men **Individual** **Road Race** **190.2 Km**	July 29				
		1	Grewal, Alexi	USA	4:59:57
		2	Bauer, Steve	CAN	G
		3	Lauritzen, Dag Otto	NOR	+0:21
		4	Saether, Morten	NOR	G
		5	Phinney, Davis	USA	+1:19
		6	Rogers, Thurlow	USA	G
		7	Ropret, Bojan	YUG	G
		8	Mora, Nestor	COL	G
		9	Kiefel, Ronald	USA	+1:43
		10	Trinkler, Richard	SUI	G

100 Km **Team**	August 05				
		1	Bartalini, Marcello	ITA	1:58:28
			Giovannetti, Marco	ITA	
			Poli, Eros	ITA	
			Vandelli, Claudio	ITA	
		2	Acherman, Alfred	SUI	2:02:38
			Trinkler, Richard	SUI	
			Vial, Laurent-P.	SUI	
			Wiss, Benno	SUI	
		3	Kiefel, Ronald	USA	2:02:46
			Knickman, Roy	USA	
			Phinney, Davis	USA	
			Weaver, Andrew	USA	
		4	Alberts, Johan	HOL	2:02:57
			Breukink, Erik	HOL	
			Ducrot, Martinus	HOL	
			Jakobs, Gert	HOL	

Equestrian Sports

Santa Anita Park
Fairbanks Ranch, Rancho Santa Fe

Individual **Dressage** **Competition**	August 10					
		1	Klimke, Dr. Reiner	*Ahlerich*	FRG	1504
		2	Jensen, Anne Grethe	*Marzog*	DEN	1442
		3	Hofer, Otto J.	*Limandus*	SUI	1364
		4	Bylund, Ingamay	*Aleks*	SWE	1332
		5	Krug, Herbert	*Muscadeur*	FRG	1323
		6	Sauer, Uwe	*Montevideo*	FRG	1279
		6	Bartle, Christopher	*Wily Trout*	GBR	1279
		8	Sanders-Keyzer, Annemarie	*Amon*	HOL	1271
		9	Stueckelberger, Christine	*Tansanit*	SUI	1257
		10	Boylen, Christilot	*Anklang*	CAN	1237

Team Dressage **Competition**	August 9					TOTAL INDIV	TOTAL TEAM
		1	Klimke, Dr. Reiner	*Ahlerich*	FRG	1797	4955
			Sauer, Uwe	*Montevideo*	FRG	1582	
			Krug, Herbert	*Muscadeur*	FRG	1576	
		2	Hofer, Otto J.	*Limandus*	SUI	1609	4673
			Stueckelberger, Christine	*Tansanit*	SUI	1606	
			DeBary, Amy Catherine	*Aintree*	SUI	1458	
		3	Hakanson, Ulla	*Flamingo*	SWE	1589	4630
			Bylund, Ingamay	*Aleks*	SWE	1582	
			Nathhorst, Louise	*Inferno*	SWE	1459	

Three-Day Event **Dressage Test** **Individual** **Classification**	July 30					
		1	Schmutz, Hansueli	*Oran*	SUI	39.80
		2	Davidson, Bruce	*J.J. Babu*	USA	49.00
		3	Stives, Karen	*Ben Arthur*	USA	49.20
		4	Todd, Mark	*Charisma*	NZL	51.60
		5	Morvillers, Pascal	*Gulliver "B"*	FRA	52.60
		6	Pettersson, Michael	*Up To Date*	SWE	54.00
		7	Holgate, Virginia	*Priceless*	GBR	56.40
		7	Stark, Ian	*Oxford Blue*	GBR	56.40
		7	Erhorn, Claus	*Fair Lady*	FRG	56.40
		10	Jonsson, Jan	*Isolde*	SWE	57.60

Three-Day Event **Endurance Test** **Individual** **Classification**	August 01					
		1	Stives, Karen	*Ben Arthur*	USA	49.20
		2	Todd, Mark	*Charisma*	NZL	51.60
		3	Holgate, Virginia	*Priceless*	GBR	56.80
		4	Fleischmann, Torrance	*Finvarra*	USA	60.40
		5	Checcoli, Mauro	*Spey Cast Boy*	ITA	62.00
		6	Morvillers, Pascal	*Gulliver "B"*	FRA	63.00
		7	Stark, Ian	*Oxford Blue*	GBR	63.60
		8	Green, Lucinda	*Regal Realm*	GBR	63.80
		9	Plumb, J. Michael	*Blue Stone*	USA	66.40
		10	Sciocchetti, Marina	*Master Hunt*	ITA	67.00

Three-Day Event **Jumping Individual** **Classification**	August 03					
		1	Todd, Mark	*Charisma*	NZL	51.60
		2	Stives, Karen	*Ben Arthur*	USA	54.20
		3	Holgate, Virginia	*Priceless*	GBR	56.80
		4	Fleischmann, Torrance	*Finvarra*	USA	60.40
		5	Morvillers, Pascal	*Gulliver "B"*	FRA	63.00
		6	Green, Lucinda	*Regal Realm*	GBR	63.80
		7	Sciocchetti, Marina	*Master Hunt*	ITA	67.00
		8	Checcoli, Mauro	*Spey Cast Boy*	ITA	67.00
		9	Stark, Ian	*Oxford Blue*	GBR	68.60
		10	Plumb, J. Michael	*Blue Stone*	USA	71.40

Three-Day Event **Team** **Classification**	August 03					
		1	Plumb, J. Michael	*Blue Stone*	USA	71.40
			Stives, Karen	*Ben Arthur*	USA	54.20
			Fleischmann, Torrance	*Finvarra*	USA	60.40
			Davidson, Bruce	*J.J. Babu*	USA	75.20
		2	Holgate, Virginia	*Priceless*	GBR	56.80
			Stark, Ian	*Oxford Blue*	GBR	68.60
			Clapham, Diana	*Windjammer*	GBR	165.20*
			Green, Lucinda	*Regal Realm*	GBR	63.80
		3	Hogrefe, Dietmar	*Foliant*	FRG	74.40
			Overesch, Bettina	*Peacetime*	FRG	79.60
			Tesdorpf, Burkhard	*Freedom*	FRG	216.05*
			Erhorn, Claus	*Fair Lady*	FRG	80.00

*Indicates not counted in team score

Individual Jumping **Competition**	August 12				TOTAL FINAL	FAULTS	TIME
		1 Fargis, Joe	*Touch of Class*	USA	4.00	0	58.06
		2 Homfeld, Conrad	*Abdullah*	USA	4.00	8	51.03
		3 Robbiani, Heidi	*Jessica V*	SUI	8.00	0	53.39
		4 Deslauriers, Mario	*Aramis*	CAN	8.00	4	57.07
		5 Candrian, Bruno	*Slygof*	SUI	8.00	8	58.10

Team Jumping **Competition**	August 07				TOTAL TEAM	TOTAL INDIV
		1 Fargis, Joe	*Touch of Class*	USA	.00	12.00
		Homfeld, Conrad	*Abdullah*	USA	8.00	
		Burr, Leslie	*Albany*	USA	12.00	
		Smith, Melanie	*Calypso*	USA	WD	
		2 Whitaker, Michael	*Overton Amanda*	GBR	8.00	36.75
		Whitaker, John	*Ryans Son*	GBR	20.75	
		Smith, Steven	*Shining Example*	GBR	27.00	
		Grubb, Timothy	*Linky*	GBR	28.25	
		3 Schockemohle, Paul	*Deister*	FRG	39.25	
		Luther, Peter	*Livius*	FRG	12.00	
		Sloothaak, Franke	*Farmer*	FRG	19.25	
		Ligges, Fritz	*Ramzes*	FRG	29.00	

WD = Withdrawn

Fencing

Long Beach Convention Center, Terrace Theater

Women **Foil-Individual**	August 03			
		1	Luan, Jujie	CHN
		2	Hanisch, Cornelia	FRG
		3	Vaccaroni, Dorina	ITA

Women Foil-Individual (cont.)	August 03			
4	Guzganu, Elisabeta		ROM	
5	Brouquier, Veronique		FRA	
6	Modaine, Laurence		FRA	
7	Bischoff, Sabine		FRG	
8	Gaudin, Brigitte		FRA	

Women Foil-Team	August 07		TD	TTD
1	Weber, Christiane	FRG	18	49
	Hanisch, Cornelia	FRG	17	
	Bischoff, Sabine	FRG	10	
	Funkenhauser, Zita	FRG	14	
	Wessel, Ute	FRG	0	
2	Dan, Aurora	ROM	10	49
	Veber, Koszto	ROM	6	
	Oros, Rozalia	ROM	15	
	Zsak, Marcela	ROM	13	
	Guzganu, Elisabeta	ROM	5	
3	Modaine, Laurence	FRA	15	64
	Trinquet-Hachin, Pascale	FRA	13	
	Gaudin, Brigitte	FRA	17	
	Brouquier, Veronique	FRA	19	
	Meygret, Anne	FRA	0	

Men Foil-Individual	August 02	
1	Numa, Mauro	ITA
2	Behr, Matthias	FRG
3	Cerioni, Stefano	ITA
4	Pietruszka, Frederick	FRA
5	Borella, Andrea	ITA
6	Gey, Mathias	FRG
7	Omnes, Philippe	FRA
8	Soumagne, Thierry	BEL

Men Sabre-Individual	August 04	
1	Lamour, Jean Francois	FRA
2	Marin, Marco	ITA
3	Westbrook, Peter	USA
4	Granger-Veyron, Herve	FRA
5	Gichot, Pierre	FRA
6	Mustata, Marin	ROM
7	Scalzo, Giovanni	ITA
8	Pop, Ioan	ROM

Men Épée-Individual	August 08	
1	Boisse, Philippe	FRA
2	Vaggo, Bjorne	SWE
3	Riboud, Philippe	FRA
4	Bellone, Stefano	ITA
5	Poffet, Michel	SUI
6	Borrmann, Elmar	FRG
7	Pusch, Alexander	FRG
8	Fischer, Volker	FRG

Men Foil-Team	August 07		TD	TTD
1	Numa, Mauro	ITA	20	60
	Borella, Andrea	ITA	12	
	Cerioni, Stefano	ITA	16	
	Scuri, Angelo	ITA	12	
	Cipressa, Andrea	ITA	0	
2	Behr, Matthias	FRG	14	52
	Gey, Mathias	FRG	12	
	Hein, Harald	FRG	17	
	Beck, Frank	FRG	9	
	Reichert, Klaus	FRG	0	
3	Omnes Philippe	FRG	12	54
	Groc, Patrick	FRG	15	
	Pietruszka, Frederick	FRG	13	
	Jolyot, Pascal	FRG	14	
	Cerboni, Marc	FRG	0	

Men Sabre-Team	August 09		TD	TTD
1	Marin, Marco	ITA	15	57
	Dalla Barba, Gianfranco	ITA	14	
	Scalzo, Giovanni	ITA	14	
	Meglio, Ferdinando	ITA	14	
	Arcidincono, Angelo	ITA	0	
2	Lamour, Jean Francois	FRA	13	44
	Guichot, Pierre	FRA	12	
	Granger-Veyron, Herve	FRA	11	
	Delrieu, Philippe	FRA	8	
	Ducheix, Franck	FRA	0	
3	Mustata, Marin	ROM	18	58
	Pop, Ioan	ROM	14	
	Chiculita, Alexandru	ROM	20	
	Marin, Corneliu	ROM	6	

Men Épée-Team	August 11		TD	TTD
1	Borrmann, Elmar	FRG	14	64
	Fischer, Volker	FRG	20	
	Heer, Gerhard	FRG	0	
	Nickel, Rafael	FRG	10	
	Pusch, Alexander	FRG	20	
2	Boisse, Philippe	FRA	13	54
	Henry, Jean Michel	FRA	0	
	Lenglet, Olivier	FRA	14	
	Riboud, Philippe	FRA	18	
	Salesse, Michel	FRA	9	
3	Bellone, Stefano	ITA	13	55
	Cuomo, Sandro	ITA	12	
	Ferro, Cosimo	ITA	0	
	Manzi, Roberto	ITA	15	
	Mazzoni, Angelo	ITA	15	

Football

The Rose Bowl
Stanford Stadium, Stanford, California
Harvard Stadium, Boston, Massachusetts
Navy-Marine Corps Memorial Stadium,
Annapolis, Maryland

Gold-Silver Match   August 11   FRA 2-BRA 0   Half Time 0-0

Rust, Albert	FRA	0	*
Ayache, William	FRA	0	*
Bibard, Michel	FRA	0	*
Bijotat, Dominique	FRA	0	*
Brisson, Francois	FRA	1	*
Cubaynes, Patrick	FRA	0	
Garande, Patrice	FRA	0	
Jeannol, Philippe	FRA	0	*
Lacombe, Guy	FRA	0	*
Lemoult, Jean-Claude	FRA	0	*
Rohr, Jean-Philippe	FRA	0	*
Senac, Didier	FRA	NP	
Thouvenel, Jean-Christoph	FRA	NP	
Toure, Jose	FRA	NP	
Xuereb, Daniel	FRA	1	*
Zanon, Jean-Louis	FRA	0	*
Bensoussan, Michel	FRA	NP	
Michel, Henri, Coach	FRA		
Rinaldi, Gilmar	BRA	0	*
Silva, Ronaldo	BRA	0	*
Brum, Jorge Luiz	BRA	0	*
Galvao, Mauro	BRA	0	*
Kaeser, Ademir Rock	BRA	0	*
Ferreira, Andre Luiz	BRA	0	*
Santos, Paulo	BRA	NP	
Verri, Carlos	BRA	0	*
Leiehardt Neto, Joao	BRA	0	*
Oliveira, Augilmar	BRA	0	*
Paiva, Silvio	BRA	0	*
Dias, Luiz	BRA	NP	
Winck, Luiz Carlos	BRA	NP	
Silva, Davi Cortez	BRA	NP	
Gil, Antonio Jose	BRA	0	*
Vidal Francisco	BRA	0	
Cruz, Milton	BRA	0	
Picemi, Jair, Coach	BRA		

Bronze Match   August 10   YUG 2-ITA 1   Half Time 0-1

YUG	ITA
Pudar, Ivan	Tancredi, Franco
Caplijic, Vlado	Ferri, Riccardo
Baljic, Mirsad	Galli, Filippo
Katanec, Srecko	Nela, Sebastiano
Elsner, Marko	Tricella, Roberto
Radanovic, Ljubomir	Vierchowod, Pietro
Smajic, Admir	Bagni, Salvatore
Gracan, Nenad	Baresi, Franco
Djurovski, Milko	Battistini, Sergio
Bazdarevic, Mehmed	Sabato, Antonio
Cvetkovic, Borislav	Vignola, Beniamino
Ivkovic, Tomislav	Zenga, Walter
Nikolic, Jovica	Fanna, Pietro
Deveric, Stjepan	Massaro, Daniele
Miljus, Branko	Briaschi, Massimo
Stojkovic, Dragan	Iorio, Maurizio
Mrkela, Mitar	Serena, Aldo
Toplak, Ivan, Coach	Bearzot, Enzo, Coach

*Starter

Gymnastics

Pauley Pavilion, University of California,
Los Angeles

Women	August 03				
Individual All-Around	1	Retton, Mary Lou	USA	79.175	
Competition	2	Szabo, Ecaterina	ROM	79.125	
	3	Pauca, Simona	ROM	78.675	
	4	McNamara, Julianne	USA	78.400	
	5	Cutina, Laura	ROM	78.300	
	6	Ma, Yanhong	CHN	77.950	
	7	Zhou, Ping	CHN	77.775	
	8	Chen, Yongyan	CHN	77.725	
	9	Kessler, Romi	SUI	77.525	
	10	Johnson, Kathy	USA	77.450	

Women	August 05				
Horse Vault	1	Szabo, Ecaterina	ROM	19.875	
	2	Retton, Mary Lou	USA	19.850	
	3	Agache, Lavinia	ROM	19.750	
	4	Talavera, Tracee	USA	19.700	
	5	Zhou, Ping	CHN	19.500	
	6	Lehmann, Brigitta	FRG	19.425	
	6	Brown, Kelly	CAN	19.425	
	8	Chen, Yongyan	CHN	19.300	

Women	August 05				
Uneven Bars	1	Ma, Yanhong	CHN	19.950	
	2	McNamara, Julianne	USA	19.950	
	3	Retton, Mary Lou	USA	19.800	
	4	Stanulet, Mihaela	ROM	19.650	
	5	Kessler, Romi	SUI	19.425	
	6	Zhou, Ping	CHN	19.350	
	7	Mochizuki, Noriko	JPN	19.325	
	8	Agache, Lavinia	ROM	19.150	

Women	August 05				
Balance Beam	1	Pauca, Simona	ROM	19.800	
	1	Szabo, Ecaterina	ROM	19.800	
	3	Johnson, Kathy	USA	19.650	
	4	Retton, Mary Lou	USA	19.550	
	5	Ma, Yanhong	CHN	19.450	
	6	Kessler, Romi	SUI	19.350	
	7	Wilhelm, Anja	FRG	19.200	
	7	Chen, Yongyan	CHN	19.200	

Women	August 05				
Floor Exercises	1	Szabo, Ecaterina	ROM	19.975	
	2	McNamara, Julianne	USA	19.950	
	3	Retton, Mary Lou	USA	19.775	
	4	Zhou, Qiurui	CHN	19.625	
	5	Kessler, Romi	SUI	19.575	
	6	Ma, Yanhong	CHN	19.450	
	7	Morio, Maiko	JPN	19.375	
	8	Cutina, Laura	ROM	19.150	

Women	August 11				
Rhythmic Competition	1	Fung, Lori	CAN	57.950	
	2	Staiculescu, Doina	ROM	57.900	
	3	Weber, Regina	FRG	57.700	
	4	Dragan, Alina	ROM	57.375	
	5	Reljin, Milena	YUG	57.250	
	6	Canton, Marta	ESP	56.950	
	7	Staccioli, Giulia	ITA	56.775	
	8	Yamasaki, Hiroko	JPN	56.675	
	9	Bobo, Marta	ESP	56.375	
	10	Simic, Daniela	YUG	56.325	

Women	August 11				
Team Competition	1	ROM		392.20	
	2	USA		391.20	
	3	CHN		388.60	

Men	August 02				
Individual	1	Gushiken, Koji	JPN	118.700	
All-Around	2	Vidmar, Peter	USA	118.675	
Competition	3	Li, Ning	CHN	118.575	
	4	Tong, Fei	CHN	118.550	
	5	Gaylord, Mitchell	USA	118.525	
	6	Conner, Bart	USA	118.350	
	7	Xu, Zhiquiang	CHN	118.225	
	8	Kajitani, Nobuyuki	JPN	117.375	
	9	Hirata, Noritoshi	JPN	117.200	
	10	Geiger, Jurgen	FRG	116.675	

Men	August 04				
Floor Exercises	1	Li, Ning	CHN	19.925	
	2	Lou, Yun	CHN	19.775	
	3	Sotomura, Koji	JPN	19.700	
	3	Vatuone, Philippe	FRA	19.700	
	5	Conner, Bart	USA	19.675	
	6	Pintea, Valentin	ROM	19.600	
	7	Vidmar, Peter	USA	19.550	
	8	Cushiken, Koji	JPN	19.450	

Men	August 04				
Side Horse	1	Li, Ning	CHN	19.950	
	1	Vidmar, Peter	USA	19.950	
	3	Daggett, Timothy	USA	19.825	
	4	Tong, Fei	CHN	19.750	
	5	Cairon, Jean-Luc	FRA	19.700	
	6	Kajitani, Nobuyuki	JPN	19.625	
	7	Gross, Benno	FRG	19.500	
	8	Zellweger, Josef	SUI	19.500	

Men	August 04				
Rings	1	Gushiken, Koji	JPN	19.850	
	1	Li, Ning	CHN	19.850	
	3	Gaylord, Mitchell	USA	19.825	
	4	Tong, Fei	CHN	19.750	
	4	Vidmar, Peter	USA	19.750	
	6	Yamawaki, Kyoji	JPN	19.725	
	7	Nicula, Emilian	ROM	19.500	
	8	Zellweger, Josef	SUI	19.375	

Men	August 04				
Horse Vault	1	Lou, Yun	CHN	19.950	
	2	Li, Ning	CHN	19.825	
	2	Gushiken, Koji	JPN	19.825	
	2	Gaylord, Mitchell	USA	19.825	
	2	Morisue, Shinji	JPN	19.825	
	6	Hartung, James	USA	19.800	
	7	Long, Warren	CAN	19.700	
	8	Wunderlin, Daniel	SUI	19.625	

Men	August 04				
Parallel Bars	1	Conner, Bart	USA	19.950	
	2	Kajitani, Nobuyuki	JPN	19.925	
	3	Gaylord, Mitchell	USA	19.850	
	4	Tong, Fei	CHN	19.825	
	5	Gushiken, Koji	JPN	19.800	
	6	Li, Ning	CHN	19.775	
	7	Winkler, Daniel	FRG	19.600	
	7	Geiger, Jurgen	FRG	19.600	

Men	August 04				
Horizontal Bar	1	Morisue, Shinji	JPN	20.000	
	2	Tong, Fei	CHN	19.975	
	3	Gushiken, Koji	JPN	19.950	
	4	Lou, Yun	CHN	19.850	
	4	Vidmar, Peter	USA	19.850	
	4	Daggett, Timothy	USA	19.850	
	7	Piatti, Marco	SUI	19.800	
	8	Wunderlin, Daniel	SUI	19.675	

Men	August 11				
Team Competition	1	USA		591.40	
	2	CHN		590.80	
	3	JPN		586.70	

Handball

Titan Gymnasium, California State
University, Fullerton
The Forum

Women	August 11				
Competition	1	YUG			
	2	KOR			
	3	CHN			

			PLAYED	WON	LOST	TIED	FOR	AGAINST	POINTS
Women	August 09								
Championship Pool	1	YUG	5	5	0	0	143	102	10
	2	KOR	5	3	1	1	125	119	7
	3	CHN	5	2	2	1	112	115	5
	4	FRG	5	2	3	0	91	100	4
	4	USA	5	2	3	0	114	123	4
	6	AUT	5	0	5	0	91	117	0

Women Championship Pool (cont.) — Tournament Progress

	YUG	CHN	KOR	FRG	AUT	USA
YUG	X	31-25	29-23	20-19	30-15	33-20
CHN	25-31	X	24-24	20-19	21-16	22-25
KOR	23-29	24-24	X	26-17	23-22	29-27
FRG	19-20	19-20	17-26	X	18-17	18-17
AUT	15-30	16-21	22-23	17-18	X	21-25
USA	20-33	25-22	27-29	17-18	25-21	X

Men Competition — August 11

1 YUG
2 FRG
3 ROM

Men Team Standing — August 11

A1-B1	YUG-FRG	18-17
A2-B2	ROM-DEN	23-19
A3-B3	ISL-SWE	24-26
A4-B4	SUI-ESP	18-17
A5-B5	JPN-USA	16-24
A6-B6	ALG-KOR	21-25

Final Standings

1	YUG	7	SUI
2	FRG	8	ESP
3	ROM	9	USA
4	DEN	10	JPN
5	SWE	11	KOR
6	ISL	12	ALG

Hockey

Weingart Stadium, East Los Angeles College

Women Competition — August 11

1 HOL
2 FRG
3 USA

Women Championship Pool Team Standing — August 10

	PLAYED	WON	LOST	TIED	FOR	AGAINST	POINTS
1 HOL	5	4	0	1	14	6	9
2 FRG	5	2	1	2	9	9	6
3 * USA	5	2	2	1	9	7	5
4 AUS	5	2	2	1	9	7	5
5 CAN	5	2	2	1	9	11	5
6 NZL	5	0	5	0	2	12	0

Pool Progress

	HOL	NZL	AUS	FRG	CAN	USA
HOL	X	2-1	2-0	6-2	2-2	2-1
NZL	1-2	X	0-3	0-1	1-4	0-2
AUS	0-2	3-0	X	2-2	1-2	3-1
FRG	2-6	1-0	2-2	X	3-0	1-1
CAN	2-2	4-1	2-1	0-3	X	1-4
USA	1-2	2-0	1-3	1-1	4-1	X

Men Competition — August 11

1 PAK
2 FRG
3 GBR

* Penalty stroke competition for the bronze medal.

Men Qualifying And Final Standing Matches — August 11

Qualifying Matches

A1-B2	AUS-PAK	0-1	
B1-A2	GBR-FRG	0-1	
A3-B4	IND-NZL	1-0	
B3-A4	HOL-ESP	0-0	P. STROKES: HOL 10-ESP 4
A5-B6	MAL-CAN	0-1	
B5-A6	KEN-USA	1-1	P. STROKES: KEN 6-USA 5

Matches for Final Standing

1-2	FRG-PAK	1-2	
3-4	AUS-GBR	2-3	
5-6	HOL-IND	2-5	
7-8	ESP-NZL	0-1	
9-10	CAN-KEN	0-1	
11-12	MAL-USA	3-3	P. STROKES: MAL 9-USA 8

Men Qualifying And Final Standing Matches — Final Standings

1	PAK	7	NZL
2	FRG	8	ESP
3	GBR	9	KEN
4	AUS	10	CAN
5	IND	11	MAL
6	HOL	12	USA

Judo

Eagle's Nest Arena, California State University, Los Angeles

Extra Lightweight — August 11

1	Hosokawa, Shinji	JPN
2	Kim, Jae-Yup	KOR
3	Liddie, Edward	USA
3	Eckersley, Neil	GBR

Half Lightweight — August 11

1	Matsuoka, Yoshiyuki	JPN
2	Hwang, Jung-Oh	KOR
3	Reiter, Josef	AUT
3	Alexandre, Marc	FRA

Lightweight — August 11

1	Ahn, Byeong-Keun	KOR
2	Gamba, Ezio	ITA
3	Onmura, Luis	BRA
3	Brown, Kerrith	GBR

Half Middleweight — August 11

1	Wieneke, Frank	FRG
2	Adams, Neil	GBR
3	Nowak, Michel	FRA
3	Fratica, Mircea	ROM

Middleweight — August 11

1	Seisenbacher, Peter	AUT
2	Berland, Robert	USA
3	Nose, Seiki	JPN
3	Carmona, Walter	BRA

Half Heavyweight — August 11

1	Ha, Hyoung-Zoo	KOR
2	Vieira, Douglas	BRA
3	Fridriksson, Bjarni	ISL
3	Neureuther, Gunter	FRG

Heavyweight — August 11

1	Saito, Hitoshi	JPN
2	Parisi, Angelo	FRA
3	Cho, Yong-Chul	KOR
3	Berger, Mark	CAN

Open Category — August 11

1	Yamashita, Yasuhiro	JPN
2	Rashwan, Mohamed	EGY
3	Cioc, Mihai	ROM
3	Schnabel, Arthur	FRG

Modern Pentathlon

Coto de Caza
Heritage Park Aquatic Center, Irvine

Individual Competition — August 01

			TOTAL	Riding	Fencing	Swimming	Shooting	Running
1	Masala, Daniele	ITA	5469	1100	956	1300	978	1135
2	Rasmuson, Svante	SWE	5456	1070	1022	1304	912	1148
3	Massullo, Carlo	ITA	5406	1100	758	1220	1066	1262
4	Phelps, Richard	GBR	5391	1100	912	1304	780	1295
5	Storm, Michael	USA	5325	1040	868	1288	1088	1041
6	Four, Paul	FRA	5287	1040	978	1204	1066	999
7	Sisniega, Ivar	MEX	5282	1070	912	1320	780	1200
8	Quesada, Jorge	ESP	5281	1060	890	1172	1000	1159
9	Hulkkonen, Pasi	FIN	5193	1010	846	1272	956	1109
10	Boube, Didier	FRA	5186	1070	890	1144	912	1170

Team Competition — August 05

1	ITA	16060
2	USA	15568
3	FRA	15565

Rowing
Lake Casitas

Women Single Sculls	August 04 Wind: 0 M/Sec Temp: 18 C			
	1	Racila, Valeria	ROM	3:40.68
	2	Geer, Charlotte	USA	3:43.89
	3	Haesebrouck, Ann	BEL	3:45.72
	4	Schreiner, Andrea	CAN	3:45.97
	5	Justesen, Lise Marianne	DEN	3:47.79
	6	Mitchell, Beryl	GBR	3:51.20

Women Double Sculls	August 04 Wind: 0 M/Sec Temp: 18 C			
	1	Popescu, Marioara	ROM	3:26.75
		Oleniuc, Elisabeta	ROM	
	2	Hellemans, Greet	HOL	3:29.13
		Hellemans, Nicolette	HOL	
	3	Laumann, Daniele	CAN	3:29.82
		Laumann, Silken	CAN	

Women Pair-Oars	August 04 Wind: 0 M/Sec Temp: 18 C			
	1	Arba, Rodica	ROM	3:32.60
		Horvat, Elena	ROM	
	2	Craig, Betty	CAN	3:36.06
		Smith, Tricia	CAN	
	3	Becker, Ellen	FRG	3:40.50
		Volkner, Iris	FRG	

Women Quadruple Sculls With Coxswain	August 04 Wind: 0 M/Sec Temp: 18 C			
	1	Taran, Titie	ROM	3:14.11
		Sorohan, Anisoara	ROM	
		Badea, Ioana	ROM	
		Corban, Sofia	ROM	
		Oancia, Ecaterina	ROM	
	2	Marden, Anne	USA	3:15.57
		Rohde, Lisa	USA	
		Lind, Joan	USA	
		Gilder, Virginia	USA	
		Rickon, Kelly	USA	
	3	Eriksen, Hanne Mandsf.	DEN	3:16.02
		Hanel, Birgitte	DEN	
		Koefoed, Charlotte	DEN	
		Rasmussen, Bodil Steen	DEN	
		Soeresen, Jette Hejli	DEN	

Women Four-Oars With Coxswain	August 04 Wind: 0 M/Sec Temp: 18 C			
	1	Lavric, Florica	ROM	3:19.30
		Fricioiu, Maria	ROM	
		Apostol, Chira	ROM	
		Bularda, Olga	ROM	
		Ioja, Viorica	ROM	
	2	Brain, Marilyn	CAN	3:21.55
		Schneider, Angie	CAN	
		Armbrust, Barbara	CAN	
		Tregunno, Jane	CAN	
		Thompson, Lesley	CAN	
	3	Grey-Gardner, Robyn	AUS	3:23.29
		Brancourt, Karen	AUS	
		Chapman, Susan	AUS	
		Foster, Margot	AUS	
		Lee, Susan	AUS	

Women Eight-Oars With Coxswain	August 04 Wind: 0 M/Sec Temp: 18 C			
	1	O'Steen, Shyril	USA	2:59.80
		Metcalf, Harriet	USA	
		Bower, Caroll	USA	
		Graves, Carie	USA	
		Flanagan, Jeanne	USA	
		Norellus, Kristine	USA	
		Thorsness, Kristen	USA	
		Keeler, Kathryn	USA	
		Beard, Betsy	USA	
	2	Balan, Doina	ROM	3:00.87
		Trasca, Marioara	ROM	
		Plesca, Aurora	ROM	
		Mihaly, Aneta	ROM	
		Chelariu, Adriana	ROM	
		Armasescu, Mihaela	ROM	
		Diaconescu, Camelia	ROM	
		Sauca, Lucia	ROM	
		Ioja, Viorica	ROM	
	3	Hellemans, Nicolette	HOL	3:02.92
		Cornet, Lynda	HOL	
		Van Ettekoven, Harriet	HOL	
		Hellemans, Greet	HOL	
		Drogenbroek Van, Marieke	HOL	
		Quist, Anne Marie	HOL	

Women Eight-Oars With Coxswain (cont.)	Neelissen, Catharina	HOL		
	Vaandrager, Willemien	HOL		
	Laurijsen, Martha	HOL		

Men Single Sculls	August 05 Wind: .5 M/Sec Temp: 20 C			
	1	Karppinen, Pertti	FIN	7:00.24
				+1:43.76
	2	Kolbe, Peter-Michael	FRG	7:02.19
				+1:46.57
	3	Mills, Robert	CAN	7:10.38
				+1:50.71
	4	Biglow, John	USA	7:12.00
				+1:46.07
	5	Ibarra, Ricardo D.	ARG	7:14.59
				+1:49.84
	6	Kontomanolis, Kostantinos	GRE	7:17.03
				+1:48.85

Men Double Sculls	August 05 Wind: .5 M/Sec Temp: 20 C			
	1	Lewis, Bradley	USA	6:36.87
		Enquist, Paul	USA	+1:38.14
	2	Deloof, Pierre-Marie	BEL	6:38.19
		Crois, Dirk	BEL	+1:41.90
	3	Pancic, Zoran	YUG	6:39.59
		Stanulov, Milorad	YUG	+1:40.05

Men Pair-Oars Without Coxswain	August 05 Wind: .5 M/Sec Temp: 20 C			
	1	Iosub, Petru	ROM	6:45.39
		Toma, Valer	ROM	+1:40.04
	2	Climent, Fernando	ESP	6:48.47
		Lasurtegui, Luis	ESP	+1:40.97
	3	Grepperud, Hans Magnus	NOR	6:51.81
		Loken, Sverre	NOR	+1:42.85

Men Pair-Oars With Coxswain	August 05 Wind: .5 M/Sec Temp: 20 C			
	1	Abbagnale, Carmine	ITA	7:05.99
		Abbagnale, Giuseppe	ITA	+1:47.80
		Di Capua, Giuseppe	ITA	
	2	Popescu, Dimitrie	ROM	7:11.21
		Tomoiaga, Vasile	ROM	+1:47.23
		Raducanu, Dumitru	ROM	
	3	Still, Kevin	USA	7:12.81
		Espeseth, Robert	USA	+1:48.08
		Herland, Douglas	USA	

Men Quadruple Sculls Without Coxswain	August 05m Wind: .5 M/Sec Temp: 20 C			
	1	Hedderich, Albert	FRG	5:57.55
		Hormann, Raimund	FRG	+1:27.25
		Wiedenmann, Dieter	FRG	
		Dursch, Mishael	FRG	
	2	Reedy, Paul	AUS	5:57.98
		Gullock, Gary	AUS	+1:29.15
		Mclaren, Timothy	AUS	
		Lovrich, Anthony	AUS	
	3	Hamilton, Doug	CAN	5:59.07
		Hughes, Mike	CAN	+1:28.56
		Monckton, Phil	CAN	
		Ford, Bruce	CAN	

Men Four-Oars Without Coxswain	August 05 Wind: 5M/sec. Temp: 18 C			
	1	O'Connel, Leslie	NZL	6:03.48
		O'Brien, Shane	NZL	1:28.59
		Robertson, Conrad	NZL	
		Trask, Keith	NZL	
	2	Clark, David	USA	6:06.10
		Smith, Jonathan	USA	1:30.16
		Stekl, Philip	USA	
		Forney, Alan	USA	
	3	Jensen, Michael	DEN	6:07.72
		Nielsen, Lars	DEN	1:28.95
		Rasmussen, Per H.S.	DEN	
		Christiansen, Erik	DEN	

Men Four-Oars With Coxswain	August 05 Wind: .5 M/Sec Temp: 20 C			
	1	Cross, Martin	GBR	6:18.64
		Budgett, Richard	GBR	+1:34.53
		Holmes, Andrew	GBR	
		Redgrave, Steven	GBR	
		Ellison, Adrian	GBR	
	2	Kiefer, Thomas	USA	6:20.28
		Springer, Gregory	USA	+1:37.15
		Bach, Michael	USA	
		Ives, Edward	USA	
		Stillings, John	USA	
	3	Lawton, Kevin	NZL	6:23.68
		Symon, Donald	NZL	+1:34.34
		Mabbott, Barrie	NZL	
		Tong, Ross	NZL	
		Hollister, Brett	NZL	

Men	August 05 Wind: .5 M/Sec Temp: 20 C			
Eight-Oars	1 Turner, Pat	CAN	5:41.32	
With Coxswain	Neufeld, Kevin	CAN	+1:24.99	
	Evans, Mark	CAN		
	Main, Grant	CAN		
	Steele, Paul	CAN		
	Evans, Mike	CAN		
	Crawford, Dean	CAN		
	Horm, Blair	CAN		
	McMahon, Brian	CAN		
	2 Lubsen, Walter Jr.	USA	+5:41.74	
	Sudduth, Andrew	USA	+1:23.26	
	Terwilliger, John	USA		
	Penny, Christopher	USA		
	Darling, Thomas	USA		
	Borchelt, Earl	USA		
	Clapp, Charles Iii	USA		
	Ibbetson, Bruce	USA		
	Jaugstetter, Robert	USA		
	3 Muller, Craig	AUS	5:43.40	
	Hefer, Clyde	AUS	+1:24.57	
	Patten, Sam	AUS		
	Willoughby, Timothy	AUS		
	Edmunds, Ian	AUS		
	Battersby, James	AUS		
	Popa, Ion	AUS		
	Evans, Steve	AUS		
	Thredgold, Gavin	AUS		

Shooting

Olympic Shooting Range, Prado Recreation Area

Women	August 05		
Air Rifle	1 Spurgin, Pat	USA	393
	2 Gufler, Edith	ITA	391
	3 Wu, Xiaoxuan	CHN	389
Women	August 05		
Standard Rifle	1 Wu, Xioxuan	CHN	581
	2 Holmer, Ulrike	FRG	578
	3 Jewell, Wanda	USA	578
Women	August 05		
Sport Pistol	1 Thom, Linda	CAN	585
	2 Fox, Ruby	USA	585
	3 Dench, Patricia	AUS	583
Men	August 05		
Rapid Fire Pistol	1 Kamachi, Takeo	JPN	595
	2 Ion, Corneliu	ROM	593
	3 Bies, Rauno	FIN	591
Men	August 05		
Free Pistol	1 Xu, Haifeng	CHN	566
	2 Skanaker, Ragnar	SWE	565
	3 Wang, Yifu	CHN	564
Men	August 05		
Running Game Target	1 Li, Yuwei	CHN	587
	2 Bellingrodt, Helmut	COL	584
	3 Huang, Shiping	CHN	581
Men	August 05		
Small-Bore Rifle	1 Cooper, Malcom	GBR	1173
Three Position	2 Nipkow, Daniel	SUI	1163
	3 Allan, Alister	GBR	1162
Men	August 05		
Small-Bore Rifle	1 Etzel, Edward	USA	599
Prone Position	2 Bury, Michel	FRA	596
	3 Sullivan, Michael	GBR	596
Men	August 05		
Air Rifle	1 Heberle, Philippe	FRA	589
	2 Kronthaler, Andreas D.I.	AUT	587
	3 Dagger, Barry	GBR	587
Trap Shooting	August 05		
	1 Giovannetti, Luciano	ITA	192
	2 Boza, Francisco	PER	192
	3 Carlisle, Daniel	USA	192

Skeet Shooting	August 05		
	1 Dryke, Matthew	USA	198
	2 Rasmussen, Ole Riber	DEN	196
	3 Scribani Rossi, Luca	ITA	196

Swimming

Olympic Swim Stadium,
  University of Southern California
Raleigh Runnels Memorial Pool,
  Pepperdine University

Women	July 29 World Record: 54.79 Olympic Record: 54.79			
100M Freestyle	1 Steinseifer, Carrie	USA	55.92	
	1 Hogshead, Nancy	USA	55.92	
	3 Verstappen, Annemarie	HOL	56.08	
Women	July 30 World Record: 1:57.75			
200M Freestyle	Olympic Record: 1:58:33			
	1 Wayte, Mary	USA	1:59.23	
	2 Woodhead, Cynthia	USA	1:59.50	
	3 Verstappen, Annemarie	HOL	1:59.69	
Women	July 31 World Record: 4:06.28 Olympic Record: 4:08.76			
400M Freestyle	1 Cohen, Tiffany	USA	4:07.10	*
	2 Hardcastle, Sarah	GBR	4:10.27	
	3 Croft, June	GBR	4:11.49	
Women	August 03 World Record: 8:24.62			
800M Freestyle	Olympic Record: 8:28.90			
	1 Cohen, Tiffany	USA	8:24.95	*
	2 Richardson, Michele	USA	8:30.73	
	3 Hardcastle, Sarah	GBR	8:32.60	
Women	July 31 World Record: 1:00.86 Olympic Record: 1:00.86			
100M Backstroke	1 Andrews, Theresa	USA	1:02.55	
	2 Mitchell, Betsy	USA	1:02.63	
	3 DeRover, Jolanda	HOL	1:02.91	
Women	Aug 04 World Record: 2:09.91			
200M Backstroke	Olympic Record: 2:11.77			
	1 DeRover, Jolanda	HOL	2:12.38	
	2 White, Amy	USA	2:13.04	
	3 Patrascoiu, Aneta	ROM	2:13.29	
Women	Aug 02 World Record: 1:08.51 Olympic Record: 1:10.11			
100M Breaststroke	1 Van Staveren, Petra	HOL	1:09.88	*
	2 Ottenbrite, Anne	CAN	1:10.69	
	3 Poirot, Catherine	FRA	1:10.70	
Women	July 30 World Record: 2:28.36 Olympic Record: 2:29.54			
200M Breaststroke	1 Ottenbrite, Anne	CAN	2:30.38	
	2 Rapp, Susan	USA	2:31.15	
	3 Lempereur, Ingrid	BEL	2:31.40	
Women	August 02 World Record: 57.93 Olympic Record: 59.05			
100M Butterfly	1 Meagher, Mary T.	USA	59.26	
	2 Johnson, Jenna	USA	1:00.19	
	3 Seick, Karin	FRG	1:01.36	
Women	August 04 World Record: 2:05.96			
200M Butterfly	Olympic Record: 2:10.44			
	1 Meagher, Mary T.	USA	2:06.90	*
	2 Phillips, Karen	AUS	2:10.56	
	3 Beyermann, Ina	FRG	2:11.91	
Women	August 03 World Record: 2:11.73			
200M Individual	Olympic Record: 2:14.47			
Medley	1 Caulkins, Tracy	USA	2:12.64	*
	2 Hogshead, Nancy	USA	2:15.17	
	3 Pearson, Michele	AUS	2:15.92	
Women	July 29 World Record: 4:36.10 Olympic Record: 4:36.29			
400M Individual	1 Caulkins, Tracy	USA	4:39.24	
Medley	2 Landells, Suzanne	AUS	4:48.30	
	3 Zindler, Petra	FRG	4:48.57	

† = New World Record
* = New Olympic Record

Women 4×100M Medley Relay	August 03	World Record: 4:05.79	Olympic Record: 4:06.67		
	1	Andrews, Theresa	USA	4:08.34	
		Caulkins, Tracy			
		Meagher, Mary T.			
		Hogshead, Nancy			
	2	Schlicht, Svenja	FRG	4:11.97	
		Hasse, Ute			
		Beyemann, Ina			
		Seick, Karin			
	3	Abdo, Reema	CAN	4:12.98	
		Ottenbrite, Annie			
		MacPherson, Michelle			
		Rai, Pamela			

Women 4×100M Freestyle Relay	July 31	World Record: 3:42.71	Olympic Record: 3:42.71		
	1	Johnson, Jenna	USA	3:43.43	
		Steinseifer, Carrie			
		Torres, Dara			
		Hogshead, Nancy			
	2	Verstappen, Annemarie	HOL	3:44.40	
		Voskes, Elles			
		Reijers, Desi			
		Van Bentum, Conny			
	3	Zscherpe, Iris	FRG	3:45.56	
		Schuster, Suzanne			
		Pielke, Christiane			
		Seick, Karin			

Men 100M Freestyle	July 31	World Record: 49.36	Olympic Record: 49.99		
	1	Gains, Ambrose	USA	49.80	*
	2	Stockwell, Mark	AUS	50.24	
	3	Johansson, Per	SWE	50.31	

Men 200M Freestyle	July 29	World Record 1:47.55	Olympic Record: 1:48.03		
	1	Gross, Michael	FRG	1:47.44	*†
	2	Heath, Michael	USA	1:49.10	
	3	Fahrner, Thomas	FRG	1:49.66	

Men 400M Freestyle	August 02	World Record: 3:48.32	Olympic Record: 3:51.31		
	1	Dicarlo, George	USA	3:51.23	*
	2	Mykkanen, John	USA	3:51.49	
	3	Lemberg, Justin	AUS	3:51.79	

Men 1500M Freestyle	August 04	World Record: 14:54.76	Olympic Record: 14:58.27		
	1	O'Brien, Michael	USA	15:05.20	
	2	Dicarlo, George	USA	15:10.59	
	3	Pfeiffer, Stefan	FRG	15:12.11	

Men 100M Backstroke	August 03	World Record: 55:19	Olympic Record: 55:49		
	1	Carey, Richard	USA	55:79	
	2	Wilson, David	USA	56.35	
	3	West, Mike	CAN	56.49	

Men 200M Backstroke	July 31	World Record: 1:58.86	Olympic Record: 1:58.99		
	1	Carey, Richard	USA	2:00.23	
	2	Delcourt, Frederic	FRA	2:01.75	
	3	Henning, Cameron	CAN	2:02.37	

Men 100M Breaststroke	July 29	World Record: 1:02.13	Olympic Record: 1:02.16		
	1	Lindquist, Steve	USA	1:01.65	*†
	2	Davis, Victor	CAN	1:01.99	
	3	Evans, Peter	AUS	1:02.97	

Men 200M Breaststroke	August 02	World Record: 2:14.58	Olympic Record: 2:15.11		
	1	Davis, Victor	CAN	2:13.34	*†
	2	Beringen, Glenn	AUS	2:15.79	
	3	Dagon, Etienne	SUI	2:17.41	

Men 100M Butterfly	July 30	World Record: 53.38	Olympic Record: 53.78		
	1	Gross, Michael	FRG	53.08	*†
	2	Morales, Pedro Pablo	USA	53.23	
	3	Buchanan, Glenn	AUS	53.85	

Men 200M Butterfly	August 03	World Record: 1:57.05	Olympic Record: 1:58.72		
	1	Sieben, John	AUS	1:57.04	*†
	2	Gross, Michael	FRG	1:57.40	
	3	Vidal Castor, Rafael	VEN	1:57.51	

Men 200M Individual Medley	August 04	World Record: 2:02.25	Olympic Record: 2:03.60		
	1	Baumann, Alex	CAN	2:01.42	*†
	2	Morales, Pedro Pablo	USA	2:03.05	
	3	Cochran, Neil	GBR	2:04.38	
	3	Cochran, Neil	GBR	2:04.38	

Men 400M Individual Medley	July 30	World Record 4:17.53	Olympic Record 4:22.89		
	1	Baumann, Alex	CAN	4:17.41	† *
		Prado Ricardo	BRA	4:18.45	
		Woodhouse, Robert	AUS	4:20.50	

Men 4 X 100M Medley Relay	August 04	World Record: 3:40.42	Olympic Record: 3:42.22		
	1	Carey, Richard	USA	3:39.30	*†
		Lundquist, Steve			
		Morales, Pedro Pablo			
		Gaines, Ambrose			
	2	West Mike	CAN	3:43.23	
		Davis, Victor			
		Ponting, Tom			
		Goss, Sandy			
	3	Kerry, Mark	AUS	3:43.25	
		Evans, Peter			
		Buchanan, Glenn			
		Stockwell, Mark			

Men 4 X 100M Freestyle Relay	August 02	World Record: 3:19.26	Olympic Record: 3:19.94		
	1	Cavanaugh, Christopher	USA	3:19.03	*†
		Heath, Michael			
		Biondi, Matthew			
		Gaines, Ambrose			
	2	Fasala, Gregory	AUS	3:19.68	
		Brooks, Neil			
		Delany, Michael			
		Stockwell, Mark			
	3	Leidstrom, Thomas	SWE	3:22.69	
		Baron, Bengt			
		Om, Mikael			
		Johansson, Per			

Men 4 X 200M Freestyle Relay	July 30	World Record: 7:18.87	Olympic Record: 7:18.87		
	1	Heath, Michael	USA	7:15.69	*†
		Larson, David			
		Float, Jeffery			
		Hayes, Lawrence Bruce			
	2	Fahrner, Thomas	FRG	7:15.73	
		Korthals, Dirk			
		Schowtka, Alexander			
		Gross, Michael			
	3	Cochran, Neil	GBR	7:24.78	
		Easter, Paul			
		Howe, Paul			
		Astbury, Andrew			

Water Polo
Top Three
Team Standings

August 10

1	Krivokapic, Milorad	YUG
2	Lusic, Deni	YUG
3	Petrovic, Zoran	YUG
4	Vuletic, Bozo	YUG
5	Djuho, Veselin	YUG
6	Roje, Zoran*	YUG
7	Bebic, Milivoj	YUG
8	Bukic, Perica	YUG
9	Sukno, Goran	YUG
10	Paskvalin, Tomislav	YUG
11	Milanovic, Igor	YUG
12	Andric, Dragan	YUG
13	Popovic, Andrija**	YUG
1	Wilson, Craig	USA
2	Robertson, Kevin	USA
3	Figueroa, Gary	USA
4	Campbell, Peter	USA
5	Burke, Douglas	USA
6	Vargas, Joseph	USA
7	Svendsen, Jon	USA
8	Siman, John	USA
9	McDonald, Andrew	USA
10	Schroeder, Terry*	USA
11	Campbell, Jody	USA
12	Shaw, Timothy	USA
13	Dorst, Christopher**	USA
1	Rohle, Peter	FRG
2	Loebb, Thomas	FRG
3	Otto, Frank	FRG
4	Hoppe, Rainer	FRG
5	Fernandez, Armando	FRG
6	Huber, Thomas	FRG
7	Schroder, Jurgen	FRG
8	Osselmann, Rainer	FRG
9	Stamm, Hagen	FRG
10	Freund, Roland*	FRG
11	Theismann, Dirk	FRG
12	Chalmovsky, Santiago	FRG
13	Obschernikat, Werner**	FRG

*Captain **Alternate

† = New World Record
* = New Olympic Record

Water Polo
Final Standings — August 10

1	YUG	9	14	5	4	0	1	47	33
2	USA	9	9	5	4	0	1	43	34
3	FRG	5	15	5	2	2	1	49	34
4	ESP	4	-4	5	1	2	2	42	46
5	AUS	3	-11	5	1	3	1	37	48
6	HOL	0	-23	5	0	5	0	25	48

Women Springboard Diving — August 06

1	Bernier, Sylvie	CAN	530.70
2	McCormick, Kelly	USA	527.46
3	Seufert, Christina	USA	517.62
4	Li, Yihua	CHN	506.52
5	Li, Qiaoxian	CHN	487.68
6	Tenorio, Elsa	MEX	463.56
7	Smith, Lesley	ZIM	451.89
8	Fuller, Debbie	CAN	450.99
9	Donnet, Jennifer	AUS	443.13
10	Jongejans, Daphne	HOL	437.40

Women Platform Diving — August 10

1	Zhou, Jihong	CHN	435.51
2	Mitchell, Michele	USA	431.19
3	Wyland, Wendy	USA	422.07
4	Chen, Xiaoxia	CHN	419.76
5	Beddoe, Valerie	AUS	388.56
6	Fuller, Debbie	CAN	371.49
7	Tenorio, Elsa	MEX	360.45
8	Canseco, Guadalupe	MEX	352.89
9	Mabuchi, Yoshino	JPN	349.95
10	Kent, Julie	AUS	346.44

Men Springboard Diving — August 08

1	Louganis, Gregory	USA	754.41
2	Tan, Liangde	CHN	662.31
3	Merriott, Ronald	USA	661.32
4	Li, Hongping	CHN	646.35
5	Snode, Christopher	GBR	609.51
6	Italiani, Piero	ITA	578.94
7	Killat, Albin	FRG	569.52
8	Foley, Stephen	AUS	561.93
9	Mondragon, Jorge	MEX	550.35
10	Doerr, Dieter	FRG	549.33

Men Platform Diving — August 12

1	Louganis, Gregory	USA	710.91
2	Kimball, Bruce	USA	643.50
3	Li, Kongzheng	CHN	638.28
4	Tong, Hui	CHN	604.77
5	Killat, Albin	FRG	551.97
6	Doerr, Dieter	FRG	536.07
7	Snode, Christopher	GBR	524.40
8	Bedard, David	CAN	518.13
9	Foley, Stephen	AUS	479.43
10	Zavala, Miguel Angel	MEX	476.82

Women Sychronized Swimming — August 12

1	Ruiz, Tracie	USA	198.467
2	Waldo, Carolyn	CAN	195.300
3	Motoyoshi, Miwako	JPN	187.050
4	Engelen, Marijke	HOL	182.632
5	Hanisch, Gudrun	FRG	182.017
6	Holmyard, Caroline	GBR–USA	182.000
7	Hermine, Muriel	FRA	180.534
8	Singer, Karin	SUI	178.383

Women Sychronized Swimming Duet — August 09

1	Costie, Candy	USA	195.584
	Ruiz, Tracie	USA	
2	Hambrook, Sharon	CAN	194.234
	Kryczka, Kelly	CAN	
3	Kimura, Saeko	JPN	187.992
	Motoyoshi, Miwako	JPN	
4	Holmyard, Caroline	GBR	184.050
	Wilson, Carolyn	GBR	
5	Boss, Edith	SUI	180.109
	Singer, Karin	SUI	
6	Eijken, Catrien	HOL	179.058
	Engelen, Marijke	HOL	
7	Besson, Pascale	FRA	176.709
	Hermine, Muriel	FRA	
8	Novelo, Claudia	MEX	176.409
	Ramirez, Pilar	MEX	

† = New World Record
* = New Olympic Record

Volleyball
The Long Beach Arena

Women Gold/Silver Game — August 07 USA 0-CHN 3 SETS (14-16, 3-15, 9-15)

1	Lang, Ping	CHN
2	Liang, Yan	CHN
3	Zhu, Ling	CHN
4	Hou, Yuzhu	CHN
5	Zhou, Xiaolan	CHN
6	Yang, Xilan	CHN
7	Su, Huijuan	CHN
8	Jiang, Ying	CHN
9	Li, Yanjun	CHN
10	Yang, Xiaojun	CHN
11	Zheng, Meizhu	CHN
12	Zhang, Rongfang	CHN
	Yuan, Weimin, Coach	CHN

1	Weishoff, Paula	USA
2	Woodstra, Susan	USA
3	Crockett, Rita	USA
5	Flachmeier, Laurie	USA
6	Becker, Carolyn	USA
7	Hyman, Flora	USA
8	Magers, Rose	USA
9	Vollersten, Julie	USA
10	Green, Debbie	USA
11	Ruddins, Kimberly	USA
12	Beauprey, Jeanne	USA
14	Chisholm, Linda	USA
	Selinger, Arie, Coach	USA

Women Bronze Game — August 07 PER 1-JPN 3 SETS (15-13, 4-15, 7-15, 10-15)

1	Egami, Yumi	JPN
2	Morita, Kimie	JPN
3	Mitsuya, Yuko	JPN
4	Hirose, Miyoko	JPN
5	Ishida, Kyoko	JPN
6	Kagabu, Yoko	JPN
7	Hiro, Norie	JPN
8	Sugiyama, Kayoko	JPN
9	Otani, Sachiko	JPN
10	Miyajima, Keiko	JPN
11	Odaka, Emiko	JPN
12	Nakada, Kumi	JPN
	Yamada, Shigeo, Coach	JPN

1	Pimentel, Carmen	PER
2	Chaparro, Ana Rosa	PER
3	Garcia, Rose	PER
4	Heredia, Isabel	PER
5	Perez Del Solar, Gabriela	PER
6	Del Risco, Cecilia	PER
7	Tait, Cecilia	PER
8	Cervera, Luisa	PER
9	Fajardo, Denisse	PER
10	Gallardo, Miriam	PER
11	Torrealva, Gina	PER
12	Malaga, Natalia	PER
	Park, Man Bok, Coach	PER

Women Semi–Final, Finals and Final Standings — August 07

SEMI-FINALS

A1-B2	USA-PER	3-0	(16-14, 15-9, 15-10)
A2-B1	CHN-JPN	3-0	(15-10, 15-7, 15-4)
A3-B4	FRG-CAN	3-0	(15-5, 15-7, 15-1)
A4-B3	BRA-KOR	1-3	(15-13, 13-15, 9-15, 10-15)

FINALS

1-2	USA-CHN	0-3	(14-16, 3-15, 9-15)
3-4	PER-JPN	1-3	(15-13, 4-15, 7-15, 10-15)
5-6	FRG-KOR	0-3	(10-15, 10-15, 2-15)
7-8	CAN-BRA	0-3	(9-15, 3-15, 8-15)

FINAL STANDING

1-CHN	2-USA
3-JPN	4-PER
5-KOR	6-FRG
7-BRA	8-CAN

Men Gold/Silver Game — August 11 USA 3 - BRA 0 SETS (15-6, 15-6, 15-7)

1	Dvorak, Dusty	USA
2	Saunders, Dave	USA
3	Salmons, Steve	USA

Men	4	Sunderland, Paul	USA
Gold/Silver	5	Duwelius, Rich	USA
Game	6	Timmons, Steve	USA
(cont.)	7	Buck, Craig	USA
	9	Waldie, Marc	USA
	10	Marlowe, Chris	USA
	12	Berzins, Aldis	USA
	13	Powers, Pat	USA
	15	Kirlay, Karch	USA
		Beal, Doug, Coach	USA
	1	Rezende, Bernardo	BRA
	2	Oliveira Neto, Mario Xand	BRA
	3	Ribeiro, Antonio	BRA
	4	Montanaro Junior, Jose	BRA
	5	Nascimento, Ruy Campus	BRA
	6	Dal Zotto, Renan	BRA
	7	Silva, William	BRA
	8	Ribeiro, Amauri	BRA
	9	Freire, Marcus	BRA
	10	Lampariello Neto,Domingo	BRA
	12	Rajzman, Bernard	BRA
	14	D'Avila, Fernando	BRA
		Freitas, Paulo, Coach	BRA

Men	August 11 CAN 0 - ITA 3 SETS (11-15, 12-15, 8-15)		
Bronze	1	Negri, Marco	ITA
Game	2	Lucchetta, Pier Paolo	ITA
	3	Dametto, Gian Carlo	ITA
	4	Bertoli, Franco	ITA
	5	Dall'Olio, Francesco	ITA
	6	Rebaudengo, Piero	ITA
	7	Errichiello, Giovanni	ITA
	8	De Luigi, Guido	ITA
	9	Vullo, Fabio	ITA
	10	Lanfranco, Giovanni	ITA
	11	Vecchi, Paolo	ITA
	12	Lucchetta, Andrea	ITA
		Prandi, Silvando, Coach	ITA
	1	Hoag, Glenn	CAN
	2	Danyluk, Terry	CAN
	3	Barrett, John	CAN
	4	Jones, Dave	CAN
	5	Gratton, Paul	CAN
	6	Coulter, Al	CAN
	7	Jones, Tom	CAN
	9	Saxton, Don	CAN
	10	Wagner, Randy	CAN
	11	Kertzynski, Alex	CAN
	12	Bacon, Rick	CAN
	15	Pischke, Garth	CAN
		Maeda, Ken, Coach	CAN

Men
Semi-Final, Finals
and Final Standings

August 11

SEMI-FINALS
A1-B2	BRA-ITA	3-1 (12-15, 15-2, 15-3, 15-5)
A2-B1	USA-CAN	3-0 (15-6, 15-10, 15-7)
A3-B4	KOR-CHN	3-1 (15-4, 15-11, 6-15, 19-17)
A4-B3	ARG-JPN	3-1 (9-15, 15-10, 15-10, 15-11)

FINALS
1-2	USA-BRA	3-0 (15-6, 15-6, 15-7)
3-4	CAN-ITA	0-3 (11-15, 12-15, 8-15)
5-6	KOR-ARG	3-1 (15-13, 9-15, 15-9, 15-7)
7-8	JPN-CHN	3-0 (16-14, 15-9, 15-6)
9-10	TUN-EGY	3-2 (15-13, 15-9, 5-15, 13-15, 15-5)

FINAL STANDING
1-USA	2-BRA
3-ITA	4-CAN
5-KOR	6-ARG
7-JPN	8-CHN
9-TUN	10-EGY

Weightlifting

Albert Gersten Pavilion
Loyola Marymount Universtiy

August 09
Up to 52 kg	1	Zeng, Guoqiang	CHN	235.0
	2	Zhou, Peishun	CHN	235.0
	3	Manabe, Kazushito	JPN	232.5

Up to 56 kg	1	Wu, Shude	CHN	267.5
	2	Lai, Runming	CHN	265.0
	3	Kotaka, Masahiro	JPN	252.5
Up to 60 kg	1	Chen, Weiqiang	CHN	282.5
	2	Radu, Gelu	ROM	280.0
	3	Tsai, Wen-Yee	TPE	272.5
Up to 67.5 kg	1	Yao, Jingyuan	CHN	320.0
	2	Socaci, Andrei	ROM	312.5
	3	Jouni Gronman	FIN	312.5
Up to 75 kg	1	Radschinsky, Karl-Heinz	FRG	340.0
	2	Demers, Jacques	CAN	335.0
	3	Cioroslan, Dragomir	ROM	332.5
Up to 82.5 kg	1	Becheru, Petre	ROM	335.0
	2	Kabbas, Robert	AUS	342.5
	3	Isaoko, Ryoji	JPN	340.0
Up to 90 kg	1	Vlad, Nicu	ROM	392.5
	2	Petre, Dumitru	ROM	360.0
	3	Mercer, David	GBR	352.5
Up to 100 kg	1	Milser, Rolf	FRG	385.0
	2	Gropa, Vasile	ROM	382.5
	3	Niemi, Pekka	FIN	367.5
Up to 110 kg	1	Oberburger, Norberto	ITA	390.0
	2	Tasnadi, Stefan	ROM	380.0
	3	Carlton, Guy	USA	377.5
Over 110 kg	1	Lukim, Dinko	AUS	412.5
	2	Martinez, Mario	USA	410.0
	3	Nerlinger, Manfred	FRG	397.5

Wrestling

Anaheim Convention Center

August 12
Freestyle 48 kg	1	Weaver, Robert	USA
	2	Irie, Takashi	JPN
	3	Son, Gab-Do	KOR
Freestyle 52 kg	1	Trstena, Saban	YUG
	2	Kim, Jong-Ku	KOR
	3	Takada, Yuji	JPN
Freestyle 57 kg	1	Tomiyama, Hideaki	JPN
	2	Davis, Barry	USA
	3	Kim, Eui-Kon	KOR
Freestyle 62 kg	1	Lewis, Randy	USA
	2	Akaishi, Kosei	JPN
	3	Lee, Jung-Keun	KOR
Freestyle 68 kg	1	You, In-Tak	KOR
	2	Rein, Andrew	USA
	3	Rauhala, Jukka	FIN
Freestyle 74 kg	1	Schultz, David	USA
	2	Knosp, Martin	FRG
	3	Sejdi, Saban	YUG
Freestyle 82 kg	1	Schultz, Mark	USA
	2	Nagashima, Hideyuki	JPN
	3	Rinke, Chris	CAN
Freestyle 90 kg	1	Banach, Ed	USA
	2	Ohta, Akira	JPN
	3	Loban, Noel	GBR
Freestyle 100 kg	1	Banach, Lou	USA
	2	Atiyeh, Joseph	SYR
	3	Puscasu, Vasile	ROM
Freestyle +100 kg	1	Baumgartner, Bruce	USA
	2	Molle, Bob	CAN
	3	Taskin, Ayhan	TUR
Greco Roman 48 kg	1	Maenza, Vincenzo	ITA
	2	Scherer, Markus	FRG
	3	Saito, Ikuzo	JPN

Greco Roman	1	Miyahara, Atsuji	JPN
52 kg	2	Aceves, Daniel	MEX
	3	Bang, Dae-Du	KOR

Greco Roman	1	Passarelli, Pasquale	FRG
57 kg	2	Eto, Masaki	JPN
	3	Holidis, Haralambos	GRE

Greco Roman	1	Kim, Weon-Kee	KOR
62 kg	2	Johansson, Kentolle	SWE
	3	Dietsche, Hugo	SUI

Greco Roman	1	Lisjak, Vlado	YUG
68 kg	2	Sipila, Tapio	FIN
	3	Martinez, James	USA

Greco Roman	1	Salomaki, Jouko	FIN
74 kg	2	Tallroth, Roger	SWE
	3	Rusu, Stefan	ROM

Greco Roman	1	Draica, Ion	ROM
82 kg	2	Thanopoulos, Dimitrios	GRE
	3	Claeson, Soren	SWE

Greco Roman	1	Fraser, Steven	USA
90 kg	2	Matei, Ilie	ROM
	3	Andersson, Frank	SWE

Greco Roman	1	Andrei, Vasile	ROM
100 kg	2	Gibson, Greg	USA
	3	Tertelje, Jozef	YUG

Greco Roman	1	Blatnick, Jeffrey	USA
+100 kg	2	Memisevic, Refik	YUG
	3	Dolipschi, Victor	ROM

Yachting
Long Beach Marina and Harbor

Windglider Class Race Summary	August 08				
	1	Van Den Berg, Stephan	HOL	44.70	27.70
	2	Steele, Randall Scott	USA	66.00	46.00
	3	Kendall, Bruce	NZL	91.40	46.40
	4	Guillerot, Gildas	FRA	97.40	52.40
	5	Maran, Klaus	ITA	69.40	54.40
	6	Hyde, Greg	AUS	73.70	55.70
	7	Meyer, Dirk	FRG	93.20	67.20
	8	Eybl, Bjoern	AUT	97.00	80.00
	9	Bonello, Peter	MLT	101.70	82.70
	10	Nystrom, Hans	SWE	129.00	84.00

Sailing Class Race Summary	August 08				
	1	Haines Jr., Robert	USA	62.70	33.70
		Tevelyan, Edward	USA		
		Davis, Roderick	USA		
	2	Grael, Torben	BRA	59.40	43.40
		Alder, Daniel	BRA		
		Senfft, Ronaldo	BRA		
	3	Fogh, Hans	CAN	63.70	49.70
		Kerr, John	CAN		
		Calder, Steve	CAN		

Flying Dutchman Class Race Summary	August 08				
	1	McKee, Jonathan	USA	31.40	19.70
		Buchan, William Carl	USA		
	2	McLaughlin, Terry	CAN	36.70	22.70
		Bastet, Evert	CAN		
	3	Richards, Jonathan	GBR	65.70	48.70
		Allam, Peter	GBR		

Star Class Race Summary	August 08				
	1	Buchan, William E.	USA	55.70	29.70
		Erickson, Stephen	USA		
	2	Griese, Joachim	FRG	67.40	41.40
		Marcour, Michael	FRG		
	3	Gorla, Giorgio	ITA	56.50	43.50
		Peraboni, Alfio	ITA		

Finn Class Race Summary	August 08				
	1	Coutts, Russell	NZL	61.70	34.70
	2	Bertrand, John	USA	72.00	37.00
	3	Neilson, Terry	CAN	57.70	37.70
	4	Blanco, Joaquin	ESP	95.70	60.70

Finn Class Race Summary (cont.)	5	Gerz, Wolfgang	FRG	101.10	66.10
	6	Pratt, Chris	AUS	86.00	68.00
	7	Mcintyre, Michael	GBR	91.70	70.70
	8	Zarif Neto, Jorge	BRA	103.70	78.70
	9	Neeleman, Mark	HOL	116.70	81.70
	10	Bengtsson, Ingvar	SWE	113.00	84.00

Tornado Class Race Summary	August 08				
	1	Sellers, Rex	NZL	41.70	14.70
		Timms, Christopher	NZL		
	2	Smyth, Randy	USA	64.00	37.00
		Glaser, Jay	USA		
	3	Cairns, Chris	AUS	77.40	50.40
		Anderson, John	AUS		

470 Class Race Summary	August 08				
	1	Doreste, Luis	ESP	68.70	33.70
		Molina, Roberto	ESP		
	2	Benjamin, Stephen	USA	78.00	43.00
		Steinfeld, H. Christopher	USA		
	3	Peponnet, Thierry	FRA	69.40	49.40
		Pillot, Luc	FRA		

Baseball
Dodger Stadium

Gold / Silver Game	August 07			AB	R	H	RBI
2B	Shoda, Kozo		JPN	3	3	1	0
C	Shimada, Munehiko		JPN	4	0	1	1
CF	Kumano, Terumitsu		JPN	3	2	1	0
RF	Arai, Yukio		JPN	4	0	2	1
1B	Hirosawa, Katsumi		JPN	4	1	2	4
LF	Morita, Noboru		JPN	4	0	0	0
DH	Hata, Shinji		JPN	1	0	0	0
DH	Wada, Yutaka		JPN	3	0	0	0
3B	Urahigashi, Yasushi		JPN	4	0	1	0
SS	Morita, Yoshihiko		JPN	3	0	0	0
Totals				**33**	**6**	**8**	**6**

				AB	R	H	RBI
CF	McDowell, Oddibe	USA	4	0	0	0	
RF	Gwynn, Chris	USA	3	0	0	0	
DH	Clark, William	USA	4	0	0	0	
1B	McGwire, Mark	USA	3	1	1	0	
3B	Snyder, James	USA	3	1	2	2	
C	Marzano, John	USA	3	0	0	0	
LF	Mack, Shane	USA	3	1	1	1	
PH	Surhoff, William	USA	1	0	1	0	
SS	Green, Gary	USA	4	0	1	0	
2B	Affaro, Flavio	USA	4	0	1	0	
Totals			**32**	**3**	**7**	**3**	

Bronze Game	August 07			AB	R	H	RBI
LF	Li, Chih-Chun		TPE	6	1	1	0
SS	Wu, Fu-Lien		TPE	6	0	1	0
3B	Lin, Hua-Wei		TPE	6	1	1	1
1B	Chao, Shih-Chiang		TPE	2	0	0	0
PR	Wu, Te-Shen		TPE	0	0	0	0
1B	Yang, Ching-Long		TPE	3	1	1	2
DH	Chiang, Tai-Chuan		TPE	6	0	1	0
RF	Lin, I-Tseng		TPE	4	0	2	0
CF	Lee, Chu-Ming		TPE	5	0	1	0
C	Twu, Jong-Nan		TPE	5	0	1	0
2B	Leu, Wen-Sheng		TPE	5	0	1	0
Totals				**48**	**3**	**10**	**3**

				AB	R	H	RBI
LF	Lee, Soon Chul	KOR	6	0	0	0	
CF	Park, Heung-Sik	KOR	5	0	0	0	
3B	Kim, Yong-Kuk	KOR	6	0	0	0	
DH	Park, Noh-Jun	KOR	6	0	0	0	
2B	Kang, Ki-Woong	KOR	5	0	1	0	
1B	Kim, Hyoung-Suk	KOR	4	0	0	0	
RF	Lee, Jong-Doo	KOR	1	0	0	0	
PH	Lee, Kang-Don	KOR	1	0	0	0	
RF	Choy, Kai-Young	KOR	1	0	0	0	
SS	Ahn, Un-Hak	KOR	3	0	0	0	
SS	Baek, In-Ho	KOR	2	0	2	0	
C	Kim, Young-Sin	KOR	4	0	0	0	
Totals			**44**	**0**	**3**	**0**	

Tennis

Los Angeles Tennis Center
University of California, Los Angeles

			Set 1	Set 2	Set 3
Women Singles	August 11				
	Graf, Steffi	FRG	1	6	6
	Goles, Sabrina	YUG	6	3	4
Men Singles	August 11		Set 1	Set 2	Set 3
	Edberg, Stefan	SWE	6	7	(8-6)
	Maciel, Francisco	MEX	1	6	

Closing Ceremonies

"In the sun that is young once only, Time let me play and be golden..." Dylan Thomas

Photo: S. Powell

Opposite Page
Photo: T. Duffy

Photo: D. Cannon

Photo: IOPP

Photo: T. Duffy

Acknowledgements

International Olympic Committee

Executive Board
 Juan Antonio Samaranch (Spain), President
 Louis Guirandou-N'Diaye (Ivory Coast),
  First Vice President
 Alexandru Siperco (Romania),
  Second Vice President
 Ashwini Kumar (India)
  Third Vice President
 Virgilio de Leon (Panama)
 Prince Alexandre de Mérode (Belgium)
 Julian K. Roosevelt (United States)
 Richard W. Pound (Canada)
 Sylvio de Magalhães Padilha (Brazil)
 Monique Berlioux (France), Director

Los Angeles Olympic Organizing Committee

Executives
 Peter V. Ueberroth, President
 Harry L. Usher,
  Executive Vice President/
  General Manager

Group Vice Presidents
 Philip N. Brubaker, Olympic Family
  Operations
 Charles G. Cale, Sports
 Priscilla Florence, Human Resources
 Edward Keen, Architecture/Construction
 Don S. Matso, External Relations
 Michael C. Mitchell, Planning & Control
 Michael C. Mount, Support Operations

Typography

Stephen B. Whipple & Associates — Utah, USA

Lithography & Binding

Paul Klein Schiphorst
Royal Smeets Offset — Weert, Netherlands

Paper

Koninklijke Nederlandse Papierfabrieken
120 grams wood free glossy coated

Photographers

C. Anderson
V. Gonzales
V. Luke
E. Rosenberger
P. Slaughter
G. Takac

Allsport:
   D. Cannon
   A. Chung
   T. Duffy
   W. Hunt
   T. Jones
   S. Powell

IOPP:
   Bashaanse
   Benoit
   Cranford
   Edmonds
   Foggia
   Heflin
   Maze
   Messerli
   Puusa
   Sinjay
   Vreeker

Special Thanks

Gregory R. Gaddie
Amy Christiansen
Laurie S. Hathaway
Gayle Petersen

Dennis Christopher
Fred Gruter
Stephen Jenson
Sandie Kesler

David Poolinger
Kathryn Thorn

Dianne Edwards
Patricia Morrow
Vivian Thorn

Margaret Brog
Ida Cowgill
Karmell Fenton
Barbara Hiatt
Gay Nickle Lauritzen
Diana Luker
Laurie Ralphs
Merrill Stanger

Kevin Gonzales
Gregory Scott Hunt
Samuel Morgan
Mary Jo Osgood
Charles Penna
Dennis Powers

Games of the XXIV Olympiad will be in Seoul, Korea.